AMERICAN MILLINERS AND THEIR WORLD

AMERICAN MILLINERS AND THEIR WORLD

Women's Work from Revolution to Rock and Roll

NADINE STEWART

BLOOMSBURY VISUAL ARTS
LONDON • NEW YORK • OXFORD • NEW DELHI • SYDNEY

BLOOMSBURY VISUAL ARTS
Bloomsbury Publishing Plc
50 Bedford Square, London, WC1B 3DP, UK
1385 Broadway, New York, NY 10018, USA
29 Earlsfort Terrace, Dublin 2, Ireland

BLOOMSBURY, BLOOMSBURY VISUAL ARTS and the Diana logo are trademarks of
Bloomsbury Publishing Plc

First published in Great Britain 2021
Paperback edition first published 2022

For legal purposes the Acknowledgments on p. xii constitute an extension of
this copyright page.

Cover design by Adriana Brioso
Cover image: Worker in factory by Lewis Hine. Photography Collection, Miriam and Ira D.
Wallach Division of Art, Prints and Photographs © The New York Public Library

A catalogue record for this book is available from the British Library.

Library of Congress Cataloging-in-Publication Data
Names: Stewart, Nadine, author.
Title: American milliners and their world : women's work from
revolution to rock and roll / Nadine Stewart.
Description: London; New York : Bloomsbury Visual Arts, 2020. |
Includes bibliographical references and index.
Identifiers: LCCN 2020035679 (print) | LCCN 2020035680 (ebook) | ISBN
9781350063754 (hardback) | ISBN 9781350203174 (paperback) | ISBN
9781350063761 (pdf) | ISBN 9781350063778 (epub)
Subjects: LCSH: Millinery–United States–History. | Millinery
workers–United States–History. | Women–Employment–History.
Classification: LCC HD9948.U62 S745 2020 (print) | LCC HD9948.U62
(ebook) | DDC 331.4/887420973–dc23
LC record available at https://lccn.loc.gov/2020035679
LC ebook record available at https://lccn.loc.gov/2020035680

ISBN: HB: 978-1-3500-6375-4
PB: 978-1-3502-0317-4
ePDF: 978-1-3500-6376-1
eBook: 978-1-3500-6377-8

Typeset by Deanta Global Publishing Services, Chennai, India

To find out more about our authors and books visit www.bloomsbury.com
and sign up for our newsletters.

To my mother, Ruth McCune Stewart

1917-2013

Figure 1 Ruth Stewart and her daughter Nadine, Easter 1951. Personal Photograph.

CONTENTS

ILLUSTRATIONS

PREFACE

Every February during my childhood my mother would inevitably ask me the same question, "What kind of Easter bonnet do you want this year?" She had to ask early because she would be making my Easter outfit, so she needed time.

There were two choices. A bonnet which was always decorated with flowers or a sailor style which always had navy blue streamers that hung down my back. After I made my choice, Mother and I would go shopping in Joseph Horne's downtown Pittsburgh. Shopping trips with my mother were a big treat. We would have lunch in the Tea Room, which made me feel so sophisticated, and then we would head up to "Young World" on the third floor to seek the right hat. If I was really lucky, Mother would take me to the Women's Millinery Department and I would get to watch her try on hats. I loved the Millinery Department. It was a secluded alcove with subdued lighting. Women sat at dressing tables and examined their reflections in the mirror. I dreamed of trying on hats there when I grew up and buying a huge black straw cartwheel hat just like Mother's.

That was not to be. Joseph Horne's is gone. Its millinery department probably vanished long before it closed. My last Easter bonnet in 1960 was actually a white straw pillbox, inspired by Jacqueline Kennedy, the new First Lady.

Years passed. I worked as a journalist, left Pittsburgh, and moved about the country. I finally settled in New York City where I worked for a while at the Lower East Tenement Museum. The museum tells the story of immigrants who lived in the Lower East Side by recreating apartments in a tenement that was built in 1863. Their stories struck a chord since my hometown also had a flood of immigrants in the late nineteenth and early twentieth centuries who came to work in the steel mills and mines. Many of the immigrants who came into New York worked in the garment industries, including millinery.

After I left the museum, I went back to graduate school to study fashion history. In my first semester, I discovered an 1864 milliner's diary and a fictionalized memoir of another. I also discovered *A Seasonal Industry*, the 1917 study of the millinery trade by a Progressive group seeking to improve the lives of these working women. My eyes glazed over when I looked at the many charts and graphs the author Mary van Kleeck had packed in the study.

But, the images in the study are another story. They are the work of Lewis Hine, a social reformer and photographer, known for his photographs of immigrants arriving at Ellis Island Immigration Station and child laborers in the mills and mines of the nation in the early years of the twentieth century. Hine's images are unlike most images of milliners in the nineteenth and twentieth centuries since they are not idealized. They put a human face on the statistics. Hine's work is an important part of the American experience and inspired me over the years as I worked on this book. I am proud to include his photographs to tell another story of milliners in the United States.

My mother died in 2013. I never got a black straw cartwheel hat, but Mother gave me a love of millinery. This book is my tribute to her.

ACKNOWLEDGMENTS

This book is the end of a long road that began with a paper I wrote in the fall of 2006, my first semester in the Fashion and Textile Studies Master's program at the Fashion Institute of Technology (FIT). Many people helped me develop my thoughts along the way. I hope I will be able to thank all of them here.

I wrote that paper for Dr. Lourdes Font, whose passion for fashion history inspired me. She was my adviser on my thesis several years later. I owe her so much for her help in shaping and honing my thoughts.

Without the rich resources of the New York Public Library and the Gladys Marcus Library at FIT, this book would not have been possible. I would especially like to thank April Calahan and Karen Trivette Cannell of Special Collections and FIT Archives. I also wish to thank Lana Bittman and her staff in Periodicals. I spent many, many hours there paging through *Vogue*, *Harper's Bazaar*, and *Life* magazines, which yielded a trove of rich material.

I also spent a week at the Kheel Center for Labor-Management Documentation and Archives at Cornell University in Ithaca, NY. I owe the staff there great thanks for their help identifying the material I needed for my chapter on the 1930s. I also owe enormous thanks to Elizabeth and Jerry Davis, who put me up and fed me that week. Elizabeth also edited the first draft of my first chapter and pointed out material I needed to write coherently about the origins of millinery.

Thanks go to Wayne E. Reilly for his careful editing of the diary of his great-grandmother, Emma Ann Foster. His work made it possible to understand the spare entries in the diary in the context of the Civil War Maine in 1864.

I took three courses in millinery to increase my understanding of this demanding craft. I wish to thank my instructor, Janet Linville, who taught me so much.

The members of the Costume Society of America have been a wonderful support network. I would especially like to thank the late Joy Spanabel Emery who recommended I contact Bloomsbury after she heard my presentation at the annual symposium in San Antonio in 2015. Another member, José Blanco, edited my book proposal. I owe him thanks for taking the time to help me clarify my thoughts. June Burns Bové, who was also one of my professors at FIT, is always there with good advice. My department head at Montclair State University, Abby Lillethun, has been a sounding board for my thoughts and worries since I started teaching there in 2013.

Still another CSA member, Janea Whitacre invited me to speak at Colonial Williamsburg in 2014 at a conference celebrating the sixtieth anniversary of the Margaret Hunter Millinery Shop. This conference inspired me to continue with my research which had stalled for a few years.

I had more editing help from Barbara Cohen-Stratyner. She edited one of my proposed first chapters and got me back on track by pointing out that I needed to focus on the milliners, not on the fascinating errata I'd found in my research on the nineteenth century.

My friend Louise Hoeller encouraged me to present that first paper at the 2008 conference of the Edith Wharton Society, which helped me start on the road to this book.

The team at Bloomsbury has been unfailingly helpful. Special thanks to Anna and Hannah, who were the first to express interest, and, later on, Frances, Pari, Yvonne, and Rebecca, who have been there with advice and help for a first-time author.

My friends have been a great source of help and support, especially Linda Ellerbee, one of my oldest friends. We've shared so much over the years. She has enriched my life with her wit and support. She has also given me so many wonderful books, including two obscure books on the Milliners' Union that formed the basis of my chapter on the 1930s. Thanks also to Rolfe Tessum who photographed my personal picture for publication.

I would like to thank my family—my mother Ruth McCune Stewart, who always made sure I had the perfect hat for Easter every year of my childhood and my late brother, Bruce, another hat lover who was an unfailing source of strength and love.

Finally, I would like to thank my husband, David Zydallis, for the love, support, and good cooking he has provided over thirty years of marriage. David believed I could write a book before I did. His faith in me sustained me through the years of research and writing needed to produce this book.

INTRODUCTION

In the early part of the twenty-first century, the woman's hat has almost disappeared as a fashionable accessory. Women wear them for warmth in winter, for shade in summer, and for traditional, usually religious, occasions. Few today remember that just fifty years ago the hat was the most essential of accessories; even fewer know anything about the milliners who toiled to make hats for the fashionable. For most Americans, the only milliner they might know about comes from fiction—Lily Bart, heroine of Edith Wharton's *House of Mirth*, published more than one hundred years ago in 1905.

Lily ends up at the milliner's table after she fails to make a good match and falls from the upper ranks of New York society. Disinherited by her aunt and scorned by fashionable society, she tries to salvage herself by training as a milliner in the exclusive shop of Madame Regine. As the scene opens, things are not going well. "Lily had taken up her work early in January: it was now two months later, and she was still being rebuked for her inability to sew spangles on a hat frame."[1]

Lily had chosen a popular profession. A study by the Russell Sage Association in 1917 reported there were 13,000 in New York City alone, 5,800 in Chicago, and 3,800 in Philadelphia.[2] Mary van Kleeck, who oversaw the Russell Sage study, wrote of millinery work: "It attracts young girls just leaving school, who look upon wage-earning as part of the natural course of events, and it is likely to be selected also by women of the so-called 'leisure class' when they are suddenly and unexpectedly forced to earn their own living."[3]

So, it was natural that Lily would turn to hatmaking, thinking it might be the one profession she might have an aptitude for. It was not to be. Depressed and drug-addicted, Lily dies shortly after she leaves Madame Regine's, a victim of the rigid society of turn-of-the-century New York.

But, what of the other women who toiled in the millinery workroom with Lily? They, too, were struggling to earn a living. As Lily rips out the spangles, she listens to the women around the table speak of the world of New York society. "Every girl in Mme. Regina's work-room knew to whom the headgear in her hands was destined, and had her opinion of the future wearer, and a definite knowledge of the latter's place in the social system."[4] This book aims to turn the focus on the vast "underworld of toilers,"[5] women who struggled to support themselves in the competitive world of fashion—a struggle that continues today. It is hard to find the stories of these milliners. Much of their lives are undocumented. Few of them left a diary. Often, we have to view them through the eyes of their customers and their bosses, men who view them with some contempt.

But, their story is part of the story of women's work in the United States. This was a nation that was rising to power in the nineteenth century, was keenly conscious of its place in the Atlantic World, relative to the fashion centers of Europe. It was also a nation that changed drastically after a bloody civil war tore apart many women's lives and waves of immigrants flooded the nation.

Milliners had special problems in American society. Though their work was considered respectable and genteel, they were hobbled by a society that did not believe women belonged in the workplace. These were problems that did not change appreciably in the twentieth century, even though making hats became big business. Milliners began to be trapped in their genteel world—seasonal work that was increasingly dominated by men. However, this is much more than a story of "women's work." Through the use of diaries, etiquette books, contemporary literature, and trade journals, this book will give an insight into the mindset of the times when women were consigned to their sphere, a state deemed assigned to them by God.[6] It will show how making hats became a big business, but milliners' working conditions did not improve. .

Ironically, milliners' concern with maintaining their genteel status in the work world kept them from unionizing to improve their conditions in the early twentieth century. They clung to the nineteenth-century perception that striking was for factory workers, not "ladies" who worked with fine materials and dealt with customers in the middle and upper classes.[7] One organizer commented, "You might as well try to direct the wind as to organize milliners."[8]

Though American milliners were leaders in establishing American style in the 1930s and 1940s, the rise of the cosmetics industry in the 1950s accelerated the trend toward hatlessness. By the 1960s the unthinkable happened—women did not long for a beautiful hat to define them, but a wonderful hairdo. This shift in fashion changed the status of the milliner from a leader of fashion and a trendsetter to an obscure craftsperson by the middle of the twentieth century. The "genteel" status had become a fashion ghetto.

But, unlike Lily Bart, the story of milliners in America is not a story of defeat but a story of perseverance and grit in the face of a society that did not value female workers. Virginia Penny, a nineteenth-century social reformer and writer, praised their special qualities, writing:

> There are comparatively few persons that make good milliners. As a milliner, one must have good taste and nimble fingers; as a sales woman, she needs to understand human nature, have activity, an honest heart, and good disposition.[9]

Those words are as true today as they were in 1863.

1
MILANERS TO MILLINERS

Today the definition of the word "milliner" seems simple and straightforward. The *Oxford English Dictionary's* definition only says:

Mil•li•ner *(mil'ə nər)*, n. A person who makes or sells women's hats.

But the roots of the word extend back to the Renaissance. While women and men have worn a wide variety of headgear over the centuries, the art of the milliner, a person who makes headgear specifically for women, is relatively new. It developed as the thirst for fashion grew along with a rise in consumerism and communication.

The word "milliner" originally referred to "Milaners," peddlers from Milan who traveled to Northern Europe as early as the 1520s to sell trims—silks, braids, ribbons, and hats of fine Italian straw. Italy was the nexus of trade in luxury items since its ports had access to the riches of the East. There was a thriving Italian silk industry that could produce the ribbons, braids, and other embellishments the rich in the courts of Northern Europe craved. The sunny climate allowed the growth of the finest straw for bonnets. Along the way, these men passed along the latest word on fashionable styles to men and women who were hungry for such news.[1]

Because milaners sold items that were associated with women, the profession became associated with effeminate men. In *Henry IV, Part 1* Shakespeare's history play written in 1597, the blunt soldier Hotspur derides another courtier by comparing him to a milaner. "Fresh as a bridegroom; and his chin reap'd / Show'd like a stubble-land at harvest-home; He was perfumed like a milliner; And 'twixt his finger and his thumb he held a pouncet-box."[2]

The portraits of Queen Elizabeth I give us a picture of the Renaissance love of trims. Dress after dress is bedecked with ribbons, lace, jewels, and fine embroidery. The queen used her dress to dazzle her subjects, so she clearly loved the goods a milaner could supply. By the time she died in 1603, she owned over 2,000 pieces of clothing.[3] Her courtiers announced their wealth through their heavily embellished clothing too. The English court was not alone. Courtiers across Renaissance Europe covered themselves in clothing encrusted with the goods of the milaners.

The thirst for magnificent embellishments grew in seventeenth-century France. Louis XIV's minister of finance Jean-Baptiste Colbert set out to make France the world leader in luxury, particularly in fine clothing. Protective laws were enacted aimed at wrestling production of luxury goods from Italy. French silk weavers and lace makers benefited and were supported by the state. Colbert also encouraged skilled artisans to move to France, sometimes arranging for them to be smuggled into the country.[4]

By the second half of the seventeenth century, the French court was the most prestigious in Europe, setting the style for most of the continent. Louis XIV dictated the dress in his court with an iron hand, making sure his courtiers supported French luxury artisans by investing heavily in fine clothes to wear in his court. Fashion historian Jennifer M. Jones points out how important trims had become to the clothing of these courtiers. "An elegantly dressed person, whether male or female, often used as much as 300 yards of ribbon on all parts of dress, including the hair."[5]

The fashion world was changing. Men had been making clothing for both men and women since the Middle Ages. They belonged to tailors' guilds that divided the work of producing garments into units that did not change with the changes in fashions. By the late seventeenth century, women began to work in secret as dressmakers though such work was risky since the tailors would break into their shops and destroy them. The new dressmakers were fined for violating guild rules, but this work continued because their women customers kept patronizing them.

In 1675, there was a breakthrough. The dressmakers petitioned Louis XIV to allow them to work legally. The king agreed. A new profession was born, the *couturière* (or seamstress in English). For the first time women were able to set up a guild of their own. They were restricted to making mourning gowns, clothes for children, and, most important, a new garment that would change women's fashions—the *manteau*. Originally, this was a simple robe-like garment that was worn at home. Because it did not have a boned bodice like the *grand habit*, the formal court dresses produced by the tailors, it was much more comfortable. Even though a corset or stays were worn underneath, the fact that the *manteau* was looser meant that comfort and ease became the new fashion. Soon women were wearing the *manteau* outside the home. The success of these *couturières* meant that the door was opened for more women workers in the fashion world.

Even though women were able to cut and stitch garments, the actual shape of the clothes did not change much from year to year. Much of what we associate today with fashionable change did not exist. Hemlines did not rise and fall. Waistlines stayed in the same place. Silhouettes stayed the same as well. Fashion historian Anne Hollander explains: "For this kind of construction work, basic technical skill but no artistic talent was required. Creative fashion instead expressed itself on the surface, and there it changed very rapidly, particularly at idle and rich courts, with the aid of certain specialized experts."[6] Those experts were the *marchandes de modes* or "fashion merchants," a new profession in the eighteenth century. They provided the trims that varied the look of a dress or a hairstyle.

The *marchandes* emerged quickly in the second half of the eighteenth century. Originally, male *merciers* (or mercer in English) had taken over the function of the original milaners, selling the trimmings and ornaments, like lace and ribbons, which added the fine decorative touch to a fashionable garment along with fine textiles for the garments themselves. Women soon began to enter this profitable business of trims and embellishments.[7] They were limited to making and trimming anything a woman wore on her head and shoulders, though they could also make belts and ruffles to decorate dresses. *Merciers* continued to sell dress fabric in precut lengths, but otherwise their involvement in the making of a dress was limited since they were prohibited from cutting cloth. In the intricate guild system, the seamstresses could cut cloth and stitch the gowns. But when it came to the crucial trims, seamstresses were restricted. They could not trim the gowns they made unless the trim was the same material as the gown itself.[8]

The *marchandes* did not have that restriction. They dictated how a gown would be decorated and, in the process, began to set the styles. The *marchande* with her bandbox of trims and measuring stick became a familiar sight in the homes of the rich, visiting her customers in the morning as they completed their toilette. The work offered an opportunity to women from the working class. No special training was needed to become a *marchande*—just a sure sense of taste.[9] The *Encyclopedie Methodique* defined the *marchandes'* work as:

> Those who arrange and sell all the little objects that aid dress, particularly, of women, taffetas, gauze, linen, lace, decorations, ribbons of all types, flowers, feathers, and so on are the items they employ. They arrange, diversify, and mix these materials according to their purpose, their fantasy, and the manner that the taste and caprice of the moment inspires and necessitates.[10]

A key part of this definition follows. "Their art is not to make anything; it consists in ingeniously furnishing a new look withal the varied and gracious ornaments of other arts, particularly that of braid and trimmings."[11]

The court began to move back to Paris in the late seventeenth century away from the rigid dress codes of Louis XIV that held sway in Versailles. A retail revolution took place in the center of Paris. Merchants established permanent shops where customers could meet and browse the latest items. By the mid-eighteenth century, *marchandes'* shops and workrooms were located in the center of Paris on the Faubourg and Rue Saint-Honore. Their wares were visible from the street through large windows—a temptation to shop after an evening at the theater.[12]

By 1776 the *marchandes* got their own guild united with the feather suppliers and flower makers. They had gained the right to decorate the *grand habit*, the formal gown required for presentation at court, but with the creation of their guild they also gained the right to make the entire garment. Before that, the process was fragmented. Tailors made the boned bodice of the court gown and seamstress were allowed to stitch the skirt.[13] With this new freedom to create, the *marchandes* established a foothold as the leaders of the fashion world. They soon appeared in other European countries from England to Italy, countries where the milaners first plied their trade.

In the second half of the eighteenth century, fashion became more ostentatious. The wide panniers expanded. Hairstyles rose to heights as high as 3 feet augmented by *poufs* which were concocted from false hair, wool, wire mesh, and gauze. The new styles allowed the *marchandes* to give free rein to their imaginations. They covered the new wider gowns with trims, but it was on the head where their creativity was really on display since the head was where the real changes in style could be seen. The *marchandes* piled on feathers, ribbons, lace, jewels, fur, and, even, fresh flowers. One baroness described the experience as "very unwieldy: small, flat bottles curved to fit the shape of the head, containing a little water for real flowers that could be kept fresh in the hairdo. This did not always work, but when it was mastered, it was charming."[14] Styles changed weekly and often featured tributes to important figures and current events, such as a high hairstyle topped with a ship in full sail in honor of the victory of a French ship over the English fleet.[15]

The leading *marchande* was Rose Bertin, who rose from humble origins in Picardy to become the head of the *marchandes*' new guild and the favorite of Queen Marie Antoinette. She was allowed to meet with the queen alone twice a week in violation of the rigid etiquette of the French court. Her position made her many enemies, but her influence was so powerful many made their way to her exclusive shop on Rue St Honore. Many more copied her work shamelessly.[16]

There were male *marchands* as well. The most famous, Jean-Joseph Beaulard, also worked for Marie Antoinette. He is known for a unique invention—the *bonnet à resort* or springed bonnet. It enabled a woman to quickly lower her towering hairstyle by a foot by simply pressing a hidden spring. This was considered a safe way to avert criticism from those who did not approve of the three-foot-high hairstyles, like grandmothers.[17] Despite Beaulard's prominence, the ranks of male *marchands* were thin. The trade was increasingly seen as a female profession. As the centuries wore on, women would work hard to keep it that way.

Hairstyles began to flatten in the 1780s, but styles did not become simpler. *La mode* still required copious amounts of ribbons, artificial flowers, and feathers in combinations that changed frequently. In addition, *marchandes des modes* began to make and sell bonnets and turbans out of straw or fabric. This was the beginning of their evolution into the milliners and *modistes* in the nineteenth century.[18]

The *marchandes* continued to work during the French Revolution even though the guild system was abolished in March 1791, and the fashion industry of France was in chaos. The *marchandes* were able to make the iconic tricolor cockades required to show support of the new order, which were required by law in 1792.[19] Some *marchandes* were even able to obtain pieces of stone from the Bastille which were placed in gold and silver settings and worn like jewels.[20] But after five years of turmoil, it was dangerous to look like a fashion follower.

Bertin along with many other fashion workers went into exile in London. The frenzy over hairstyles had been less powerful across the English Channel and the Atlantic. But, the influence of the French court was strong despite the Revolution. Bertin's fashion dolls circulated even during her exile.[21]

Bertin returned to France in 1795 after the excesses of the Revolution were extinguished.[22] However, the fashionable world had moved on. There was a radical change in women's dress. The silhouette was simple, echoing Greek and Roman columns, made of sheer white fabric like muslin. Gowns had low necklines with high waists under the breasts and short puffed sleeves that revealed the arms, while the skirt fell to the feet in straight folds. Hairstyles were far simpler as well, upswept with ringlets surrounding the face. There was no need for the excessive embellishments of the past.

The "Minister of La Mode" died in 1813.

In England, there were fewer rules and regulations and a different name for the trade. *Marchande de modes* were known as milliners, who could sell every conceivable type of accessory and the materials as well as garments like petticoats and cloaks. As the *London Tradesman* noted in 1747,

> The Milliner is concerned in making and providing the Ladies with Linen of all sorts, for wearing apparel, from the Holland Smock to the Tippet and Commode . . . the Milliner furnishes them with Holland, Cambrick, Lawn, and Lace of all sorts and makes these Materials into Smocks, Aprons, Tippets, handkerchiefs, Neckaties, Ruffles, Mobs, Caps, Dressed-Heads with as many Etceteras as would reach from Charing-Cross to The Royal Exchange.
>
> They make up Cloaks, Manteels, Mantelets, Cheens and Capucheens, of Silk, Velvet, plain or brocaded and trim them with Silver and Gold Lace or Black Lace. They make up and sell Hats, Hoods, and Caps of all Sorts and Materials; they sell quilted Petticoats and Hoops of all Sizes. . . . The Milliner . . . imports new Whims from Paris every Post. . . . The most noted of them keep an Agent at Paris, who have nothing to do but watch the Motions of the Fashions, and procure Intelligence of their Changes.[23]

There were male milliners on both sides of the English Channel and in the Netherlands early in the eighteenth century. Historian Randolph Trumbach describes them as part of a group that emerged in the early eighteenth century — men who were only interested in sex with other men and who exhibited effeminate mannerisms. In Britain, 500 legal cases document their appearance along with several plays and satirical prints.[24] Because these men were feminine in behavior they gravitated to selling women's clothes and were apprenticed to milliners. By the mid-eighteenth century leading clergyman Josiah Tucker called men who made women's clothing sinful, "Ye men milliners, ye pretty boys, placed behind counters, artful spruce, decoys tempting the fair to spend cash with grace."[25] Another writer went further, calling one of these men a "damned insignificant he-she thing."[26] By the end of the century, "man milliner" had a derogatory connotation, as the *Webster's Revised Dictionary* definition explains, "A male milliner. Hence *derogatory* [emphasis in original]: a vain, trifling, or effeminate man."[27] Such a man would not be welcome in the new culture of the emerging American nation, already obsessed with discarding what was seen as the frivolous culture of the Old World that would sap republican values.

Across the ocean in the British colonies, milliners linked with manufacturers and merchants in England for goods to sell. English and French fashions were reported in American magazines and newspapers.

The diary of an early merchant Elizabeth Murray, who kept a shop in Boston, in the late eighteenth century, shows that keeping a millinery shop was a business that could be very rewarding, especially in port cities like Boston, New York, and Philadelphia. Indeed, at least ninety women had such shops in Boston from 1740 to the American Revolution.[28] Murray did so well she was able to help her daughters, relatives, and the daughters of friends set up a business like hers over the years.

> Shops were comfortable, familiar spaces for them, places of feminine interaction and conversation where the latest fashion might be discussed and gossip exchanges. For women, shops may have been the equivalent of taverns and coffeehouses, the typical sites of male consumers.[29]

Another milliner, Sibylla Robertson Masters of Pennsylvania was able to develop "a new way of working and staining in straw, and the plat, and the leaf of the palmetto tree, and covering and adorning hats and bonnets in such a manner as was never before done or practiced in England or any of our plantations."[30] She was able to apply for and get a patent for her process from King George III in February 1716 — the first colonist to receive a patent from the king, which makes her the first American woman to be recognized as an inventor.[31]

Further out in the country, there was also demand for fashionable clothing. Analyzing records from the Connecticut River Valley, historian Marla Miller describes how making clothing became exclusively work for women. Just as in Europe the milliner, who was trained in the use of trims, had the highest status and received the highest income of all the occupations available to women. As the eighteenth century wore on women became associated with the making of women's clothing more and more. Working with a needle was not just a respectable female trade but also an "innate female skill," work women were born to do.[32]

But how did young women learn the specialized skills required to function effectively as a milliner? The answer can be hard to find. Traditional studies of apprenticeships in the United States focus on contracts which bind a novice to an experienced artesian for a number of years. During that period the novice could gain the skills required for work such as printing and furniture making by working with the master. However, Marla Miller points out such an arrangement often did not exist for young women. Most records that have survived only specify that young women learn "housewifery." As Miller points out, "This stipulation can be misleading. Eighteenth-century households did not draw distinctions between domestic and craft labor as sharply as we do today."[33] To truly find out about the training of young women workers, a historian must comb through records in women's diaries, accounting lists, and logbooks. She cites four examples of diaries that contain fleeting references of an apprentice in the house.

Miller points that "In none of these cases do documents survive that affirm a legally binding relationship of the kind traditionally understood as an apprenticeship. . . . Unknown numbers of young women, then, completed periods of training in the clothing trades that, while acknowledged as apprenticeships by participants and observers alike, left no paper trail."[34]

The onset of the American Revolution complicated Americans' view of the world of fashion. "The popular press shrilly insisted both before and after the war that American women were excessive in their consumption of British goods and books; the critics held that by indulging in British products, American women were undercutting the efforts of American men to develop a fully independent national culture."[35] Women were urged to wear homespun and encouraged to spin the thread needed for clothing themselves.

Hostility to fashions from Britain continued throughout the war. One target was the exaggerated poufs of the Old World. In 1778 Philadelphia's Fourth of July celebration featured "a very high Head dress . . . exhibited thro the Streets this afternoon on a very dirty Woman with a mob after her, with Drums &c by way of ridiculing that very foolish fashion."[36]

After the war, anti-fashion pressure continued. Women were told they should not, as citizens of a newly independent republic, allow themselves to be ensnared by milliners and other fashion makers from abroad, but strive to support new, vulnerable American manufacturers.[37] The ambivalent attitude toward fashionable dress was succinctly expressed by Dr. Benjamin Rush, a signer of the Declaration of Independence and a leading supporter of education for citizens of the new republic.

> I have sometimes been led to ascribe the invention of ridiculous and expensive fashions in female dress entirely to the gentlemen in order to divert the ladies from improving their minds and thereby to secure a more arbitrary and unlimited authority over them.[38]

Rush was an early believer in educating women for the new American society. His Thoughts on Female Education delivered to an audience at the Young Ladies' Academy in Philadelphia in 1787 expressed the ideal of "republican motherhood." Women needed an education to raise their sons to be virtuous citizens of the new nation. That education should include the traditional skills of sewing and housekeeping, and training to be efficient stewards of their households through skills like reading, spelling, math, and even, science to "prevent superstition" and enable the women to assist in nursing the sick.[39] Even more important, women should learn about history and government, so they could help the new nation avoid the corruption Rush felt infected British society.[40] With an education like this, women would not be mere ornaments of fashionable society like the British women he despised.

Despite the new nation's ambivalent attitude, milliners were important transmitters of the latest fashions from France and England.[41] One early observer of American society commented on the milliners' power acknowledging they "have more influence in regulating [dress] than the court of Washington. . . . [Milliners] keep up a regular correspondence with Europe, and import new dresses into Charleston [port city of South Carolina] as soon as they are introduced in the capitals of France and England."[42]

Bonnets were still in demand though the Revolution made it difficult to get the right kind of straw from Europe. The need for fine straw bonnets inspired several American women to invent better ways of making them. A breakthrough came in 1798 when twelve-year-old Betsy Metcalf of Rhode Island devised a new method of braiding straw while she was trying to copy an expensive straw. She used local oat straw which she smoothed with scissors and then split with her thumbnail. Metcalf taught her technique to other young women and the craze spread all over New England. Women braided in their sewing circles instead of knitting and crocheting, while children braided in school. The new industry gave thousands work, so many that whole towns in New England were known as "straw towns." Metcalf could have gotten a patent from the newly formed Patent Office but resisted going public with her idea.

> I learned them to braid from nearly all the towns around Providence and never received compensation for it. I learned all who came to make bonnets free of

expense. Many said I ought to have a patent but I did not want my name sent to Congress. I could easily earn a dollar a day and sometimes one dollar and fifty cents for several weeks at a time.[43]

Though Metcalf was reluctant to go through the process of obtaining a patent, Mary Kies of Connecticut was not. She developed and patented a method of braiding straw with silk or thread in 1809, which was simpler and made a more affordable bonnet. Shortly after that, the new nation embargoed the importation of European goods in an attempt to keep the country out of the upheaval of the Napoleonic Wars. The First Lady herself, Dolley Madison, commended Kies for an invention that enabled the New England hat industry to continue on. The hat industry continued to provide work for thousands during the War of 1812, when so many of the nation's nascent industries foundered.[44] Unfortunately, the fashion for straw bonnets changed, so Kies never profited from her invention. She died a pauper in 1837.[45] Today there is a monument to her in South Killingly, Connecticut, placed there in 1965 to honor the first woman in the country to apply for and receive a patent.[46]

A few years after Kies's invention, another Connecticut woman gained notice for her work in straw. Sophia Woodhouse used a native grass instead of straw for a bonnet and won a local award in 1819 and again in 1820. The bonnet was sent to England where the British Society of Arts proclaimed it superior to the finest Leghorn straw bonnets from Italy and awarded her a silver medal. The British wanted to import her seed and produce the grass themselves, but since Woodhouse had a patent, the deal fell through. However, Woodhouse did achieve some fame. One of her bonnets was sent to Louisa Adams, wife of President John Quincy Adams. The president confided to his diary that the bonnet was "an extraordinary specimen of American manufacture." Woodhouse was able to establish a successful business in Wethersfield, Connecticut. One of her employees produced 300 bonnets in a single summer![47]

The inventions in the straw braiding industry gave thousands of American women work. As they entered the new century it seemed possible that women would continue to be valuable contributors to the work of building the new nation's economy. But, the founders of the new nation drafted a constitution that did not mention women at all. As historian Linda Kerber observed, "They [white male landowners and businessmen] found it impossible to imagine respectable adult women as anything other than wives. They could not separate the sexual monopoly which a man exercised over his wife from the political monopoly which he exercised over her property. They could not imagine an adult woman with her own obligation to the state."[48] Women were not the only group the framers of the Constitution ignored. The nation's slaves were only mentioned for the purpose of determining the number of members of Congress (Article I, Section 2). These omissions would create schisms that would tear the nation apart in the new century.

2
THE WOMAN'S SPHERE

Figure 2 Milliner and her daughter, *c*. 1854. Library of Congress.

I ask no favors for my sex. I surrender not our claim to equality. All I ask of our brethren is, that they will take their feet from off our necks, and permit us to stand upright on that ground which God designed us to occupy.

SARAH GRIMKÉ, LETTER 2 (JULY 17, 1837)[1]

These powerful words were written by Sarah Grimké, a crusader for women's rights and a passionate advocate for the end of slavery in the years before the Civil War. Grimké, who came from a slave-owning family in South Carolina, signed her letters "Yours in the bonds of womanhood," an indication that she equated women's "bonds" with the bonds of chattel slavery.

Grimké was writing about a shift that began in the late eighteenth century. The revolutions and subsequent challenges to the accepted social order at the end of the eighteenth century had shaken the world. In addition, the rapid pace of industrialization and invention added to anxiety about the future. Inventions like the cotton gin, the steam engine, the Jacquard loom, and the sewing machine, all of which were devised before 1860, speeded up production and created jobs in cities. The nature of work changed too. In the early years of the Republic, life was lived according to the seasons with both men and women sharing responsibility for work and family life. Though men were considered the heads of households, the entire family worked together as a unit. With an increase in production, the dynamic changed. Work went from tasks that were seasonal and flexible to jobs ordered by the demands of time. Men increasingly went out of the home to work in factories or businesses, while women were expected to stay at home and create a safe haven for the husband to return to and raise their children. Under the new system, merchants dispersed materials to people who worked in their homes. The workers were paid by the piece, giving rise to the nickname "piecework." This was the beginning of the "putting out" system. One of the important industries affected was the straw braiding business, which went from using native grasses, a technique patented by Mary Kies before 1800, to imported Cuban palm leaves. By 1830 thousands of home workers were using these materials, diminishing the innovative methods devised by women earlier.[2]

By the beginning of the nineteenth century, the world was changing around women. Society's view of women and their proper role in the world was hardening. Women were increasingly expected to live in their "sphere," a domestic world, while their husbands went out into the world of work. Under the legal doctrine of "femme couverte" that came from English common law, "by marriage, the husband and wife are one person in the law, the very beginning, or legal existence of woman is suspended during the marriage."[3] That meant married women were effectively noncitizens. All property rights belonged to the husband, which meant adult married women could not own property, divorce their husbands, sign contracts, or be guardians of their children. A woman had to get her husband's approval to obtain an education or go to work. Her money, whether inherited or earned, belonged to her husband as well. Since women were not mentioned in the Constitution of the United States, the founding document of the nation, the increasing rigidity of the doctrine of femme couverte restricted women's lives severely. This was reflected in the etiquette books of the time, which decreed a wife also had to be careful to address her husband properly. "A lady will not say 'My husband,' except among intimates; in every other case she should address him by name, calling him Mr. It is equally good tone, when alone with him, to designate him by his Christian name."[4]

Sarah Grimké saw clearly that women were not privileged or protected by the women's sphere: "Woman, instead of being elevated by her union with man, which might be expected from an alliance with a superior being, is in reality lowered. She generally loses her individuality, her independent character, her moral being. She becomes absorbed into him, and henceforth is looked at, and acts through the medium of her husband."[5]

In this stratified world, the position of an unmarried woman was tenuous at best. The author of the *Female Instructor* acknowledged as early as 1811 that there was no safety net in the woman's sphere:

I must confess when I see many of the sex, who have lived well in the time of their childhood, grievously exposed to many hardships and poverty upon the death of their parents, I have often wished there were more of the callings and employments of life particularly appointed to women, and that they were regularly educated in them, that there might be better provision made for their support.[6]

Despite society's glorification of the women's sphere, thousands of young women moved from rural homes to cities to find work beginning in the 1830s. They were considered a problem. Often, they worked in the new textile factories, like the Slater Mill in Rhode Island, but these jobs were dangerous and difficult with no real future prospects. Most of these women left and married to assume what society considered their proper role. Educating women for new careers was beyond the scope of Victorian social policy. It was commonly understood that a working life would lead to only bad ends—disease, death, and prostitution.

There was also a strong feeling in society that women simply did not have the qualifications to run a retail business. *Frank Leslie's Ladies Gazette of Fashion* summed up the prevailing opinion in 1857. "Women haven't developed the qualifications—1) they are timid and 2) they are jealous and exclusive. Won't advertise their wares, for fear their names may be placed next to some plebian dealer in the same linen, who sells at a better article at more reasonable price, but in a less aristocratic locality."[7]

Appearances were even more important. "They [middle-class women] also consider if unladylike to have it known, except among friends, that they are obliged to work for a living, and therefore affect an exclusiveness to which few of them have any right, excepting that give them by an overweening pride and vanity."[8]

Not everyone agreed with the tenets of the "women's sphere." Virginia Penny, a former teacher and social reformer, pointed out that society was not looking at women realistically. "Socially, morally, mentally, and religiously, she is written about; but not as a working, every-day reality, in any other capacity than pertaining to home life."[9] She added scornfully:

It is very easy to obtain book after book on "The Sphere of Woman," "The Mission of Woman," and "The Influence of Woman." But to a practical mind it must be evident that good advice is not sufficient. That is very well, provided that the reader is supplied with the comforts of life. But plans need to be devised, pursuits require to be opened, by which women can earn a respectable livelihood. It is the great want of the day.[10]

The author Louisa Mae Alcott would have agreed with Penny. The women of her family spent years struggling at menial jobs to support the idealistic schemes of their philosopher father, Bronson. Years later, in her 1873 novel, *Work*, Alcott looked back at years spent as a paid companion, governess, seamstress, and teacher, jobs she gave to her heroine, Christie, and commented bitterly:

> There are many Christies, willing to work, yet unable to bear the contact with coarser natures which makes labor seem degrading, or to endure the hard struggle for the bare necessities of life when life has lost all that makes it beautiful. People wonder when such as she say they can find little to do; but to those who know nothing of the pangs of pride, the sacrifices of feeling, the martyrdoms of youth, love, hope, and ambition that go on under the faded cloaks of these poor gentlewomen, who tell them to go into factories, or scrub the kitchens, for there is work enough for all, the most convincing answer would be, "Try it."[11]

Since many women knew how to sew, dressmaking and millinery were obvious choices for women who had to work. The author of the *Female Instructor* (Charles Williams Day) suggested this could be the solution for these women. "What if all the garments which are worn by women, were so limited and restrained in the manufacture of them, that they should all be made only by their own sex? This would go a great way toward relief in this case: and what if some of the easier labors of life were reserved for them only?"[12]

Millinery was one of the best of the few jobs a woman could have in the nineteenth-century America. It offered the chance to make a living without sacrificing one's respectability, which made it an acceptable occupation for middle-class or lower-middle-class women, much better than factory work or domestic service.[13]

It was also viewed as work only women could do since it involved the making of decorated, fashionable hats for female customers which meant close contact that would be improper for men to engage in. By the nineteenth century, the work was firmly anchored in the women's sphere. A guide to working women from the 1850s pointed out that this was logical given the nature of the two sexes:

Figure 3 New England bonnet makers, 1866. Picture Collection, The New York Public Library.

Fancy a man making a bonnet—above all, fancy him putting on the trimming. A pretty mess he would make of it! No, a bonnet in all its aspects, is feminine, and should be made and sold as it is worn, solely by the sex for which nature designed it. The proper sphere of women may involve a doubt; but there is no question that millinery, in all its branches, belongs to it. It is just as absurd for a man to engage in any part of it, as it would be for him to parade on Broadway as a gipsey [*sic*].[14]

In the sex-segregated world of fashion, men made hats only for men. Hatters made blocked felt top hats for middle-class men,[15] while cap makers made cloth caps for the men of the working class.

Virginia Penny wrote a milliner needed a special combination of skills: "There are comparatively few persons that make good milliners. As a milliner, one must have good taste and nimble fingers; as a sales woman, she needs to understand human nature, have activity, an honest heart, and good disposition."[16]

Milliners, then, were exalted as creators of works of art, makers of one of the "great wants of civilization."[17] William Burns, the author of a guide to the working women of New York published in the 1850s, called a woman's bonnet "one of the most beautiful of created things, save the face of which it is the

La Modiste. Dessin d'Eugène Lami.

10-937(876-78)

Figure 4 *La Modiste*. Society's ideal, 1876–8. Picture Collection, The New York Public Library.

setting." He added that a milliner needed the skills of an artist, an architect, and a sculptor, which meant that "the milliner shines forth in all the dignity and beauty of a handmaid of Nature, and a priestess of decorative Art. It is her mission to embellish the most charming portion of humanity and to fascinate the other. She bends over her tasteful task during long and weary hours, sustained by the consciousness of the happiness that her labor will impart."[18]

Though most women could sew in the antebellum period, making women's hats was a job that required specialized training.

Milliners . . . possessed skills that distinguished them from the ranks of plain sewers. They transformed a variety of materials—straw, buckram, wire, and silk—into an equally varied number of hat and bonnet shapes. Charged with the task of arranging numerous trimmings in pleasing and ever-changing combinations, they were designers as well as craftsman, artist as well as artisans.[19]

The workroom labor was described in *Godey's* in an August 1834 story.

It was a fine spectacle to behold these active workwomen emulating one another in the dispatch of their task—tilting with their long needles and long scissors. For it may not be useless to remark, in passing, that—distinguishing themselves, also in that matter, from the common herd of workwomen, as the cavalry are distinguished from the infantry, by their long sabers and tall lances—the *modistes* use only scissors and needles of prodigious length.[20]

An apprenticeship was necessary to learn these special skills. During the eighteenth century, young women could board with a milliner and train while assisting the family with other household jobs. In the early nineteenth century, apprenticeships in millinery as in the other needle trades usually stretched over three years. The family of the apprentice, a girl in her early teens, paid a fee to the milliner for this training. If they were lucky, these young women were also taught to read and write, an important part of their training since milliners had to keep accounts, order goods, and keep track of customers' often long overdue payments.[21]

In the 1820s an established milliner like Eliza Oliver Dodds of Washington, DC, carefully kept track of the work of her assistants and apprentices. Two young women came to her as apprentices for a three-year term in 1821. Once they completed their unpaid training, they were hired at $4 a month.[22]

But by the 1840s the apprentice system was breaking down. Apprentices did not live with their bosses anymore but were expected to live at home while they trained or pay for a place to stay, like a boarding house. One proprietor commented: "I don't want a girl who hasn't a good home . . . a girl can't live on $6 a week. It worries me to turn her off in the dull season."[23] This meant that white native-born women predominated in the field since their families could afford to support them through a training period that lasted at least two seasons—spring and fall.[24]

Often employers were reluctant to take new apprentices since it took valuable time to train them, time regular workers could use to turn out more hats. In addition, new inexperienced workers often wasted costly material, which would be a loss a small business would find difficult to sustain. When the apprentice acquired the skills she needed, she would demand to be paid, instead of working "to repay the time and effort expended on teaching her."[25]

The information we have today comes largely from the account books of the head of the millinery shop, like Eliza Dodds, not from the young apprentices themselves. Clearly, many of them would have been victims of cheating and graft by employers who took advantage of their youth and inexperience. An example of this comes from Williams Burns's guide to the New York working woman written around 1850. Burns's guide purports to be a truthful record of their lives with "no namby-pambyism about them; no mawkish sentiment, revamped from the penny-a-line publications of London."[26] He writes of the travails of a young worker in a trade closely related to millinery—a young flower maker who described how she was conned by a male employer:

> They advertise in the papers for girls to learn to make artificial flowers, describing it as a good business. The girls apply and are told that they must work for six months for nothing.[27]

The girl describes how she learned the trade quickly in less than a week, but honored her agreement and worked for six months without pay, only to be fired at the end of her term.

> The man told me that he had no more work for me—that when he had, he would send for me, and he turned me away and engaged six new apprentices before my very face. I understood the trick in a moment.[28]

For the new worker, there was a danger of exploitation. "The cruelty exercised by some milliners and dress makers toward those in their employ, by requiring of them too long and severe application, is very great. Many girls suffer, as the effect, diseases of the spine and the eyes."[29]

Milliners and flower makers had another problem no one anticipated—exposure to arsenic. A bright green pigment containing arsenic was developed by a chemist named Carl Wilhelm Scheele in 1778. The color was vivid, much brighter than the green previously produced by natural dyes, so it soon became a sign of high fashion. It was perfect for coloring bright green leaves on artificial flowers. Flower makers who worked with it developed scabs and ulcers on the skin. Exposure also turned fingernails green. In extreme cases, women died horrible deaths convulsing and vomiting green fluid. The solutions used to color the leaf fabric were so strong milliners were in danger from it too.[30] Milliners were also exposed to arsenic through the birds used throughout the nineteenth century to decorate hats. Taxidermists cured the skins of the birds with arsenic soaps to preserve their underlying tissue, resulting in trims that produced toxic fumes that are still dangerous today.[31]

Observers of the trade fretted about the moral atmosphere of the workroom:

> Often the moral atmosphere of the workroom is not desirable. The work is not of sure nature as to demand the entire attention of the worker, and the opportunities for conversation, except in the height of the rush season, are

many. The older worker has had sufficient experience to be able to discriminate between the true and the false, and to have formed her moral concepts; but the younger worker may be injuriously affected by this atmosphere and should not be exposed to it until she has developed sufficient stamina to resist it.[32]

There was enormous anxiety in society at large about women working in the fashion trades. There was a fear that fashion was becoming too powerful, that middle-class women would ruin their homes and marriages in pursuit of it, not to mention the innocents who slaved to produce it. As one writer put it,

Hard-hearted fashion struts abroad in her plumes, her trains and her mantles forgetful of the famished hands that weaved the woof, and sewed the seams. My lady lives happily in her palatial home, unmindful, if not in ignorance of the wretched dwellings, and the half starved countenances of those martyrs of the needle, who contribute so much to her comfort and adornment.[33]

Women, like milliners, who worked in the fashion trades were often portrayed as merciless exploiters and their workers were drawn as their pathetic victims. Even Virginia Penny cautioned: "The making and selling of bonnets has long been one of the few employments open to women in the United States. If a milliner gets a good run of fashionable women, she can do well. Most proprietors of millinery establishments make a handsome profit on their goods, but some of the girls employed receive but a pittance."[34]

Since they were the workers that many middle-class people came in contact with regularly, the seamstress and milliner became the objects of fascination. They were depicted in the penny press art of the day as pale figures with downcast faces and eyes turned up to heaven working in miserable, dark garrets.[35] It was assumed such a life would lead to only bad ends, disease and death or prostitution. One of the most popular poems of the day, Thomas Hood's "Song of the Shirt" which reinforced these fears with stanzas like:

With fingers weary and worn,
With eyelids heavy and red,
A woman sat in unwomanly rags,
Lying her needle and thread—
Stitch! Stitch! Stitch!
In poverty, hunger and dirt,
And still with a voice of dolorous pitch
She sang the "Song of the Shirt!"[36]

The poem continues for eleven more stanzas rich in Victorian images of death including the line: "Sewing at once with double thread, / A Shroud as well as a Shirt."[37]

Milliners were the subject of a vast amount of literature for the upper and middle classes. These tales had the same basic plot—a virtuous, beautiful young woman leaves home for the city where evil awaits her. One example from the 1840s is *The Milliner's Girl; or Authentic and Interesting Adventures of Fanny Bilson, a Country Clergyman's Daughter*. It is worth examining its convoluted, preposterous plot to understand the level of controlled hysteria and worry these unattached young women provoked.

Fanny Bilson is the beautiful, innocent fifteen-year-old daughter of a poor Welsh clergyman who can give her no dowry. So, she sets out for London to learn the millinery trade. Fanny learns the millinery trade well. Soon she is assigned to work in the shop where she immediately attracts admirers, who she finds "impertinent and troublesome."[38] But, one of them, Sir William, persuades her to go to Vauxhall Gardens, a pleasure garden with many lovers' lanes. Fanny finds herself alone and unchaperoned with Sir William after dark. He tries to "take liberties with her."[39] The stakes are high. She turns his advances down and pleads with him, "I shall be quite ruined; my mistress will not receive me again; my character will be lost; and no people of reputation will receive me into their homes."[40]

Salvation of a sort appears. Mr. Johnson, the brother of a family friend, pulls up in a hackney and challenges Sir William. Relieved, Fanny gets in his carriage, only to find out that he thinks she is a fallen woman too. In an incredible plot twist, it turns out she already spent the night with him on her trip to London! He was disguised as a woman because he shot a lord. That means that Fanny actually spent the night with a man, even though she didn't know it! The two then have a debate about Fanny's innocence (since any lapse would be considered her fault). It is worth quoting the logic here: "And why must I spare you. . . . I considered you sufficiently when I had you entirely at my mercy. I then spared you, merely from compassion to your youth and inexperience; but as Sir William has reaped the fruits of my consideration for you; there is no occasion that I should submit to your toying it with me."[41]

Her rescuer takes her to his home and tries to get her drunk. Finally, she persuades him to let her sleep alone. The next morning, she goes back to Mrs. T's in disgrace and asks to return home.

The assaults on her virtue aren't over yet. Sir William shows up and offers to make her a kept woman with a settlement of 500 pounds a year for life. Finally, Mr. Johnson appears again and offers to go home with her because he is convinced of her chaste nature. After all this, Fanny confesses her love for him. They go home to her father where they will be married. After all the trials of working life, Fanny has achieved the only safety available—marriage.

Fanny Bilson's virtue was threatened no matter what she did. The simple fact that she could be compromised by her night with a man disguised a woman is strange enough to us today, but she was threatened at every turn. The fact that she is out late at night meant she could never go back to Mrs. T's who will not protect her. Strolling in Vauxhall Gardens makes her suspect. The entire story is a warning of the dangers of being young and alone in the world outside the home. It was a lesson repeated over and over.

On the other hand, women who owned millinery shops were often portrayed as old women who were merciless exploiters. "Miss. Slimmens' Window," which appeared in *Godey's* on January 1859, tells the story of a milliner who is past the bloom of youth and "has been compelled, for the last ten years at least, to resort to 'artificials,'"[42] such as fake hair, false teeth, and a back brace. Miss S. seems to do her work well, but there her shop is not an inviting place. "Some of her neighbors have been heard to insinuate that the smell of brimstone [sulphur was used to clean old hats] about her premises did not proceed entirely from the covered barrel which set in the backyard."[43] In short, Miss Slimmens is an old hag, even though the story tells us she is not yet thirty years old. The whole story is devoted to her ridiculous efforts to snare a husband. One young man steals $700 from her and runs off with one of her apprentices. Another disappears after she has paid his debts. The cruel humor of this story makes it very clear society's view of an unmarried older woman who must work for a living. Miss Slimmens is the reverse side of the beautiful, young Fanny, a lone woman who was not saved by marriage.

Even Virginia Penny cautioned the snares of fashion could lead to a bad end. "A love of dress is said to be created by working at such articles. Many bad effects must result from the indulgence of such a taste by those who receive the small wages of most girls working at the millinery and dress-making business."[44]

Despite such fears, women continued to seek millinery work. By 1871 the Beecher sisters complained this lure was contributing to the shortage of domestic servants:

> Young women are eagerly rushing into every other employment, till feminine trades and callings are all overstocked. We are constantly harrowed with tales of the sufferings of distressed needlewomen, of the extractions and extortions practiced on the frail sex in the many branches of labor and trade at which they try their hands; and yet women will encounter all these chances of ruin and starvation rather than make up their minds to permanent domestic service.[45]

It can be difficult to determine exactly how many women worked in the millinery trade in the early part of the nineteenth century since the census did not list women by occupation. When that information was finally included in 1870, millinery was fourth in the list of occupations for women with domestic service first.[46]

New York City was preeminent in the American fashion world. Its huge harbor did not freeze in the winter so the city dominated the Atlantic trade. Fashions from Europe arrived quickly in the city and were dispersed throughout the country via the Erie Canal. All this business activity spurred manufacturing, including a large garment trade. A decade before the Civil War, one writer commented caustically on how long it took new fashions to arrive in the land across the Hudson:

> It is strange, but no less strange than true, that though the distance between New York and Philadelphia is reduced to less than a half a day's travel, it takes a year or more for the New York fashions to get to Philadelphia, and many of them never arrive at all. . . . Our American ladies derive all their ideas of costume from France; and as New York rejoices in the most extensive and the most speedy intercourse with that land of taste and elegance, the French fashions always get there first.[47]

Virginia Penny reported by 1863 there were 450 millinery establishments in the city with 1,800 workers toiling in shops and 900 at home turning out 35,000 bonnets in the fall and spring seasons. "Of straw bonnets, one million two hundred thousand are sold annually to the milliners of New York for the trade alone."[48] Millinery work was spread out over the city from high-end shops on Broadway to places further downtown where conditions were much worse. "On back streets and avenues in New York, women work longer, and the stores are kept open later than on Broadway. On Division Street,[49] large cases of bonnets are exposed for sale in summer on the sidewalks. In the poorer parts of a city, people live much and sell mostly out of doors. Their crowded apartments and the high price of rent account for it."[50]

Despite the difficult conditions, the young milliners were often a feisty lot. If we look carefully behind the main characters of the tales of milliners in the popular press, we see young women in the millinery workroom engaging in behavior that is decidedly unladylike, "laughing unrestrainedly, singing and talking wildly."[51] In New York, these young working women were most visible promenading along the Bowery, a street lined with dance halls, theaters, and oyster wagons. Here they could meet and mix with young working-class men. The "g'hals" who had the skills to produce their own clothes rejected the ladylike modest style of the antebellum era. They wore bright colors and bonnets tilted back on the heads leaving their faces exposed.[52] The Bowery groups were so well known they became the lead characters in a series of plays featuring Mose, the brave "b'hoy," and his loyal girlfriend, Lize, working-class figures that attained semi-mythic stature in theaters nationally.[53]

William Burns, who wrote a study of working women in New York in the 1850s, told of another advantage of becoming a milliner which would have appealed to middle-class Victorians. A milliner would be more likely to find a husband. As evidence, he describes how Ellen Stanley, whose father lost his fortune, managed to become a fashionable milliner. Even more important, she was able to meet and "marry a man worthy of so much prudence, energy, beauty, and virtue."[54] Burns

POSITION OF A WIRING HALL.

Figure 5 Milliners in the wiring hall. Picture Collection, The New York Public Library.

also includes examples of other women workers whose work leads to their ruin. The artificial flower maker was not only cheated by her employer but pursued by loose men in her shabby rooming house. Many of his examples like an umbrella maker and a straw braider and a widowed dressmaker ended up as prostitutes. In this depressing picture, only the milliner seems to have any hope of rising and marrying, perhaps because of her exposure to men in classes above her.

Though there was work available, working women faced the problem of extremely low pay. Women earned 50 to 60 percent less than men. Indeed, a study in 1833 from Philadelphia found three-quarters of the working women there had to work seventy-eight hours a week to equal what a man earned for a ten-hour day.[55] "The time milliners and dressmakers spend at their work is such as to preclude (except in a few first-class establishments) any time for exercise and mental culture. Their wages are so low that they could not indulge in any recreation if they had the time."[56]

Sarah Grimké commented on the discrepancy acidly,

In those employments which are peculiar to women, their time is estimated at only half the value of that of men. A woman who goes out to wash, works as hard in proportion as a wood sawyer, or a coal heaver, but she is not generally able to make more than half as much by a day's work. . . . All these things evince the low estimation in which women is held.[57]

Women workers could not expect support from the male working class either. In 1833 craftsmen from nine trades attempted to form a union. The General Trades Union of the City of New York or GTU grew quickly, so quickly that by 1836 it staged a rally of 30,000 workmen to protest the sentencing of 20 tailors who had gone on strike. By 1834, the union made a national push, forming the National Trades Union (NTU). The GTU and NTU even opened up to immigrant workers in the drive for fair wages, but blacks and women were excluded. When tailoresses attempted to join their ranks, they were told to return to the home. The women attempted to form their own union, which collapsed without male support. The solution to low wages for women was the "family wage"; that is, working men should be paid enough to afford to keep their wives at home, like the wives of the middle class. Then, the Panic of 1837 shattered the nascent labor movement.[58] It revived in the 1850s—for men only. Trade unionism would not be possible for women until the twentieth century.

Upper-class women attempted to speak for women of the lower classes, but the divide was just too wide. A "Mrs. Jenkins" wrote in *Godey's Ladies Book* in 1852 about a Bible class she taught in the crowded working district of Manhattan: "It was very easy for me to go round in my silk dress and white kid gloves, and preach up self-denial and industry to them, out of our Sunday's lesson, and they practicing it all the time, in those dark filthy alleys swarming with pigs and children."[59] Mrs. Jenkins could see that the poor working and living conditions her Bible students lived in undid the effect of her lessons.

> One of them [a milliner] sewed straw bonnets; . . . no wonder they can sell them so cheap, when they only get ten cents apiece for them! . . . Others worked in crowded milliner shops from Monday morning till Saturday night, for a dollar and half, mixing with good and bad—the Monday's talk with their comrades undoing all the good of Sunday's lessons. . . . A girl could hardly have a worse moral atmosphere than one of those work-rooms.[60]

Concern for the hard-working milliners faded when customers wanted their orders on time as one observer discovered.

> "But I suppose they don't work all night," said I, with a surprised accent. "I should think all day was sufficient."
>   "But indeed they do, Miss May. In the season they sit up all night." "How cruel of their employers," cried I indignantly, "to treat them so. Why they are worse off than slaves."

"Ah! That they are," said she, "but it is not the fault of the milliners and dressmakers, it is the fault of the ladies, who want their things made in such a hurry. They never give time enough; that's where the fault lies."[61]

No matter how hard women worked, their employers often looked down on them. A good example is Mr. D, a manufacturer of straw goods on Broadway. Mr. D. complained his employees spent all the money they earned on clothes. "He has two forewomen, to each of whom he pays $500 a year. They never save a cent. He has one to whom he paid $1,000, but she never laid by a dollar."[62] Most of D's workers were paid $3 to $8 a week, but only after they spent four months training without pay and committed to working ten- to twelve-hour days.

Still, D complained that his workers did not take the time to keep up with the current styles.

Women, he thinks, have not as much originality of thought as men. . . . He walks on Broadway, and studies the fashion of bonnets; but none of his women ever do. (Perhaps they have no time.) He goes on to put forth a common complaint about women workers. Women, he thinks, never acquire such proficiency as men. They advance to a certain degree in the art, and ever after are stationary. He thinks it is partly because the majority looks forward to marrying, and partly because they are so constituted that they are not susceptible of acquiring the highest degree of excellence.[63]

Virginia Penny saw through this prejudiced point of view, writing: "I fear D. does not consider that women have not had as much time not so many opportunities for improving themselves as men."[64] Not many others in Victorian society did.

Milliners faced another problem—layoffs. Workers would be hired for the busy seasons, preparing hats for spring and fall. Most would be laid off in late summer and after Christmas with no prospect of being rehired when the next season approached.

With wages so low women were unable to provide basic necessities like food and shelter, it is no surprise some women drifted into prostitution. This was backed up by a survey by Dr. William Sanger in 1858 who found that a quarter of the 2,000 women he surveyed in New York's House of Refuge were victims of low ages and irregular employment. Sanger was unusual for this time because he did not blame the women. He cited male employers who "drive a woman into starvation by refusing her employment, and then condemn her for maintaining a wretched existence at the price of her virtue."[65] Milliners were linked in the public mind to prostitution along with others in the garment trades, including dressmakers, tailoresses, and artificial flower makers, even though Sanger found that 47 percent of the prostitutes he studied were former domestic servants. Articles in the flash press, the gossip sheets of the day, were full of stories about milliners who picked up men in millinery shops and took them to a nearby brothel. Illustrations showed milliners in sexually revealing poses. These stories reinforced the prevailing view in society that the fault lay in the lax morals of the milliners. The fact that some women did turn to prostitution, which Victorians viewed as a danger to the moral fiber of the entire society, lead to the conclusion that women should not work since they would inevitably succumb to temptation.

But even with all its problems, the millinery business was considered work that would always be needed as long as women loved fashion. "With 2000 women here, wearing bonnets, and in a nation of ten millions of bonneted women, millinery looms up, an extensive and important business. Here is one of the great wants of civilization supplied by a female industry; for this is essentially feminine employment."[66]

Those words were written in the 1850s. By the end of the decade, it seemed women were well settled in their "proper" place. Women were becoming more active in the public sphere, agitating for property rights of married women, temperance, and abolition of slavery. As society became industrialized and more complicated, the need for some relief from coverture led to women's conferences for rights, most notably at the Seneca Falls conference in 1848.

But, leading opinion writers like Catherine Beecher argued right-thinking women knew their place:

> I never observed that the women of America considered conjugal authority as a fortunate usurpation of their rights, nor that they thought themselves degraded by submitting to it. It appears to me, on the contrary, that they attach a sort of pride to the voluntary surrender of their own will and make it their boast to bend themselves to the yoke, not to shake it off. Such, at least, is the feeling expressed by the most virtuous of their sex; the other are silent; and in the United States it is not the practice for a guilty wife to clamor for the rights of woman, while she is trampling upon her holiest duties.[67]

The influential editor of Godey's Ladies Book, Sara Josepha Hale, seemed oblivious to her own active work life when she wrote: "In civil governments the laws must, in the last resort, be upheld by material force. This duty women could not perform; nor could they share in the government, unless the other sex permitted."[68]

But the prevailing feeling about women's rights came from "Miss Leslie" in an 1853 etiquette book for ladies: "Men make fortunes, women make livings. And none make poorer livings than those who waste their time, and bore their friends, by writing and lecturing upon the equality of the sexes, and what they call 'Women's Rights.' How is it that most of these ladies live separately from their husbands; either despising them, or being despised by them?"[69]

By the middle of the century, women in the millinery trade had carved out what historian Wendy Gamber calls "a female economy," an exclusively female world that enabled women to establish work lives and businesses that may have been precarious and subject to failure, but allowed women entry, much like Rose Bertin in eighteenth-century France. There was the alluring possibility of great success and the attraction of the beautiful which drew women to the trade. The business of millinery was viewed as a constant need of women of all classes.

The Civil War would crack the antebellum world in ways they could not have anticipated. When it ended in 1864, thousands of women had been forced to work in new jobs, such as farming, clerical help, and nursing simply because so many men died on the battlefield or were so badly injured they could no longer work. The production of fashion would begin to change too. The war drove the development of ready-made clothing, initially for men. The fashion world would begin to expand faster and faster, moving away from the production of one-of-a-kind custom products, like women's hats. The changes were far in the future, but the wheels had been set in motion.

3
WAR AND MILLINERY

In the beginning, no one expected the war that exploded in 1860 to last long. Southerners in the newly formed Confederate States of America did not think the states remaining in the Union would contest their secession. In the North, it was felt that the region's industrial superiority would enable its army to triumph quickly. Instead, the war was the most destructive in the nation's history. Between 1861 and 1865, 620,000 soldiers and 50,000 civilians died, a figure equal to the total of all the American dead in the Revolution, the War of 1812, the Mexican War, the Spanish-American War, the First and Second World Wars, and the Korean War.[1] The impact of these deaths of young men in their prime affected the lives of women and children on both sides. The next decade would change women's lives profoundly. The Civil War was a destructive force on the home front as well as the battlefield.

This war has often been cited by historians as one which gave women more opportunities to move into the wider world, but that was often traumatic as Virginia Penny pointed out:

> At no time in our country's history have so many women been thrown on their own exertions. A million of men are on the battlefield, and thousands of women, formerly dependent on them, have lost or may lose their only support. Some of the mothers, wives, sisters and daughters of soldiers, may take the vacancies created in business by their absence—others must seek new channels of labor.[2]

The call to arms affected women on both sides of the Mason-Dixon line. The absence of men threw women on both sides on their own resources. Before shots were fired at Fort Sumter, the battle that launched the war, those in the North had already experienced the beginnings of the Industrial Revolution. Factories had been established. Some women and children were some of the first to be employed in them. Transportation had been improved. The region had a thriving commercial economy. Yet, most of the population was still rural, living and working on farms and in small shops.[3] Women had grown up conditioned to believe in the domestic sphere. Little in their background prepared them for the often crushing responsibilities the war would bring to their homes and families.[4] Women had to take on new roles to replace the absent men. They often worked their farms, filled men's places in government offices, and volunteered to go into the field and nurse the wounded.

Since the army did not have a medical corps, the Sanitary Commission was formed. Supervised by mental health reformer Dorothea Dix, women were enlisted to run kitchens in army camps, run hospital ships, administrate soldiers' homes, and make uniforms. Dix only wanted middle-aged white women. She felt younger women might be husband-hunting in the hospitals. Her directive specifies, "All nurses are required to be plain looking women. Their dresses must be brown or black, with no bows, no curls, no jewelry, and no hoops."[5] But when the commission sent out a call for volunteers to serve as nurses, hundreds showed up in Washington to apply.

The army also needed new bedding, uniforms, and tents, all articles made of textiles that women could produce since many of them had been working on piecework before the war. One hundred thousand jobs opened up for seamstresses. Often, these women were exploited by male bosses who sought to pay them as little as possible and packed them into cramped work spaces.[6]

A few women had worked in the Patent Office and the US Mint before the war. More were hired to fill men's vacant places in the Treasury, War Department, and the Post Office.

None of these jobs were open to African American women, who faced even more pressing needs when their men entered the service. African American soldiers were paid less and often paid late. The decreased income of white women meant they had less money to spend on extra help.[7]

Many of the white women engaged in volunteer work to help the troops. To support the work of the Sanitary Commission, women formed Soldiers' Aid Societies where they collected and sent supplies, like handknit socks to replace the uncomfortable machine-made socks issued to soldiers by the army. There were thousands of these relief organizations. The New England Women's Auxiliary Association alone received donations from fifty-two towns across the state in 1863.[8] African American women in the North formed their own societies. Their priorities were somewhat different since they sent help to former slaves in the South as well as soldiers.[9]

Women also held fundraising fairs, which successfully raised large sums for the Sanitary Commission. A fair in Chicago in 1863 raised more than $100,000. The amounts raised escalated. A fair in Cincinnati raised $280,000, while one in Pittsburgh took in $320,000. The largest fair by far was held in New York City in April 1864, which pulled in close to two million dollars.[10] These were just a few of the fairs that were held across the North, all organized and staffed by women.

Some husbands objected to their wives working in "trade." General William Tecumseh Sherman wrote to his wife, "I don't approve of ladies selling things at a table. So far as superintending the management of such things, I don't object, but it merely looks unbecoming for a lady to stand behind a table and sell things. Still, do as you please."[11] Most men accepted the new roles since they were for the Commission and the war effort.

Enough women were working by 1863, the same year Virginia Penny published her huge compendium on jobs for women, *The Employments of Women*; she was able to list 519 occupations ranging from professional women like astronomers to rag and cinder gatherers. The pragmatic Penny saw beyond the need to fill wartime vacancies. She observed:

> There is a large amount of female talent in the United States lying dormant for want of cultivation, and there has been a huge amount cultivated that is not brought into exercises for want of definite plans and opportunities of making it available. . . . Widen, then, the theatres of notion and enterprise for women. Throw open productive fields of labor and let her enter.[12]

The situation in the South was quite different since most of the war was fought on its land. Southern women were subjected to the destruction of their property and a lack of consumer goods due to the weak Confederate economy. But, there was another problem. Southern women were not prepared to work for the war effort. While women in the North were exposed to the discussion of women's rights and an examination of the women's sphere before the war, the question of women's rights had virtually no impact in the South. Indeed, Southern women were convinced their system was superior and that they occupied a class that continued the tradition of the chivalry. One writer proclaimed: "The people of our Northern States, who hold that domestic slavery is unjust and iniquitous are consistent with their attempts to modify or abolish the marriage tradition."[13] This elite tradition depended on slaves to do the work of the household and the farm, so when the system began to crumble, white women were poorly prepared to cope. Historian Drew Gilpin Faust writes that the hard work of the household, like laundry, cooking, and childcare, had been handled by slaves. When these slaves departed, women were thrown on their own resources to do jobs they had never done before. "Socialized to believe in their own weakness and sheltered from the necessity of performing even life's basic tasks, white women felt almost crippled by their unpreparedness for the new lives war had brought."[14]

A few well-connected women were able to get patronage jobs in the Confederate Treasury Department, where fine handwriting was the prime requirement.[15] Other women of the lower classes worked in the Clothing Department making uniforms. As for nursing, few actually volunteered despite the Confederacy's efforts to recruit them.[16]

There were groups formed to supply the troops, but the effort was not nearly as well coordinated as it was in the North. The efforts were hindered by lack of supplies due to a naval blockade imposed by the Union. A notice in a Savannah (Georgia) paper shows the need for hand-knitted socks: "Ladies Knitting Society: Having been unable for sometime past, to supply the demand for thread for Soldiers' socks, we would inform our lady friends, that we have now enough thread for two or three hundred pairs, and they are greatly needed. The cold weather will soon be upon us, and we must not forget our soldiers."[17] Though many women tried to make these practical goods, knitting socks and making bandages for soldiers was a new skill for many of them. In the years before the war elite Southern women restricted their handwork to embroidery and fancywork, skills that were useless in time of war. There were fundraising fairs too, but none on the scale of the Sanitary Fairs in the North.

Not all men in the North served and not all women suffered. Some Northern men were able to pay another man to fight in their place. That freed many of them to engage in wartime profiteering, producing inferior goods, underpaying workers, like the seamstresses mentioned earlier, and making huge profits. They were derisively nicknamed "The Shoddy Aristocracy"—a name that grew out of term for inferior cloth made of waste wool that many war profiteers used to make soldiers' uniforms.

The Shoddies spent their money lavishly on fashion. In 1863, the newly wealthy promenaded down New York's Fifth Avenue in their new finery and spent their money at A. T. Stewart's "New Store," a five-floor shopping palace with rows of displays of tempting textiles like silks and fancy goods for the many balls of the social season. The store not only sold fine goods—it produced them. Five hundred women and girls worked on the fourth floor turning out clothing on the new sewing machines, while 300 more women worked in the linen department on the fifth floor.[18] That was just one example. Shoddies appeared in cities like Philadelphia and Cincinnati, any city that was geared up for military production. Their showy wealth produced a backlash. *Harper's Weekly* published several satirical stories featuring "Mrs. Clementina Shoddy" and her mother "Mrs. Shoddy" who entertained themselves "by dancing and making merry, and throwing away fortunes on diamonds" at the same time "our brothers and sons are dying on battle-fields."[19] In 1864 a group of wealthy women in New York City formed the Women's Patriotic Association for Diminishing the Use of Imported Luxuries in an effort to deflect the charges of extravagance. They signed a pledge to boycott imported fashions for three years or the duration of the war.[20] They were ridiculed since most women in the North had already given up much more than fashion. Clara Barton, who nursed soldiers on the battlefields of Antietam, Fredericksburg, and Cold Harbor, commented acidly: "They must go beyond wearing apparel before it will reach me, when they get down to bread and water, I will listen to them. . . . I have no time to join in dress festival."[21]

But, the war did not stop the desire for fashionable, acceptable dress. Women's fashion magazines like *Godey's* and *Petersen's* were published throughout the war. Neither magazine mentioned the war at all except for references to the business climate, like "The season is unusually late in opening, owing to the financial embarrassments of midwinter, the time when most of our large importing houses are beginning to receive their goods."[22] The styles shown were taken directly from French plates and showed dresses made with lavish amounts of material, decorated with expensive trims. Each outfit on the plate showed the proper headgear for each outfit trimmed with the same expensive materials as the dresses.

Milliners would have had plenty of work since styles of headgear changed throughout the 1860s. Women's hats were shown in the newest shape made to accommodate the new hairstyles which often used hairpieces which enlarged the head size. Hats and bonnets were smaller and perched on the head rather than encircling it. A woman from Ohio wrote delightedly about the new bonnet she bought in New York in 1863: "I have purchased my winter bonnet—it is green velvet with plumes to match and pink face trimming. The bonnets are not so large as they were last winter. I shall be sorry if large bonnets go out of style for I think they were so pretty."[23] Many women probably modified their old hats and bonnets to fit the new styles, but milliners would still have had a market for new trims to change the look of the hat. They would also be enlisted to clean and recondition last season's chapeaux. Women in the North had to be careful since they could be the subject of malicious gossip if they followed fashion too closely: "A new frock, a fancy hat, an unguarded comment to another man: all these could be, and often were, taken as indications of the unchaperoned woman's moral depravity."[24]

Of course, following fashion was a problem in the South. Women with means tried to get fashionable clothing from Europe or the North that was smuggled by blockade-runners.[25] Most women had to rely on recycling their dresses and hats. There was an effort across the region to produce cloth and clothing from scratch, which was promoted as a woman's patriotic duty. This work had previously been the work of slaves, so many women had trouble adjusting to the change in their status and to the amount of work involved in textile production.[26] They were hindered further by a lack of equipment, such as combing cards and spinning wheels.[27]

Women's hats and bonnets were still custom made by hand. Women still needed hats, war or no war, as going out without the proper head covering was unimaginable. This was true not just for the elite but for working-class women too. Fashion historian Valerie Steele points out how important accessories, like hats, were for women of the time: "Accessories had considerable significance as indicators of class, age, and occupation. Hats (and gloves) were crucial to a 'respectable' appearance for both men and women. It was not fear of cold or sunstroke that kept hats on, nor even the longstanding association of uncovered female hair with eroticism. To go bareheaded was simply not proper."[28]

As the war raged on and men on both sides died from wounds on the battlefield or from disease, the need for proper mourning attire, which included the correct bonnet and veil, arose. *Godey's* published illustrations of proper mourning dress for all occasions throughout the war. They were shown next to other fashionable dress and echoed them in cut and silhouette. Hats and bonnets had to follow fashion too. To follow the rules of etiquette properly, new millinery was needed for each stage of mourning from deep black to lilac, gray, and purple. Since the construction of bonnets required skills most women didn't have, a milliner would have been needed to produce the right hat or bonnet. The right materials and craftswomen were available in the North, but they still required an extra expense at a time when budgets were tight. In the South, acquiring the proper mourning dress was expensive and difficult since materials had to come through the blockade. But the need for proper mourning dress went beyond the demands of rigid Victorian etiquette, so women struggled to wear the right bonnet and all-encompassing veil of heavy crape to give their sorrow a visible form.[29]

So, milliners still worked, as women struggled to maintain the proper ways of dressing on the home front, since "it was something more than an industry, . . . this creation of ever-varied settings for the face of fortunate womanhood."[30]

Making a hat was complex work. Though the onset of the Industrial Revolution meant that machines did more and more mechanical work for trades like dressmaking, the skills involved in making custom millinery did not change appreciably until the late 1910s. Elizabeth Beardsley Butler in her 1907 study of the millinery trade in Pittsburgh pointed out: "The progress of a hat, in all its absurd contortions of shape, from factory workroom to wearer, through the hands of shaper, maker and trimmer, has given rise to a set of trade conditions in some respects unique, and a group of workers unlike in training and in opportunity to the workers in the other needle trades."[31]

By the 1860s, work at the millinery table in most shops was a complex hierarchy best described in Edith Wharton's *House of Mirth* published in 1905. Lily Bart, Edith Wharton's feckless heroine, sets out to acquire a trade and learns becoming a milliner will not be easy. At first, Lily dreamed of her own shop where her good taste would bring her a living:

> Here was, after all, something her charming listless hands could really do; she had no doubt of their capacity for knotting a ribbon or placing a flower to advantage. And of course, only these finishing touches would be expected of her: subordinate fingers, blunt, grey, needle-pricked fingers, would prepare the shapes and stitch the linings while she presided over the charming little front shop—a shop all white panels, mirrors, and moss-green hangings—where her finished creations, hats, wreaths, aigrettes and the rest, perched on their stands like birds just poising for flight.[32]

Figure 6 Foreman criticizing work. Photography Collection, Miriam and Ira D. Wallach Division of Art, Prints and Photographs, The New York Public Library.

But that dream shop was not to be. Lily had no one to back her. Her friends prevailed on Mme. Regina to employ Lily. "Even this arrangement was not effected without considerable negotiation, for Mme. Regina had a strong prejudice against untrained assistance."[33] So, Lily ended up at a workroom table with twenty other young women desperately trying to sew with the neat invisible stitches required for fine millinery. She was an apprentice, the bottom of the complex pecking order. Apprentices started by learning to bind brim edges, which was monotonous, but taught the fundamental millinery stitches and familiarized the worker with the handling of wire and buckram, materials that are difficult to handle. In the next phase, the apprentice learned hat lining, wire bows, hemming silks and velvets, shirring materials, making folds and facings, sewing on braids—all work that had to be done so stitches were invisible. Another study of the industry wrote: "Ability to sew firmly and to tack is a prime requisite in millinery."[34] Finally, apprentices learned the crucial process of making wire frames, the foundation of the hats of the time. None of this work was considered creative, but it was essential.

Handling millinery materials so as to obtain an artistic appearance requires practice, and while it is not surprising that an apprentice often complains that she did nothing but make bands or folds, she thus shows that she fails to realize that these afford practice in a b c's of her trade which should be learned with as little expense as possible to her employer. Much of the work is difficult and hard to "pick up," so that the making processes as a rule must be learned.[35]

Apprenticeships usually lasted two seasons, so the beginner could learn summer work which would involve working with straw and winter work which would entail working with heavier materials like velvet. Lily Bart would never make it that far.

Lily had taken up her work in January: it was now two months later and she was still being rebuked for her inability to sew spangles on a hat-frame. As she returned to her work she heard a titter pass down the tables. . . . Remote was the day when she might aspire to exercise the talents she felt confident of possessing; only experienced workers were entrusted with the delicate art of shaping and trimming the hat, and the forewoman still held her inexorably to the routine of preparatory work.[36]

Next in the chain of production was the "maker" who took the frames made by the apprentices and covered them with materials ranging from straw, velvet, chiffon, or silk. This work required great attention to detail since a wrong cut ruined expensive fabric. The maker was usually only guided by a sketch and a few measurements.[37] Covering a frame was not a simple process since the frames came in every conceivable shape. Fashions changed quickly from season to season, so covering them required great skill and attention to detail.[38] Because of the precision involved an apprentice could not expect to move up into such a position quickly.

Most shops of any size employed a copyist, who copied the frame and trimming of a model hat from fashion centers like Paris or New York. This was considered more creative work than that of the maker. Often the copyist changed the color, size, and materials of the model, but she was not able to initiate any new designs. Her work was imitative. The final product had to resemble the original, which the shop owner had paid a hefty sum to procure. Considerable skill was needed to produce a copy that was beautiful and well crafted. However, the copyist did not have the creative latitude given the worker at the top of the workroom pyramid, the trimmer.[39]

The apprentices, makers, and copyists were the first parts of the process. The next steps were considered the artistic jobs, the ones that transformed the hat into a thing of beauty. The trimmer was the head of the "table." It was difficult to rise to this level from an apprenticeship since it was a maxim of the millinery that "a good maker is never a good trimmer."[40] Trimmers seemed to learn their work by careful observation and practice and probably a great deal of good luck and timing. Trims gave each hat the distinctive custom touch. Each trimmer headed a table of three to eight makers and apprentices. She was not just responsible for the artistic finish of the hat but had to make sure each customer was properly fitted and had to keep a sharp eye out for poor workmanship.[41] The job was made more difficult by the fact that millinery styles were constantly changing, requiring new skills.

Larger, very exclusive shops were able to employ a designer, whose job involved coming up with new styles and shapes, then making models of them for display. The designer was not responsible for helping with customers' orders, so her work was an expensive luxury most shops could not afford.[42]

Because there was such need for a large number of workers to turn out the basic product, it was difficult to move up.

Unless a girl has taste and talent, she is not likely to be benefited even by a year's apprenticeship, for it is rarely the case that they are instructed in what is becoming or stylish, what shades are most harmonious, how to make a graceful bow, and turn out a well-trimmed end, to arrange a face trimming, and render attractive the *tout-ensemble*.[43]

Lily Bart worked for a high-end milliner who could afford to have a table of twenty milliners. Not all aspiring milliners worked at such a large, profitable shop. Many in small cities and towns eked out a living attaching themselves to employer

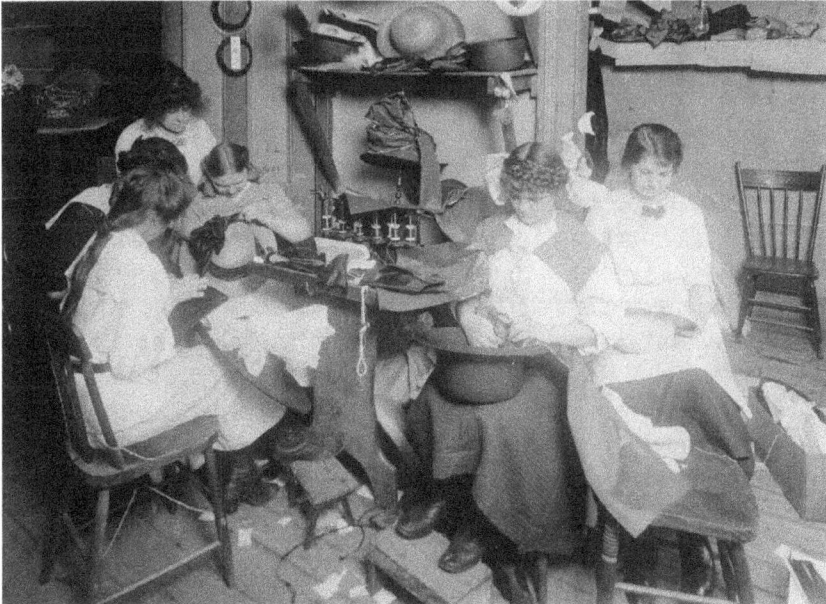

Figure 7 Training an apprentice. Photography Collection, Miriam and Ira D. Wallach Division of Art, Prints and Photographs, The New York Public Library.

after employer season after season. There are few records of these women's lives, so it is worth examining the diary of one young Maine milliner to gain an understanding of daily work life during the war. Emma Ann Foster of Gray, Maine, began to write in her new diary along with her sister Sarah Jane on January 1, 1864. Both sisters knew they were living in turbulent times. Faraway on the battlefields of Louisiana, their brother Howard was fighting in the Thirtieth Regiment Maine Infantry.[44] Controversy over the war and President Abraham Lincoln swirled around them, yet both sisters were deeply concerned about something else—their own independence. The chief topic of each girl's diary is work. There was endless work at home. But, in 1864, both would struggle to establish lives for themselves away from home. Sarah Jane longed to be a writer and crusader for the rights of the downtrodden,[45] while her worldlier sister, Emma, sought to get the training to become a milliner.

At the beginning of the year, eighteen-year-old Emma was still in school, helping with her father's shoemaking business and with many, many household jobs that kept a household running in the nineteenth century—ironing, cleaning, washing laundry, and chopping wood. There was limited opportunity in rural Gray for a young woman. Emma would have to move 23 miles to Portland, the biggest city in Maine, to get the right training.

Finding an apprenticeship was not easy since the Fosters did not want their daughter to run into danger in the big city of Portland, Maine, 23 miles away. This was made even more complicated since apprenticeships did not pay. A young woman apprentice usually had to pay for the privilege of training in a milliner's shop. By the 1860s, apprentices did not get free room and board from their masters, so they were faced with the additional burden of finding a place to live and paying for that too.[46] Emma apparently had enough sewing experience that she could seek a paying job, but it still was not easy to find a "respectable" one that would please her parents.

On April 27, Emma wrote, "I got a letter from Caleb [her older brother] today he says Sweetsir [a Portland bonnet manufacturer] will hire me if I will come down and work on trial, but as I can't see it in that light I shant [sic] go til [sic] I hear from them again."[47] Since this meant Emma would have to work a month without pay, she declined. Finally, a deal was worked out. On May 6, Emma moved to Portland to learn the millinery trade. She would sew straw at Sweetsir's Bonnet Bleachery and help out in the millinery shop with Mrs. Sweetsir.[48] She seemed to be glad to get away from her father's shoe business since she wrote, "Father paid me 50 cts [ ] all that he has paid me $3.50 and he now owes me $3.20. It is for work and stitching."[49]

The next day Emma wrote of her new job: "Rather dull work like mending."[50] However, she adds, "If I can only learn to work fast if I can I think I shall do well."[51] Straw bonnet making was demanding work, but it paid better than many other jobs for women in 1864. An employer told *Harper's*, "The girls in straw shops earn more than in most other kinds of business, they being, as a general thing, smarter girls, and such as would not work in cotton and other large mills."[52] In her first week of work, Emily was paid $1.10 as a beginner. The next week she received $3.50. By September 10, when she left she was making $4.50, but her board was $2.50 a week, which left little for clothes and food. When Emma paid $6.00 for a cloak and $6.77 for a nice dress, she used nearly three weeks' wages.[53] Hours were long. She worked six days a week, ten hours a day, often taking work home at night to finish it as she did on June 11: "I had to do some shopping and did not get home till quite late, then I went to work on Mrs. Varney's bonnet. I worked on it till twelve o'clock, and did not get it done."[54] Most of the time she reports being very tired. On July 17, she went to hear a preacher, "I was so sleepy and tired I did not enjoy it. I ought to have gone to bed instead."[55]

In her new life, Emma Foster was not in fear of falling into prostitution. She lived in the same boarding house as her elder brother, Caleb, and received many visits from family and friends. Like many girls of her day, her social life revolved around the Casco Street Freewill Baptist Church. Even with her full work schedule, she regularly attended lectures, picnics, and cruises all arranged by the church, like the one to an island in Casco Bay. "Had a pleasant sail down first went and saw the Indians then had a swim, then went after shells got a nice lot. Then we charged on the Chowder and our baskets. After dinner we went out fishing about two miles had a beautiful sail. Played Copenhagen."[56]

Since 1864 was an election year, Emma saw political rallies and celebrations, the most notable being the parades and speeches in November celebrating the election of Abraham Lincoln, a late night for Emma. "I went out till nine, then came home but did not retire till eleven. Our house was all lit up the Bands were out and the Procession."[57]

Emma was probably well aware that her apprenticeship was not going to be enough to ensure that she would become a successful milliner. At the Sweetsirs' she learned basic bonnet making, but she had no part in designing. This was a problem for millinery apprentices; it was hard to move up.[58] "No pains are taken to instruct them in what is becoming or stylish, what shades are most harmonious, how to make a graceful bow, and turn a well-trimmed end, to arrange a face trimming and render attractive the tout-ensemble."[59]

By June, she was having problems with her boss, Mr. Sweetsir. On June 7, she wrote, "Did not get to the shop until quite late. I felt very tired all day. I wish I could work for a decent man."[60] In August, she was fired. The Sweetsirs decided they wanted a worker who could live at home and, thus, take less money. Emma returned home briefly, but quickly found work with Aunt Hannah Humphrey, an established milliner in Portland for $4 a week. This was a move up. Humphrey was willing to train her as a trimmer, the most important job in a millinery shop. This opportunity probably developed because Emma had acquired experience trimming bonnets for her friends. "Unless a girl has taste or talent, she is not likely to be benefited even by a year's apprenticeship, for it is rarely the case that they are instructed in any but the mechanical work."[61]

On September 3, worries about the war and her brother overshadowed her problems at work. She wrote, "Caleb [her brother] got a letter from Howard tonight he has been sick and abused by drunken doctors and officers. He is real discouraged. I wish he were home."[62] Later in September, she wrote of another Maine man killed in Virginia. "Caleb came in the stage and found me tonight, he told me that Luther Lawrence is dead and was buried yesterday with military & masonic honors. Sarri Humphrey was engaged to him and went as a mourner to the grave."[63]

Though the war and its tragedies played on around her, Emma wrote about more immediate problems. Work in Hannah Humphrey's shop during the high season of the fall was exhausting. By October 25, Emma was already lamenting, "I fealt [sic] pretty blue sometimes today. I am very tired and I cannot turn off the work as fast as I want to."[64] She celebrated her nineteenth birthday in the shop, praying, "God grant that I may make great improvement,"[65] but by December she was further discouraged when she learned she would not be able to go home for Christmas, so she could finish the bonnets for Portland's Christmas partygoers. On December 14 she wrote: "I had a regular Hannah backache all day it has felt so weak it has made me feel so faint I could hardly work. I have been almost discouraged sometimes, I could feel that it was all for the best."[66] After all the hard work, Emma's job ended on New Year's Eve. She faced 1865 with no idea where she would work next. After all her hard work, she was only able to scratch out a meager existence in the millinery world.

The hard work was not over for Emma. We can picture her workdays as much like those of the Bunner Sisters, subject of an 1891 short story by Edith Wharton. Their humble shop was in a rented basement room. The front portion was their shop while the back room was where they lived and worked in the evening. Wharton describes the sisters in their tidy home pinking (cutting bands of trimming), making flowers, trimming hats, and even sewing for extra money, while also doing all their own household work. Emma's diary shows she was used to working this way too. That pattern probably continued. But, we hope she would feel as the Bunners did, "proud of the neatness of their shop and content with its humble prosperity. It was not what they had once imagined it would be, but though it presented but a shrunken image of their earlier ambitions it enabled them to pay their rent and keep themselves alive and out of debt."[67]

In 1876 when she was thirty, Emma married Elisha Thompson, who had returned to Maine after more than ten years in the California goldfields. They settled in Gray where they raised their family. She left us a rare, valuable glimpse into the life of young milliner, one whose life contradicts the stereotypes of the nineteenth century. Because of the valuable insights her diary gives, we can agree with Emma Foster's conclusion at the end of 1864 that it's wise to keep a diary.[68]

A treaty to end the war was signed on April 9, 1865, but it would be sixteen more months before the war was officially declared over. Southern women realized the world had changed but were still reluctant to completely abandon the illusion of white male protection and strength that had seemed so unchangeable before the war. White women in the prewar South had worked for wages only if that male support had vanished. The feeling still lingered that those who did work lost their status in society and were viewed by others as disreputable. This feeling applied to teachers, shopkeepers, and, of course, milliners.[69] Raised to expect marriage and the establishment of their own "sphere," young unmarried women like Emmala Reed of South Carolina bemoaned the lack of young men to meet. She was twenty-five at the end of the war, too old for marriage. On April 11, 1866, she wrote about the destruction of her world:

> Our whole country turned topsy-turvy. The revolution reached a dreadful crisis. Our cities & forces all gone it seems. No money, no stores—no ammunition—guns—no salt—or anything. It cannot last much longer, surely! How sudden and dreadful this crisis—what a fall for Carolina—Virginia & all. Devastated [sic] by the foe, negroes on a equality, Lee's [emphasis in original] grand army whipped & demoralized. We fear thousands killed & wounded & no hospital arrangements made for them I fear—or broken up—defeat everywhere—Providence is against us, but we still hope![70]

Black women in the South faced a rocky path as they negotiated the world of emancipation. Teachers on Georgia's Sea Islands did open sewing schools and encouraged their former slaves to sew for money,[71] but the piece work they could find exposed them to often unscrupulous contractors. The most common jobs were laundry and domestic work which put them in contact with the very people who had enslaved them. The opportunities for more creative work in the millinery or the other needle trades would not develop until the next century.[72]

Women in the North emerged from the war facing a new world too. Many still had to work since their husbands were dead or so badly injured they could not work. Even though the war had underlined the hollowness of the doctrine of the "women's sphere," historian Nina Silber points out that few of these women became active in the suffrage movement. Instead, many chose to become involved in the newly formed Women's Christian Temperance Union (WCTU) in an effort to curb men's drinking that surged in the postwar world. But, most widows simply had no time for meetings.[73]

Few women, surrounded by the war's devastation and loss, could have imagined how quickly the fashion world would expand in the late nineteenth century. Demand for fashionable dress would explode as the nation entered a period dubbed "The Gilded Age" by American author Mark Twain. There would be many more jobs for milliners, but their influence would diminish. The postwar fashion world would be run by men.

4
THE GILDED AGE

Sarah Josepha Hale campaigned tirelessly for a Thanksgiving holiday before the outbreak of the Civil War. The editor of the influential *Godey's Ladies' Book* felt the nation needed a holiday that would bring it together even as the deep differences between North and South grew larger. In 1859 she wrote, "Everything that contributes to bind us in one vast empire together, to quicken the sympathy that makes us feel from the icy North to the sunny South that we are one family, each a member of a great and free Nation, not merely the unit of a remote locality, is worthy of being cherished."[1] Hale firmly believed in the power of the women's sphere to influence men on the right path.

She continued her crusade even while the Civil War raged, writing countless editorials, writing letters to political and civic leaders, and urging her more than 350,000 readers to do the same. Finally, in October 1863, President Lincoln proclaimed a national holiday to be celebrated on November 26. The holiday was made a permanent one in the last week of Lincoln's life in 1865. But though the holiday was viewed as a celebration to strengthen the bond between God and the newly reunited nation, the war had cut deep and left the nation with scars that a holiday would not heal.

Initially, the economy expanded. Women, who had been in the workforce during the war, entered the workforce in greater numbers, not just in the fashion trades. New professions like nursing and teaching were open to them. There was an expansion in educational opportunities as well, despite the fear that women who studied for long periods of time would endanger their health. Doctors of the time felt that women's health was controlled by their reproductive organs, so a "woman who read, wrote, or studied for long periods of time could become insane or infertile or produce sickly offspring."[2]

The end of the war led to another push for the eight-hour day. Workers formed the National Labor Union, which was the first national organization of unions. Out of the thirty-two unions, only two—the Cigarmakers and the Typographers—admitted women for the first time after pressure from an organization of women workers called the Daughters of St. Crispin. In 1869 women who worked in the grueling job of washing and starching detectable men's collars in Troy, New York, went on strike for higher wages. At the beginning, 7,000 people rallied to support them, but as the strike went on, that support dwindled even though the women formed their own plant to provide the work for the strikers. The strike was doomed to fail when the employers began making paper collars which required fewer workers to clean them.[3]

The nation also had to reckon with a huge new workforce—newly freed black slaves. They were largely excluded from the new labor movement unless they formed their own unions.

The fashion trades were still major employers of women, but these women were conspicuously absent from the labor activity. There are a few organizations in the historical record, but they do not have seemed to have survived long. The milliners particularly viewed themselves as apart from workers in other fields. Before the war milliners had been the most respectable job a woman could have—one that required training in special skills. In reality, the profession was only open to white native-born women whose families could afford to pay for their apprenticeships. There was an exception—French immigrants who were considered born with innate talents to work in the fashion world. The image of the milliner had been idealized in nineteenth-century literature, so it was hard to shake the feeling that this work was safe for women to engage in. The new labor unions held the same view of women who worked in the fashion trades as the rest of society and offered little support.

The nature of millinery work was small scale. They often worked in small shops, which were competitive with each other, so workers did not form bonds with each other. Even more of a problem was the fact that millinery work was seasonal. Emma Ann Foster's experience was typical. She would work hard till Christmas when she lost her job. Millinery shops did not hire again till the spring rush, so she had to start over again to find work. No wonder a labor organizer years later in the early twentieth century vented his frustration at the task of bringing these workers into union saying, "You might as well try to direct the wind as to organize milliners!"[4] Reformer Virginia Penny was realistic. In 1869 she wrote,

> The reason women do not have strikes in the United States, like men, and demand higher wages, is, that many are ignorant; many cannot afford the time and the money; some are so despairing they think it useless; some have a false pride about the matter; they think it would look unwomanly; but the principal reason is, they have no one to lead them, on whom they can rely.[5]

A good view of the milliner's world comes to us from the *Diary of a Milliner* by Caroline H. Woods, an effusive account of life in a millinery shop published in 1867. The book tells the story of a widow who entered the millinery business

Figure 8 Presenting hats to the customer, 1905 (Wisconsin Historical Society via Getty Images.)

after the death of her husband. The stories Woods tells through her pseudonym. "Belle Otis," ring true. If Woods did not experience each of the incidents she describes, she was a keen observer of life in a millinery shop and the difficulties of making a living as a single woman. At the beginning, she apologizes for the stories she is about to tell: "If I haven't extenuated the faults of my customers, I have set down naught in malice' again them. I can say, almost unexceptionally of them, 'With all thy faults I love thee still.'"[6]

Woods's writing makes us keenly aware of the limited choices she faced as a widow who suddenly had to earn a living and her conflicted feelings about women's rights:

But to do something which earns a living will mark me as masculine and vulgar. I can live with my relatives, and retain my standing in society. Eat the bread of dependence? No! No! The bread of honest industry, or vulgarity, is preferable. But the world! But society! Bah! What is society? I am society. If I can't make myself the best of society for myself I shall be of all women most miserable.[7]

Though she is no feminist, she finds herself questioning her place in society:

I begin to see some point to the women's rights question. Why is there a masculine monopoly of business? Why shouldn't woman compete with man in the race for earning money and getting a living? There are certainly no legal objections to her doing it; no moral ones that I can see. The chief difficulty appears to lie in her own capacity, or rather lack of capacity, physical and mental, and in the social atmosphere with which she is surrounded.[8]

Her resolve fades in the next paragraph, as she acknowledges the limitations women operate under in nineteenth-century society:

To be sure woman in her present status is not fitted to undertake all kinds of business. Her manner of dress, and other habits, would make it rather inconvenient for her to go to the mast-head in a gale, or handle goods in a wholesale grocery establishment. She has as much as she can attend to out-of-doors to hold up her trailing garments, adjust her sun-shade, and make a graceful appearance in the eyes of the other sex.[9]

Even though milliners served women, creating a feminine world where customers and workers could interact, the relationship between customers and milliners was often fraught with tension. Woods gives us a vivid picture of how difficult it was to make a living as a small business person, especially one who was a woman. She called bad customers "Whited Sepulchers,"[10] meaning they had to whitewash over the rottenness inside them. This description fits the many customers who complain about the price, such as a woman she meets early in her training who complained about the price of her bonnets ending with the stinging comment: "Was there ever any reason in the price of a milliner?"[11]

Woods reflects tartly: "It is our business; and your object, just now, to attend to the adorning of your earthly tabernacle. As for the tricking out of your immortal soul, it will take something more than flowers and laces and ribbons to make it presentable in the society of those who will be judges of its beauty."[12]

Church attendance was almost mandatory for women in the nineteenth century. It was not only a place to nurture the "immortal soul" but also a stage to display a woman's latest hat. Milliners often had trouble satisfying customers' demands especially demands for new hats to wear to church on Sunday. Woods tells of losing customers because she is not open on Saturday evenings, a common practice among milliners who sought to fill as many orders as they could each season. Another woman insists on a bonnet delivery on Sunday before church, a demand Woods refuses since Sunday is her day of rest. The customer argued without the proper bonnet she could not go to church. Woods was unmoved, observing: "The last argument, no doubt, Mrs. Mann [the customer] thought irresistible. She couldn't present herself in God's house to perform His worship unless she and I both violated His laws. The mockery, the sham of worship could not be performed before the All-seeing Eye without the aid of a new bonnet!"[13]

Relations between customers and milliners could be friendly, but often there was an underlying tension in the relationship. Customers felt socially superior to women who had to work. Flaunting new clothes was one way for women of the new middle class to assert their new status.[14] Often, milliners had to contend with late payment for their goods. This was especially difficult for milliners who had to keep a stock of basic materials and trims like feathers, flowers, ribbons, and lace on hand at all times.

Even more tension came from the fact that their customers were dependent on their husbands for the money to pay for their finery. These men often resented the outlay of money for fashions they considered frivolous, even though they wanted their wives to be well turned out—but at the least cost. Virginia Penny observed: "the spirit that prompts a married woman to beat down prices, and contend for a bargain . . . arises mostly from the consciousness that her husband, in whose hands the purse is very likely to be, will expect the ultimatum of the money's worth."[15] So, when a husband was generous, Woods was delighted.

When Mrs. Stebbins, a rich customer comes in with her husband to buy a bonnet, we get Woods's view of the perfect marriage in keeping with nineteenth-century ideals. Squire Stebbins buys the most expensive bonnet in the shop because he wants the world to know he can afford it. "What mattered it that his vanity in Squire Stebbins, and his purse, and his position in the world, and all of his surroundings shone forth through Mrs. Squire Stebbins's new bonnet? His wife was a part of himself, a part of all these things, vanity included, and, most wonderful announcement of all, his wife was the sharer of his purse."[16]

Yet for all her complaining, it is clear that Woods loves her independence and remembers how restrictive married life could be: "I did love you dearly, Will; but I will own to one decided objection to married life. I was often obliged to go one way when I wished to go another."[17] She makes it clear she does not intend to marry again: "Plodding women may sit down to the restraints of married life in order to obtain the remuneration of a living, and a poor one at that, without the power of making it better; but as for me, instead of marrying again I choose business."[18]

Laws were beginning to change, so a woman's assets were not entirely controlled by her husband. New York State's Married Women's Property Act of 1848 was a model for change in the rest of the country. Still, the concept of women in business bothered many men, including the editors of the new trade magazine for male wholesalers of millinery goods, *The Millinery Trade Review*. In 1877 an article titled "Should Milliners Marry?" claimed single milliners could contract debts and then refuse to pay.

> We can see but one way out of this difficulty: absolutely refuse to sell a married woman unless for cash, or compel her husband to guarantee the bills.
>
> This is indeed a sad state of affairs, and if not soon mended may operate in such a manner to seriously interfere with the matrimonial market. Young ladies engaged in the pursuits of the business, with good credit so long as they remain spinsters, will have to refuse all offers of marriage, or else take the chances of resigning their business and losing their credit.

Single women, even those who were working, posed another problem to a society deeply concerned about "racial purity." Middle- and even upper-class women who did not marry were considered a danger to white society. The enormous flood of immigrants which dominated the end of the nineteenth century until the beginning of the First World War evoked fear in the native-born, who feared their influence would decline. "At a time when many Americans were concerned about 'racial purity' and the perceived decline of the Anglo-Saxon race, emancipated women were accused of selfishly denying their biological destiny and martial duties. Not only were they perceived as jeopardizing the well-being of the family, but they were also implicated in the pervasive fears about the future of white society."[19]

Caroline Woods wrote in the wake of the Civil War about a milliner's world which was primarily a women's enclave. But as the nation sought to heal its deep divisions, a new age was emerging, one dubbed by Mark Twain and Charles Dudley Warner as "The Gilded Age." The merchants who mobilized the nation's vast resources to manufacture materials to sustain the armies now focused their energy and invention on producing consumer goods. The fashion world was no exception. The public's demand led to pressure for the production of goods on a massive scale. More and more ready-made clothing was manufactured, a development that grew out of more efficient production of uniforms during the Civil War. Men's clothing with its simpler, more standardized construction was the first clothing a customer could buy read-made. Women's clothing was much more complicated, so only garments that did not need to be fitted were mass-produced, such as cloaks and shawls plus underpinnings like bustles, hoops, and corsets.[20]

Respectable women needed clothing for every occasion—morning, afternoon, and evening, all of it intricate and embellished with trims. There was plenty of work for milliners too since each hat required hours of custom work. At the time it would have been inconceivable that hats and bonnets could ever be mass-produced since they were piled with feathers, flowers, ribbons, and lace. But, though the new drive toward ready-to-wear did not seem to have any relation to millinery, the seeds of change were planted that would lead to the devaluing of the special skills of millinery later in the century.

Unlike dressmakers, who relied on their customers to provide material and trim for their gowns, milliners had to have ample stock on hand to entice their customers. All the flowers, feathers, fabric, millinery wire, and other supplies came from wholesale suppliers, all of whom were men. They demanded payment. Even though this payment might be on a delayed basis, milliners were submerged in a world of credit to a greater degree than before the Civil War.

The male editors of the newly minted trade magazine, *Millinery Trade Review*, chided milliners about late payment in March 1876:

> Advice to Milliners—As a matter of principle and prudence then, it is clearly the duty of the retailers to insist upon prompt cash for all their sales. A woman who has not the ready money with which to buy a bonnet, cannot afford one, and certainly the milliners cannot afford to take the risk of trusting her, unless they wish to act in a manner dishonorable to themselves and unjust to their creditors.[21]

The progression toward ready-to-wear would affect dressmakers first. The availability and increasing affordability of the sewing machine lead to the publication of sized paper patterns which could be ordered by mail from companies, such as Demorest, Butterick, and McCall's.

Though this made fashionable clothing available to more women across the country, it also devalued the carefully developed skills of the dressmaker and the milliner. Making clothing was viewed as something anyone could do. Milliners were pressed to convert bonnets to a new style. Cleaning and adapting an older bonnet was less costly, which meant less profit for the milliner than she would get from creating a custom design.

Caroline Woods described how milliners were on the alert for amateurs who would undercut their business. When a young girl came in and examined the shop's bonnets carefully, Woods knew immediately she was going to copy her work. Then, when she saw the young lady go across the street and buy the trims for less, she was outraged:

> I don't object to the girl making her own bonnet, if she does so honestly. It was the filching of our time and skill that was objectionable. One who has little or no practice may be able to make a tolerable bonnet, but the touch which a milliner inscribes upon her handiwork is wanting. Unpracticed hands, however Nature may have endowed them with skill, can never impart the ease and elegance of finish which characterize cultivated aptness.

Another young girl tried to return goods cut especially for her and was told: "It is one of my rules never to take a piece of cut goods back. If I were to do it, my ribbons and laces would be separated into inch bits, and left on my hands. Inexperienced as you are, you can see that that wouldn't do."[22]

Increasingly men, who controlled the wholesale supply of millinery materials, would begin to dominate. The Gilded Age would change the fashion industry, but would not increase opportunities for the women who worked in it.

Demand for fashionable products surged in the latter half of the nineteenth century. Demand was driven by the new department stores across the country. By the 1870s these stores offered a wide variety of merchandise all under one roof, so shoppers could go to one place to buy instead of many small shops that specialized in one thing. To entice shoppers even more the department stores were palatial palaces, often featuring dramatic central staircases, Grecian-style pillars, all lit by the most elegant lighting fixtures and, outside, lavish window displays behind the new plate glass.

In New York, new competitors bypassed A. T. Stewart's prewar store and moved uptown to Union Square, Madison Square, and Sixth Avenue. Lord and Taylor's cast-iron building featured carpeted steam elevators to enable shoppers to move quickly through its five floors. Macy's on Sixth and 14th Street expanded rapidly, taking over nearby buildings quickly. The founder Rowland Macy used his flair for showmanship by creating huge Christmas spectaculars that included a store Santa to attract children and special holiday-themed window displays as early as 1874.[23] The new shopping district with its huge cast-iron palaces attracted legions of shoppers, most of them women. The area of Broadway and Sixth was soon dubbed the Ladies' Mile.

New York was not unusual. Department stores in other parts of the country were just as lavish.

The department store giants vied for the distinction of providing their customers the most extraordinary surrounding. The 6,000-square foot Tiffany mosaic dome of Marshal Field in Chicago was described in 1910 as the "Largest single piece of Favrile Mosaic glass in the world" with 1,000,000 pieces. At the opening of Wanamaker's new store [in Philadelphia] in 1911, 30,000 guests, including President Taft, were entertained in the "great Court" and on the open galleries rising seven stories above, as they listened to the music produced by the "great organ—the largest in the world."[24]

Inside the stores, customers could browse the goods on display without feeling pressured to buy. "A certain heady democracy obtained: the humblest daughter of the working class could rub shoulders with the city's wealthiest grand dames— both would of course not be equally courted by managers, but there were few other places where it was possible or even likely for the two to meet."[25]

Caroline Woods's millinery shop could not equal what historian of fashion Philippe Perot calls "an unprecedented spectacle of permanent temptation."[26] Department stores could show and keep a stock of many, many more hats than a small millinery shop.

The department stores fueled the increasing demand for more and more fashion with rapid turnover of their stock. Production of goods had to be streamlined to make items faster and faster. "Mass production, which involves both an industrial multiplication of standardized, identical units and the consumerism that would create the 'department store' life-style, appeared with large scale production of finished products during the last third of the nineteenth century."[27]

The first sales clerks were men, but women were increasingly hired. The figure jumped from less than 8,000 in 1880 to more than 58,000 in 1890, part of the increasing number of jobs available to women by the end of the century. Men remained in the managerial, higher-paid jobs. Indeed, the fact that it was cheaper to hire women probably contributed to the increase.[28] Saleswomen did not make the hats offered for sale in the millinery department, so the milliners were relegated to the back rooms where they were invisible, which increased the devaluation of the skills of millinery.

The department store, for all its wonders, was an urban phenomenon, but there was a vast market in the small towns and farms of the nation. In 1872, a merchant set out to reach those consumers. Aaron Montgomery Ward sent his first one-page list to an association of farmers. By 1875, the list had expanded to a seventy-two-page catalog full of items farmers could buy for their wives, like hoop skirts, corsets, jewelry, fabric, and gloves. Business developed rapidly with the development of efficient means of transportation, better postage rates for packages, and Rural Free Delivery, which delivered packages to the farm families, so they didn't have to go to the nearest town to pick them up. Business was so good Montgomery Ward was followed in by May, Stern and Company in 1882 and Sears, Roebuck and Co. in 1893. Sears was a boon to black farm families, who faced discrimination in small-town stores run by white merchants. Since Sears offered these farmers credit, they could purchase the same goods as whites at lower prices than the local general store. No one required them to get permission to buy these goods. The catalogs offered a view of the big city department store and exposed sharecroppers and their wives to the new fashions of the day, including hats.[29]

Mail order catalogs were especially vital to settlers in the rapidly expanding West. Before the Civil War, there were already new states on the Pacific coast, California, admitted in 1850 and Oregon admitted in 1859. But, the latter half to the nineteenth century was a time of unprecedented expansion. The Homestead Act of 1862 encouraged this expansion be granting 160 acres of cheap public land in the nation's new territories to settlers who would live on and farm the land for five years. Nine new states were admitted to the union beginning with

Nebraska in 1867 and ending with Utah in 1896. Most of these new states were in the middle of the country filling in the space between the coasts. A transcontinental railroad was completed in 1869 linking the two coasts. The journey overland once took as long as four months using wagons drawn by oxen, horses, or mules. Trains could take passengers from coast to coast in as little as three and a half days.[30]

Men were encouraged to move to this new land in 1850 by New York newspaper publisher Horace Greeley. After the Civil War women were encouraged to go west too. Nineteenth-century society simply didn't know how to solve the "problem" of single working women and the danger moralists of the day felt they posed to the fabric of society. One radical solution was simply to get rid of them—encourage them to migrate to the West.

Even Virginia Penny thought migration might be the answer for working women, writing, "those women in the crowded thoroughfares of the eastern United States, who by their hard labor scare earn a pittance, that they might do much better by going into the plenteous West, and engaging in the capacity of seamstresses in families, dairy maids, and similar offices."[31] No one proposed going as far as some in Great Britain where the Fund for Promoting Female Emigration paid to help over a thousand women emigrate to far-flung parts of the Empire like Australia and New Zealand from 1849 to 1853.[32] The Fund was shut down after its treatment of these women was exposed in a parliamentary inquiry, but that did not end the efforts to save working women from disgrace and ruin.[33]

A New York businessman echoed the popular sentiment when he told social reformer Helen Stuart Campbell the solution to the "problem" was simple: "The amount of it is, there are too many women. The best thing to be done is to ship them West. They say they're wanted there, and there is certainly not room enough for them here. . . . Machinery will soon take their place anyway."[34]

However, the millinery shop was still a small business that a woman could run. As the country expanded westward, small millinery shops sprang up in new towns across the country, affording women a chance to make a living in an increasingly industrial America. The *Millinery Trade Review*, trade magazine for the male wholesalers of millinery supplies, joined the chorus in 1880 with an article titled "Go West, Young Woman":

> There are East many young woman who find it extremely difficult to gain a livelihood; they labor industriously for wages that barely buy the necessities of life. Should they emigrate West they would find better opportunities for improving their condition both financially and socially.
>
> It is well known that in our Eastern cities there is a preponderance of women, while in the West the balance is in favor of the man. The cry of "Go West young man," has stimulated the young men of the country to seek their fortunes towards the setting sun. We now take up the cry and substitute

women for men: therefore, go West, for by doing so you improve the business prospects of those of your own sex whom you leave behind, while improving your own at your new destination.[35]

The editors of *The Millinery Trade Review* were so bullish on the prospects of business in the West that they even predicted millinery could affect social change, even end polygamy in Utah, headquarters of the Mormon Church. An article in 1886 acknowledged that church officials had discouraged the wearing of anything but sunbonnets for many years.

It was one of the sights worthy of remembrance to see five thousand women and children attend one of the semi-annual conferences in the tabernacle, old and young dressed in the regulation sunbonnet. Here and there a stray bonnet could be seen that had made its journey across the plains clandestinely, What heart-burnings these few bonnets occasioned at that time can to-day hardly be imagined.[36]

As the older generation passed on and more non-Mormons or "gentiles" moved into the territory, the demand for fashionable bonnets increased, which meant a Mormon man must provide each of his wives with the proper bonnet, so she could be properly dressed.

From the moment the demand for millinery and dry-goods was created, it became obvious that a man who wanted to support more than one wife and family, and dress them respectably, would have more than his hands full. It is conceded by a great many old residents that the millinery and dry-goods trade has struck the practice of polygamy a harder blow than any measure that has ever been devised for the suppression of this evil.[37]

Whatever the effect of millinery on Mormonism, there was a thriving business in Utah by 1886. Ten shops in Salt Lake City, the capital, sold half a million dollars of millinery a year, while in the smaller towns, "Every season saw a demand for a better grade of goods, until to-day the remotest town has a millinery-shop and demands first-class-articles."[38]

The move west did not turn out to be a golden opportunity for most young milliners since government studies in 1887 and 1888 showed that women in Colorado and California were earning wages just as low as the wages earned in the East.[39]

For young men, it was a different story since they could travel easily from town to town without danger. An article titled "Trade in the Far West" cited the need for a new supply center in Denver, where "The merchants are doing well, the milliners are content and in good standing. Fair prices prevail, and a good quality of goods is used."[40]

By contrast, women were barred from moving into more profitable jobs like "drumming." A woman in Michigan asked about this in 1881, in a letter to the "Business Notes" section of the *Trade Review*: "It seems to me that it wouldn't be any harder to go from town to town with samples than it would be to stand behind a counter and sell goods, or run a sewing machine from dawn until dark. I know no reason why a merchant would not just as soon give his order for goods to a lady as to a gentleman."[41]

Of course, the editors viewed this as unthinkable:

> What lady would travel all night after working all day? What lady would swagger around hotel bar-rooms talking in high tones about the qualities of various hotels in the United States and Canada, or telling anecdotes of her various love affairs? What lady, on meeting a rival drummer, would spend two hours in trying to pump him as to his proposed route, and then skip a city to cut into his trade? What lady, after being kicked out of one establishment for her persistence, would pick herself up cheerfully and skip into another?[42]

The optimism of the subscribers to *The Millinery Trade Review* was boundless. Their faith in industry and their products was rock solid. They clearly felt they could use their products to solve many problems, including bleaching elephants for the circus of P.T. Barnum. In the 1880s Charles Marchand and Co., produced a special mixture of hydrogen peroxide, usually used to clean and refurbish old bonnets. Its fifteen-volume strength fluid was so strong it could "knock the spots out of a leopard, but its use would easily enable the King of Abyssinia to pose as an Albino and restore Captain Costentenas, the tattooed man to the normal condition of whiteness which characterized him before the South Sea savages fixed him up in the dime museum as a specimen of the skill in the art of exterior decoration."[43]

Barnum wanted Marchand to bleach an elephant because a rival circus was featuring an albino pachyderm. The showman did not want to scour Thailand for another one; so he found the Marchand ad in *The Millinery Trade Review* and selected "a mild-eyed and pious-looking beast on which to try the experiment."[44] Marchand enlisted his entire staff for the bleaching and proclaimed it a complete success when finished. Unfortunately, the new star had some bad habits:

> While the employees of Marchand & Co were engaged in bleaching out square yards of his tawny hide, he deliberately placed his trunk in the tub and drank off several gallons of the peroxide of hydrogen as gaily as an ordinary circus elephant drinks up a half-barrel of whiskey which is the standard remedy for the colic not infrequently engendered by a too unlimited indulgence in the pop-corn and peanuts which the small boy delights in feeding to these epicures of the sawdust arena.[45]

The elephant did not live long. Barnum went to Burma and found Toung Taloung, the real thing. Marchand and Co. received no more orders from the circus, but the episode probably advertised the effectiveness of his special brew for bonnet bleaching.

The nineteenth century's fears about the "problem" of single working women reached its peak in 1886, when feminist reformer Helen Campbell published *Prisoners of Poverty*—an expose of women's working conditions in the *New York Herald Tribune*. Mrs. Campbell was very clear about the reasons women work. First, she acknowledged some work because they want to become experts in a field that requires much education, which eliminated most women. Next, she stated many women must work because of the death of a husband. Campbell conceded many women had to work to escape poverty. Finally, what she clearly felt was a hopeless group of women have "no other life but work, they don't try to rise above a certain level."[46] Though Campbell's articles and books brought the attention of the public to the lives of the poor crammed into New York's tenements, she offers few solutions for solving the "problem" of women workers, whom she describes as an "army of incompetents."

Campbell does not exclude native-born women from her horror stories. She tells of a young milliner from New England who made a living until she made the mistake of coming to New York where her life swiftly went downhill in the

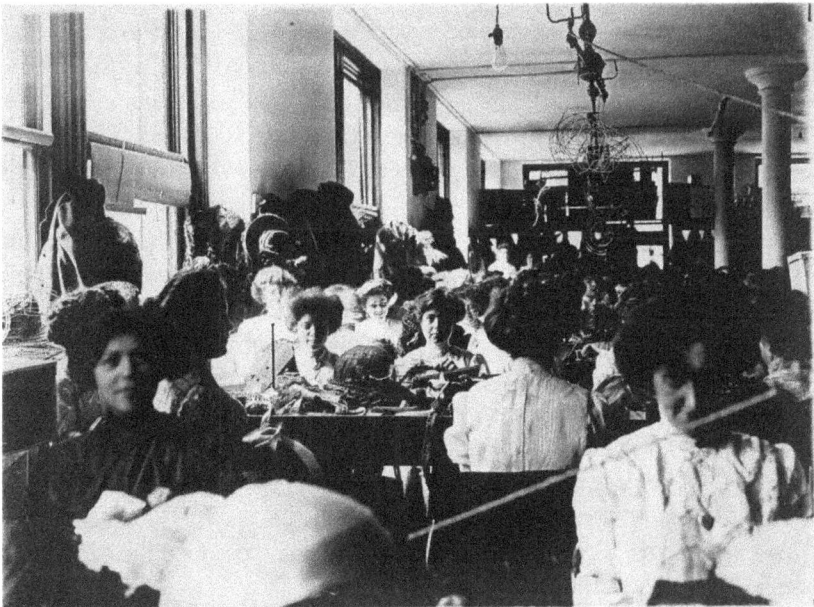

Figure 9 Crowded workroom on Broadway. Photography Collection, Miriam and Ira D. Wallach Division of Art, Prints and Photographs, The New York Public Library.

cutthroat world of commerce. Campbell does concede that millinery is a trade that is "regarded as a steady one, for spring and summer straws give place to felt, and a certain number of hands are sure of employment,"[47] but is quick to point out that the twists and turns of fashion can throw many out of work at any time.[48]

Campbell was writing at a time when immigrants were flooding the country. The United States had experienced large groups of migrants before most notably from Germany and Ireland, but this new wave of immigrants from Eastern Europe and Southern Italy was so large the federal government assumed control of immigration in 1890 and built a new station to process the immigrants on Ellis Island in New York's harbor in 1892.

One of the largest groups of immigrants were Jews from the Pale of Settlement, an area in Czarist Russia that extended from the Black Sea to Lithuania on the Baltic, where Jews were allowed to live. They were driven by persecution after the assassination of Czar Alexander II in 1881. They flooded into New York's Lower East Side, displacing the earlier immigrant group—Germans, including German Jews. The 1880s were a time of change in the garment industry since women's clothing was transitioning to ready-to-wear as men's clothing had in the mid-nineteenth century. Clothing was cut in bulk using the new rotary cutters and sent in bundles to small lofts or tenement apartments. Work would be divided up in assembly-line style with each worker performing a task like basting, pressing, machine sewing, and finishing. The work would be sent back to the contractor for payment and the finished garments would be sent uptown to the department stores on the Ladies' Mile, where merchants were hungry for new garments to entice their middle-class customers. By 1895, there were approximately 6,000 of these "sweatshops" in New York City where an additional 900 in Brooklyn, another center of Jewish settlement. The close to 80,000 workers working in these shops made New York the center of the garment industry for the entire nation.[49]

Making women's hats was still the work of many hands. The styles of the Gilded Age were not pieces that could be stamped out. Bonnets and hats were covered with plumes, ribbons, flowers and leaves made of velvet, silk, or cotton; and, even, small stuffed birds. The trims were so profuse that they often obscured the actual shape of the hat itself.[50] Hats became available at all price points, including the new immigrant workers who adopted hats as a way to adapt to American values. Immigrant women were often taken directly to shops in Lower Manhattan to rid themselves of the *sheitals* (wigs) of the Old World and buy them a new American-style hat.[51]

Sophie Abrams, a young Jewish garment worker, described the experience well:

My first day in America I went with my aunt to buy some American clothes. She bought me a shirtwaist, you know, a blouse and a skirt, a blue print with red buttons and a hat, such a hat I had never seen. I took my old brown dress and shawl and threw them away! I know it sound foolish, we being so poor, but I didn't care. I had enough of the old country. When I looked in the mirror, I couldn't get over it. I said, boy, Sophie, look at you now. Just like an American.[52]

According to historian Nan Enstad, "American hats had multiple meanings for these women. First, they were now earning money, unlike most women in the Old Country, they could spend money for things they wanted just like men did."[53] Anzia Yezierska, an immigrant, wrote about this new freedom in her novel *The Breadgivers* set on New York's teeming Lower East Side. Masha, the youngest daughter, spends her few remaining pennies on some pink roses to decorate her hat, even though she hasn't found a job yet. She justifies this act to her sister Bessie: "Give a look on these pink roses for me hat . . . like a lady from Fifth Avenue I look, and only ten cents from a pushcart on Hester Street."[54]

Initially, many Italian women remained at home with their families, but the lure of new clothing was a strong one. Millinery was only for the upper classes back home in Italy, the women of the peasant class covered their heads with shawls when they went out.

The Italian daughters or sisters, who in Italy worked around home, never receiving compensation, see the 'girl on the lower floor' [Irish or American working girl] go out every day and earn good money that gives her, what appears to the newcomer, not only splendid independence, but even the undreamed-of joy of wearing Grand Street millinery. The home became hateful.[55]

A second reason for adopting fashionable American dress was a natural outgrowth of the tension between immigrant parents intent on preserving the traditions of their native land and young women who did not want to look like "greenhorns," the insult that tagged newly arrived immigrants. Style was especially important since employers often did not hire workers who dressed in the old ethnic clothing of Europe.[56]

Inevitably, there was conflict between the generations. Social worker Lillian Wald tried to quell an argument in one family which involved another extravagant hat. A daughter had spent her overtime pay on a hat with an enormous plume. "The hat itself became a white elephant, a source of endless embarrassment, but buying it had been an orgy."[57] Wald was able to calm this mother by pointing out that the money spent on the hat was extra money earned over several weeks that did not drain the family coffers, but disputes like this one were common.

Finally, the young women were able to challenge the middle-class reformers who came to the Lower East Side with plenty of advice for them based on the new "science" of home economics. For these reformers, the new immigrants' clothing made them look cheap, and therefore, it was morally suspect. They urged spending on simply practical clothing, not silk petticoats and fancy hats. As one etiquette book decreed in 1879, "Love of dress has its perils for weak minds. Uncontrolled by good sense, and stimulated by personal vanity it becomes a temptation at first, and then a curse. When it is indulged in to the detriment of better employments, and beyond the compass of means, it cannot be too severely condemned. It then becomes criminal."[58]

The author went on to explain that fashion was not for the working class:

> It is unfortunate that in the United States, too much attention is paid to dress by those who have neither the excuse of ample means nor of social culture. The wife of a poorly paid clerk, or of a young man just starting in business, aims at dressing as stylishly as does the wealthiest among her acquaintances. The sewing girl, the shop girl, the chambermaid, and even the cook, must have their elegantly trimmed silk dresses and velvet cloaks for Sunday and holiday wear, and the injury done by this state of things to the morals and manners of the poorer classes is incalculable.[59]

But it was difficult to limit hat wearing at a time when, as historian of fashion Valerie Steele points out, "more and more middle and working class people imitated current fashion to the extent that they could afford to. The materials they used were cheaper and the designs simpler and sometimes clumsy, but to a considerable extent they work the style of the day."[60]

In the workrooms, the division of labor was much the same as it had been in the earlier part of the century with trimmers overseeing a table of four to six workers who created the shape of the hats and apprentices who labored on the mundane tasks. Shapes were constructed by sewing fabric over a wire frame. Since the frames varied considerably in shape and size, great skill was required.

The work in the custom millinery shops was dominated by white, native-born women. However, a shift was developing as more and more hats were manufactured in factories where the workers were predominately immigrants whom the customer would never see. Production in male-owned establishments was dictated by quick turnover and the ability to copy a model hat from Paris as exactly as possible.[61]

Only men could obtain the funds to invest in such a factory and employ a large number of workers to turn out hats that could be sold across the country. These millinery factories had three divisions: a jobber, who only sold millinery supplies. Many of these jobbers would hire workers before the season started to produce sample styles that would be shown to buyers. Only the styles that sold were placed into production.[62] Another part of this new division of trade was the wholesale milliner, who produced hats and also sold millinery supplies, and finally, the wholesale manufacturing milliner who only produced ready-to-wear hats and did not sell millinery supplies. Wholesale hats were still produced by hand, but the hats were not created individually. Because they were turned out in such large quantities, their price undercut the prices asked by the smaller custom millinery establishments. Millinery shops felt pressure to stock some of these lower-priced hats to compete and please customers, who were always on the alert for a better price.[63] This was a problem since manufacturers would not allow the purchase of just one hat but only allowed them to be bought in quantity, usually a "lot" of twelve.[64] If the milliner guessed wrong and picked a style that did not sell, she was left with excess dead stock on hand. Department stores had the advantage here. The large millinery departments had the floor space and the resources to purchase and display large numbers of hats that they could sell more cheaply than their custom competitors.

Invariably there was pressure to cut corners in order to produce hats even more cheaply. By the turn of the century, instead of using innumerable tiny, invisible stitches demanded in custom millinery that secured the covers of the wire frames and made the many trimmings look as if they had been blown onto the hats by favorable breezes, milliners and the wholesale factories began to use glue-like Snow-White Millinery Cement, who advertised that it "made millinery without sewing most practical and profitable."[65] The Radium Dye Company[66] of Kansas City offered a new dye that could make it much easier to freshen up old stock with new, fashionable colors. The kit contained twenty-four colors in neat glass jars along with an airbrush and compressed air tank to spray the new shade on the hat. (No protective gear like gloves or a mask was included.) A milliner could do it herself and save.[67]

Profit, not craftmanship, was the main driver in the millinery trade now the men were in charge.

The increased trend toward the mass-produced hat limited the opportunities for new workers to apprentice in the trade. As Lorinda Perry observed, "In wholesale millinery where speed is essential, only experienced workers are wanted. Furthermore, pieceworkers object to losing valuable time in teaching learners."[68]

For both custom and wholesale milliners, the work remained seasonal, much as it had been in the days of Emma Ann Foster. From February to May, work was plentiful as women bought for the spring season. Milliners faced layoffs in June and July and had to manage till August when the millinery world began to gear up for fall and winter sales. After the Christmas holiday season, milliners were laid off again.[69]

Mechanization was also creeping into work that had been dominated by hand. *The Millinery Trade Review* reported in 1880 that straw hat manufacturers in New England were using hat blocks made of plaster of Paris to stamp out hat forms. The use of these forms was accelerated by the invention of hydraulic

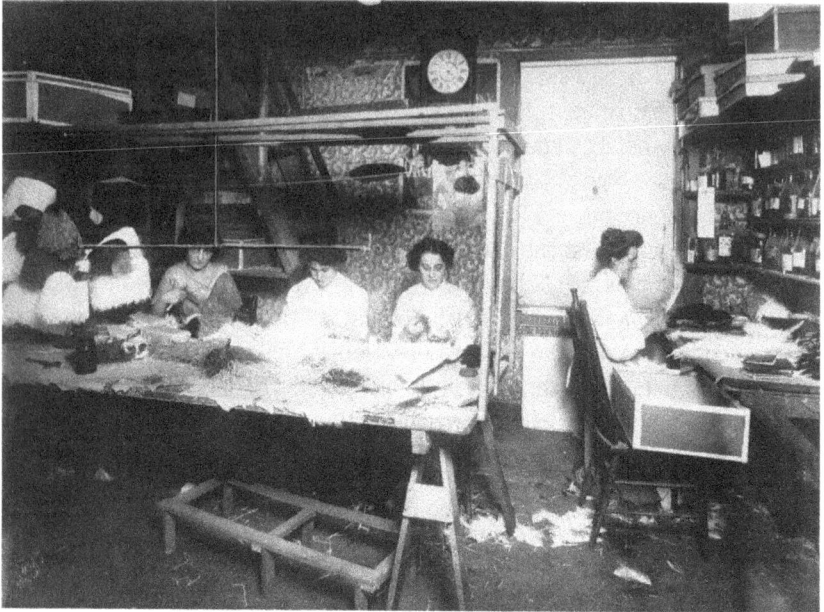

Figure 10 Process of feather making. Photography Collection, Miriam and Ira D. Wallach Division of Art, Prints and Photographs, The New York Public Library.

presses to produce shapes of buckram, straw, and felt. Running these presses and making these blocks was considered men's work since it was felt women did not have the strength or skills to run the new machines.[70] Indeed, the next year *The Review* reported on a young woman named Ellen Belcher whose scalp was torn off by a revolving shaft in a Brooklyn hat factory. After painful attempts to restore her scalp failed, Belcher had to have skin grafts and was doomed to wearing a wig for the rest of her life.[71]

Another problem for the millinery business was the use of feathers. This was just beginning to become controversial in the late nineteenth century. Millinery trade magazines were full of advertisements for feather trims of every imaginable kind, such as this one from Thomas E. Hanson's company in 1882:

> Long Amazon plumes, ostrich feathers are preferred in all kinds of combinations; cock's feathers, guinea fowl, wild pigeons, pheasant, lophophore with head cut in two, and fastened half on one side, half on the other., the neck inserted in a cockade made of pheasant's plumage, the fine tail feathers of many tropical birds little known, blue-jays, real owl's heads and vulture.[72]

The editors at the *Millinery Trade Review* sought to defuse the arguments against excessive use of animals and birds by pointing out the hypocrisy of the women who crusaded against it. One such article described the efforts of Mrs. Francis Power Cobbe against the vivisection of animals. Mrs. Cobbe made the mistake of visiting a scientist to argue her point wearing an ostrich feather hat, a muff decorated with bird of paradise, and an umbrella with an ivory handle. The scientist was not won over:

> Madam, charity begins at home. When you have given up wearing ostrich feathers, which are plucked from the live bird causing the most exquisite pain, and birds-of-paradise, which, in order to enhance their beauty and luster, are skinned alive; when you have adjured the use of ivory, because you know that the tusks are cut out of the dying elephant's jaw, then, and then only, come and upbraid me with the cruelty of my operations. The difference between us is, Madame, I inflict pain in the pursuit of knowledge and for the ultimate benefit of my fellow-creatures; you cause cruelty to be inflicted merely for your personal adornment.[73]

As the effort to curb "Millinery Murder" of birds intensified in the early twentieth century, the industry would turn this argument on its head while still mocking the motives of the female reformers behind the effort.

Figure 11 Immigrant family making flowers. Photography Collection, Miriam and Ira D. Wallach Division of Art, Prints and Photographs, The New York Public Library.

Elaborately trimmed hats would remain in fashion into the next century, but even late in the Gilded Age there were signs of change. One reason was the increasing number of women in the workforce. The attitude toward working women was slowly changing. Caroline Beecher had urged single women to go into teaching in 1845, arguing that the work was a natural fit since women were considered the "appropriate guardian of childhood."[74] Women dominated the teaching profession by the second half of the century. The attitude toward married women working underwent a change after the Civil War as *A Guide to the Manners, Etiquette, and Deportment of the Most Refined Society* decreed in 1879:

> Owing to the changes to social and industrial life which have crowded many women from their homes into business and political life, women must train for their branch of labor as men train for their work, if they wish to attain any degree of success. . . . A young woman who is able to support herself, increases her chances for a happy marriage, for, not being obliged to rely upon a husband for support or for a home, she is able to judge calmly of an offer when it comes, and is free to accept or decline, because of her independence.[75]

The invention of the typewriter enabled women to move into office work in the 1890s. It was thought they could learn to type easily since women were supposed to have more nimble fingers than men. Office work was cleaner than working in a factory, so it appealed to white native-born women who did not want to work next to immigrants in factories. By 1900, 10 percent of the office workforce was female.[76]

Another field opening to women was retail sales in department stores. Shortly after the Civil War ended 80 percent of the workforce was female. Conditions for these women were similar to these workers in the garment trades. Managers liked to hire women because their female customers were more comfortable with them, but even more important, they worked for less pay than men. An investigation by Working Women's Society in the 1880s found one New York store fired women after five years, so they wouldn't ask for more money. The workers who were able to hang on were subject to frequent layoffs. Working conditions were difficult too. Women were forbidden to sit down even if they worked a sixteen-hour day.[77]

Still, women in these jobs needed a proper dress for work. An 1879 etiquette book prescribed the right style, which was different from the upholstered look of middle- and upper-class women's afternoon walking clothes.

> The dress should be somewhat different from the ordinary walking costume. Its material should be more serviceable, better fitted to endure the vicissitudes

of the weather, and of quiet colors, such as brown or gray, and not easily soiled. Which the costume should not be of simplest nature, it should dispense with all superfluities in the way of trimming. It should be made with special reference to a free use of the arms, and to easy locomotion.[78]

Millinery for these women would be much simpler. "The hat or bonnet should be neat and tasty, with but few flowers or feathers."[79]

The bicycling craze of the 1890s changed women's clothing too. Dress reformers had been calling for more practical, comfortable clothing in the late 1800s much like reformers in the early part of the century had advocated what came to be known as the bloomer dress, but cycling brought change in dress to many more women. Women loved the new sport because it gave them the freedom to travel alone, but riding in a long skirt and corset could actually be dangerous if the skirt caught in the gears and wheels. Divided skirts began to appear.[80] The new more tailored look extended to the head. A large elaborately trimmed hat would make it difficult to balance, so women began to wear blocked hats like men. *The Millinery Trade Review* noted this development as early as 1881:

The dealers in men's hats in New York and the other large cities of the country have within the past few years added the sale to specialties in ladies' millinery. Their business has steadily increased until now the show windows of these establishments are largely given over to the display of ladies' goods. Formerly the traffic was confined to ladies riding-hats, but now it seeks to embrace the various styles of head-gear that more legitimately belong to the lady milliners.[81]

As the new century approached, men in the millinery industry looked forward to a future with new ways to profit. There was a surge in interest in training in the 1890s resulting in the establishment of schools to build a workforce of more qualified milliners.[82] However, conditions for the milliners themselves had not changed since the beginning of the century. They were still subject to low pay, seasonal layoffs, and cramped working conditions.

But, even in the pages of *The Millinery Trade Review*, there were signs the new century would bring change. In 1901, an article noted with alarm:

There is an individual somewhat known as an agitator among the working people, better known, however, as an anarchist of the East Side, who is endeavoring to organize the male and female workers in bonnet frames, straw and felt-hat factories, and other factories making materials utilized in millinery lines, into a labor union. This individual has no motive but to obtain a little more newspaper notoriety and to line his own pockets with dollars at the expense of those he makes a feint of helping. . . . This is but a small matter, yet manufacturers should take a firm stand when this man's efforts are brought to their notice, and his game should be blocked in its incipiency. They should brook no outside interference with their business or the treatment of their help. A little firmness exercised when the occasion arises will nip this agitator's influence in the bud.[83]

5
THE PROGRESSIVE ERA

The fight for shorter working hours was not the only battle being fought by progressive reformers in the early twentieth century. The dictates of the women's sphere placed women in charge of overseeing the morals of their families. Women expanded that role to oversee the morals of society as a whole. They honed their organizational skills backing causes like the temperance movement, women suffrage, and anti-lynching crusades. As the new century arrived, new causes came to the fore.

The nation's resources had seemed limitless in the nineteenth century, but by the twentieth, it was becoming clear that care had to be taken to preserve these resources, including migratory birds whose feathers were prized as decorations for women's hats. The carnage was enormous. Five million birds were slaughtered annually by 1886. Entire colonies of birds were being wiped out, not just in North America but worldwide.[1]

The National Audubon Society, named for a painter and naturalist who devoted his life to painting the birds of North America, was founded in 1905 aiming to stop "millinery murder." The new organization enlisted society women who organized women to challenge fashion and boycott feathered hats. Eventually, the first federal conservation laws were enacted—the Lacey Act of 1900, which prohibited illegal trade in wildlife and plants, the more far-reaching Weeks-Mclean Act of 1913 which protected domestic migratory birds and prohibited the importation of wild bird feathers for fashionable dress. Finally, the Migratory Bird Treaty of 1918 made it "unlawful to pursue, hunt, take, capture, kill, possess, sell, purchase, barter, import, export, or transport any migratory bird."[2]

Reformers also turned to examine the problems of working women, particularly the women in the fashion trades who clustered in New York's Lower East Side. Inspired by the home economics movement upper- and middle-class women ventured down to the heavily populated district to instill principles of housekeeping based on the latest scientific findings. They taught sanitary cooking and cleaning methods at a time when the relationship of germ to the spread of disease was developing. They advocated healthy eating which often put them at odds with the immigrants whose traditional food, such as olive oil and garlic, was quite different from the standard American diet.

Figure 12 Shaping feathers for hats. Photography Collection, Miriam and Ira D. Wallach Division of Art, Prints and Photographs, The New York Public Library.

But the real battlefield was clothing. To the reformers, money spent on fancy dress like hats and high heels was money wasted. The immigrants' clothing appeared gaudy and cheap to these women from uptown.

They felt it made the women themselves look cheap and without virtue. Underneath this concern was a deep class divide. For the reformers dressing fashionably was a mark of privilege, part of their carefully cultivated status as a "lady." Consumption of fashion was only acceptable if it was accompanied by a middle-class level of "taste." If anyone from another class could dress fashionably, standards would be lowered.[3]

Sarah Josepha Hale had expressed this fear of class blending in the nineteenth century: "O the time! O the manners! Alas! How very sadly the world has changed! The time was when the lady could be distinguished from the no-lady by her dress, as far as the eye could reach; but now, you might stand in the same room, and judging by their outward appearance, you could not tell 'which was which.'"[4]

Indignation was compounded in the early twentieth century when Bertha Richardson went to the Lower East Side to uplift women there. After one trip in 1904 she wrote angrily:

Did you ever go down to one of our city settlements full of the desire to help and lift up the poor shop girl? Do you remember the chill that came over you?

There must be some mistake, you thought. These could not be poor girls, earning five or six dollars a week. They looked better dressed than you did! Plumes on their hats, a rustle of silk petticoats, everything about them in the latest style. You went home thoughtful about those girls who wasted their hard-earned money on cheap imitation, who dressed beyond their station, and you failed to see what enjoyment they got out of it.[5]

For immigrant women, dressing well was a way to show they were truly Americans. One woman remembered that when she arrived in New York from Ellis Island, the first thing her brother did was take her to a store and buy her a new hat.[6]

Anzia Yezierska, an immigrant herself, wrote compellingly of the immigrants' longing to dress well. In *Salome of the Tenements* her heroine, desperate to escape the poverty of the Lower East Side, visits Division Street, the center of the millinery trade, and finds its wares wanting. Disgusted she throws the hats away. Later, she expresses her need for beautiful clothes: "The hunger for bread is not half as maddening as the hunger for beautiful clothes. Why, day after day, for years and years, I used to go from store to store, looking for a hat, a dress that will express me—myself. . . . Sometimes I'm so infuriated by the ugliness

Figure 13 Milliners in their creations. Photography Collection, Miriam and Ira D. Wallach Division of Art, Prints and Photographs, The New York Public Library.

Figure 14 Night class in millinery. Photography Collection, Miriam and Ira D. Wallach Division of Art, Prints and Photographs, The New York Public Library.

that I have to wear that I want to walk the streets naked—let my hair fly in the air—out of sheer protest."[7]

It was in this period that Mary van Kleeck, director of Industrial Studies at the Russell Sage Foundation, set out to study the working conditions of milliners. Van Kleeck's study was done for the Manhattan Trade School for Girls to learn "whether seasonal conditions made the earning of a livelihood so precarious that the majority of the girls applying to the school should be discouraged from aspiring to be milliners."[8]

By the early twentieth century, trade schools emerged to train young women for the workplace. There was an explosion of such schools. In 1908–9 Van Kleeck's investigators visited sixty-two of them in New York City alone.[9] These schools trained young women for twelve months in courses that met five days a week. Students received instruction in sewing, including stitches used in millinery; after that, they spent four months working on skills for summer millinery and four on winter millinery.[10]

Opinion varied in the industry about the worth of this training. Many milliners complained the new workers could not keep up with the speed required in commercial production. Also, prospective employers felt the schools were hopelessly behind the times since their instructors did not keep up with the rapid

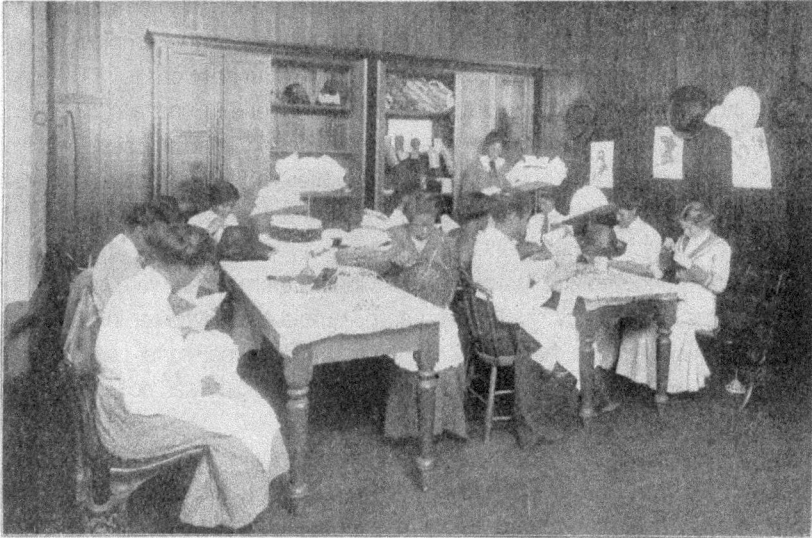

INDUSTRIAL TRAINING FOR WOMEN
Developing talent and taste in the art of millinery, an industry for women. A class at
Spellmans Seminary, Atlanta, Ga.

Figure 15 Millinery training in the South, 1917. Photography Collection, Miriam and Ira D. Wallach Division of Art, Prints and Photographs, The New York Public Library.

swings of fashion.[11] An inspector from Boston conceded there were problems but pointed out that many workrooms exploited young workers:

> If every millinery shop in Boston has a workroom so managed that its girls could be conscientiously trained—not exploited and used as errand girls— one would have not hesitancy in recommending shop training as the best introduction to the trade. Unfortunately, there are not enough of these workrooms to accommodate all the would-be milliners, and the tendency is increasingly opposed to offering training in the workroom.[12]

Van Kleeck expressed the hope that her study would help find answers to the problems of what she conceded was a field with too many workers.

Millinery had long been known for huge swings in employment. Milliners were hired for the fall season and usually laid off after the Christmas rush. Work was scarce until the spring rush began. Then, milliners were laid off again for the summer slack season. These cycles of unemployment were a constant in the industry. Emma Ann Foster dealt with this during the Civil War years as had milliners before and after her in the nineteenth century. The Manhattan Trade School had recently added a course in lampshade making, hoping to give its graduates a skill that would tide them over during the slack seasons. But, the lampshade industry was a small one, not nearly large enough to employ legions of out-of-work milliners. Van Kleeck hoped a survey of the employers and workers in an organized, systematic way would yield an answer.

The industry was not cooperative, so her caseworkers had a difficult time getting data. None of the employers wanted to be regulated. Indeed, one firm told a caseworker the millinery industry was different from all others because it was so subject to seasonal swings in employment, adding, "It's worse than playing the stock market!"[13] Often, the shop and factory records on pay were nonexistent or incomplete. Inevitably, the milliners themselves were blamed for the problems in the industry. One woman boss told a caseworker investigation of wages would make her workers demand higher pay and become too independent. Her remedy for low pay was simple. "If a girl does not like her pay in one shop, she can go to another."[14]

Viewed from the perspective of the early twentieth century, the millinery industry was worth investigating because hat wearing was mandatory for all respectable women. It was impossible for anyone at that time to imagine a time when women would go without them. "The millinery trade. . . . has become an integral part of the business of clothing the world and his wife, with a legitimate claim as such to recognition as a fundamental industry supplying one of the necessary elements in a proper standard of living."[15]

One thing that had changed with the expansion of the fashion industry in the late nineteenth century was the type of shops. The small retail shop which made hats by hand was a rarity only available to the wealthy. By this time department stores had millinery production units. There was also a new place of production—the wholesale factory which employed a larger workforce. It could be connected to a jobber, who sold millinery supplies and supervised the making of sample models to display their wares or a "wholesale milliner who combined the making of handmade hats with the sale of supplies. Finally, there was "wholesale manufacturing milliner" who churned out ready-to-wear hats only.[16] Many retail shops now sold hats turned out in these wholesale factories. "The small neighborhood shop tends to become a distributing center for the wholesale factories, performing the task of the middleman, with one or two milliners to adapt the style to the taste of individual customers."[17] Division Street on New York's Lower East Side catered to buyers in search of cheap goods, often produced by contractors who trimmed ready-to-wear hats for sale uptown. These contractors paid the lowest wages, just as the contractors who produced clothing in the sweatshops that lined the neighborhood. Those who ventured down to Division Street had to face down the pressure tactics of the "pullers-in," aggressive, burly men and women who were stationed outside the doors of each millinery shop and literally tried to pull women into their store by force. The pullers-in harassed men too, calling out to them loudly urging them not to be cheap, but to buy a hat for their lady.[18] A vivid description of

THE LITTLE CHICAGO MILLINERY, HELENA, ARK.
Miss Hattie W. Hatton, Milliner

Figure 16 Miss Hallie Hatton in her shop, Arkansas, c. 1902–3. Photography Collection, Miriam and Ira D. Wallach Division of Art, Prints and Photographs, The New York Public Library.

their pressure tactics appears in Anzia Yesierska's *Salome of the Tenements* when the main character Sonya Vrunsky, a young Jewish immigrant, sets out to buy a new hat:

> "Step right in! Selling-out Sales! Bargains!" Sonya's arm was seized by a puller-in who dragged her down from romance to Essex Street.
>
> "Who wants your bargains? Have you no eye? Have you no ears?" Shaking herself free of the obnoxious hand, she picked up the littlest of them all and waltzed him around the lamp-post.
>
> "Holiday hats! Shine yourself out for Passover! Everything marked down cheap!" Another importunate puller-in reached out for her coat sleeve.
>
> "Worms should eat you and your cheapness." She hurled at the offender. The sordidness of haggling and bargaining—all she had ever known till now—broke in upon her high mood.[19]

The world of millinery on the Lower East Side was not genteel.

Van Kleeck was not the only researcher looking into the problems of milliners. They were included in a survey of working women in Pittsburgh conducted by Elizabeth Beardsley Butler in 1907–8. Butler found there were an increasing number of jobs open to women, but they were restricted by nationality.

Telephone and telegraph work, like "clerking," is socially desirable, and by reason of this, claims the American girl. The same is true of the millinery workroom in spite of irregular hours and short seasons. . . . Surveying the city, then, we see English-speaking girls holding positions for which a few month's training and some intelligence are needed, a knowledge of English, or of reading or writing. The Italian girl, hindered by tradition, scarcely figured, but within a limited circle of industries, immigrant Jewesses hold positions beside girls of native birth.[20]

Across the state in Philadelphia, Lorinda Perry, a doctoral candidate at Byrn Mawr College, examined milliners in Boston and Philadelphia. Perry was trying to find a way to improve the wages of what was one of the largest employers of women in 1916. Her thesis is full of charts comparing the wages of different categories of milliners—copyists, trimmers, beginners. Inevitably though, stereotypical assumptions about the nationalities of the workers are presented as established fact. Perry found most of the milliners in the two cities she studied were "American," which we can assume meant they were native-born, white women, or Irish, a nationality that had been immigrating the United States since before the Civil War, so was more accepted than immigrants who arrived later. Fifteen percent were Jews from Eastern Europe, who Perry found had unique skills: "It was frequently stated that Jewish girls were the best millinery workers, since their work usually bore a distinctly 'French' touch. It may be true that they possess the artistic ability demanded of trimmers, but few of them were found in the higher division."[21] Perry attributes the inability of Jewish women to be hired for the best paying job of trimmer to their youth, not to any prejudice against them.[22] Van Kleeck also links the workers' abilities to their ethnicity. At the top of her ranking are the French. "We were told that the French are born with a knowledge of millinery and that an American can never equal them."[23] Italians are characterized as hard working and quiet, while Russian Jewish workers are "often a disturbing element."[24] Van Kleeck continues her characterization of Italian and Jewish workers in her second study *Artificial Flower Makers*: "It follows that the Italian girl is more willing than the Jewish girl to accept conditions as she finds them. The owner of a large flower factory says that he prefers to employ Italians because they are 'more tractable.'"[25] Many Jewish workers looked down on the Italians. One observed snidely, "If they were more civilized, they wouldn't take such low pay. But they go without hats and gloves and umbrellas."[26]

Employers blamed the new immigrants crowding their workrooms for a decline in the quality. "Formerly Americans and Germans worked at the trade," said one employer, "and then the Italians and Jews came in and killed it. It has changed the class of work. We cannot compete with them in cheapness of product. The only way out is for us to make higher class goods, not cheaper, and for this we need a better class of workers and we cannot seem to attract them."[27]

Figure 17 Table in a flower factory. Photography Collection, Miriam and Ira D. Wallach Division of Art, Prints and Photographs, The New York Public Library.

The influx of immigrants may have changed the "class of work" as the employers claimed, but immigrants and native-born workers struggled to keep themselves afloat. Not only were they subject to waves of unemployment at the end of every season; but when they were working, they were paid wages so low that it was impossible to save for slack times, much less have a sustainable lifestyle. Van Kleeck cites numerous examples amid the copious charts and graphs in her report that show just how dire earning a living was for these women. "The ways of living in order to make the wages go as far as possible are not always comfortable," the report points out.

> Three dollars a week for sleeping on a couch in the dining room of the family with whom she boarded, with the privilege of keeping her clothes in a closet in another room, was all the one girl could spare, even though she earned $12 a week. She had lost seven weeks because of slack season and twenty-three through illness, and her income had been $185 in the year. She was in debt for part of her board.[28]

Van Kleeck's data showed the median for milliners was $365 per year,[29] but acknowledged this figure was difficult for many to achieve. Many young women lived at home, which was expected in the industry. Lorinda Perry discovered employers "don't want a girl who hasn't a good home . . . a girl can't live on $6 a week."[30]

A paragon of thriftiness was a German immigrant who made $512 a year and managed to save some money through stringent discipline. She paid only $2 a week for a room and never more than $4 a week for meals.[31] She also saved money by making all her own clothes and underwear, walking to work, doing her laundry herself, and cooking her breakfast.[32] Another worker points out her income is not enough to cover health care. "She suffered from eye strain and had no proper examination or care, this made machine operating as well as millinery work especially difficult."[33] This worker did admit to buying small luxuries like pictures for herself and small gifts for friends. To offset that she did her own laundry after work. "In addition, experience had taught her that some money should be set aside for eyeglasses which she needed, but could not buy, for medicines, for dental care, and doctor's bills."[34] This woman only had a third of a room in a place she shared with friends. At the end of the year, she had only $80 left. One other worker told investigators she could not afford to pay someone to do her laundry, but was often much too tired to do it herself after working all day.[35]

Even sadder was the case of workers sharing their job to prolong work in the slow season. "In a wholesale shop the girls at one table had worked out a plan whereby they took turns in coming to work in the dull season, two appearing one day, and two other the next. They divided their earnings at the end of the week, having saved time and carfare by this co-operative arrangement."[36]

Working conditions were another problem. Many employers kept costs down by cramming the milliners in badly lit workrooms. In 1901, Mrs. Z.B. Dexter wrote an article pleading for better working conditions. She cited one company who kept its workers in the basement of its building:

> A few years ago, a large wholesale house which gave employment to nearly fifty trimmers provided as their workroom a space directly under the pavement, down in the dark chilly basement, where only artificial light could be sued successfully, and where perfect ventilation was very difficult to secure. How few pedestrians hurrying over those glass-filled gratings in the sidewalk realized they were trading above the heads of women making millinery for one of the most prosperous houses in New York.[37]

Dexter wrote that this particular company improved working conditions when it was proven to the managers that unhealthy conditions were bad for business, but Van Kleeck pointed out that working conditions in the industry varied widely, even though New York State had recently passed legislation that dictated minimum standards for sanitation and limited women's working hours. During the busy season, milliners were crammed into workrooms and pushed hard.

It [the millinery industry] does not yield readily to state regulation. Its hours of labor are oftentimes not limited; overtime is not restricted; sanitation, light, and ventilation are not insisted upon; the worker is not guaranteed comfort in the workroom as to seats, tables, and cleanliness; regularity of pay; permanence of contract, and due notification of dismissal are not required.[38]

Many shops stayed open late on Saturday nights in the hope of pulling in as much business as possible. One employer told Van Kleeck's investigators his store showed a loss five days a week, so "he counted on the Saturday night rush to make good this loss and to yield a profit."[39] Overtime was out of the question.

Many working women undoubtedly faced sexual harassment on the job and on the streets going to and from work. The problem rarely appears in the reformers' studies since the burden of preventing harassment fell on women's shoulders. Women were expected to control the urges of men through virtuous behavior.[40] Lorinda Perry worried that gossip in the workroom would weaken the resolve of young workers and make them vulnerable.

Often the moral atmosphere of the workroom is not desirable. The work is not of sure nature as to demand the entire attention of the worker, and the opportunities for conversation, except in the height of the rush season, are many. The older worker has had sufficient experience to be able to discriminate between the true and the false, and to have formed her moral concepts; but the younger worker may be injuriously affected by this atmosphere and should not be exposed to it until she has developed sufficient stamina to resist it."[41]

Despite the pressure women workers faced from employers who justified underpaying them because they believed these women were only working to supplement the income of their husbands, women shirtwaist workers went on strike. Shirtwaist worker Clara Lemlich expressed the need for better working conditions during the Strike of 20,000 in 1909. For her, one demand was simple—a place to hang her hat.

Sometimes a girl has a new hat. It is never much to look at because it never costs more than 50 cents, but it's pretty sure spoiled after it's been at the shop. There are no dressing rooms for the girls in the shops, no place to hang a hat where it will not be spoiled by the end of the day. We're human, all of us girls, and we're young. We like new hats as well as other young women, Why shouldn't we? And if one of us gets a new one, even if it hasn't cost more than 50 cents, that means that we have gone for weeks on two-cent lunches—dry cakes and nothing else.[42]

But for most milliners, the decision to strike was not a simple one. Many of them shared the same view of unions as dressmakers studied in May Allison's

1909 work for the Department of Labor. Allison found workers in the fashion trades often looked down on women who worked in factories where unions had gained the strongest foothold. Few understood the benefits of unionization, seeing only the disorder and strife women workers faced on the picket line. Often women strikers were considered as low as prostitutes and were attacked and beaten by the police. Adding to the problem of unionizing these women was their isolation caused by their irregular employment. It would be too easy to be blackballed and not find work for the next season in this precarious world.[43]

Nor did women find natural allies from the unions themselves. The concept of a "living wage" was considered a male prerogative. Even reformers of the time thought men, who were citizens and voters, had "higher" needs than women who did not have the right to vote yet. Women, who could not vote, should receive a separate, respectable "women's wage," just enough to support themselves, but not enough to waste on frivolous items like fashionable clothing. Men worried that higher wages for women would mean less money available for men.[44] For their part, women fought to keep men from working as milliners, largely through refusing them work or segregating the few who tried to learn behind screens so they wouldn't mix with young women in the workroom and ruin their moral character, but this strategy did not increase women's power in the industry.

Historian Nan Enstad points out that male unionists and upper-class female reformers looked at milliners wearing hats they concocted themselves bedecked with inexpensive feathers and flowers and concluded these women were not serious workers since they were wasting their wages on frivolous fashions. They felt serious union women should dress in plain, practical clothes. Indeed, one women labor leader suggested her organization should mandate that no member should spend more than $2 a week on clothing.[45] Backlash was swift and came from Mary Anderson, a labor leader from Chicago:

> It is almost wicked to speak of dress when one remembers the thousands that sit up at night making their own clothes, and if the girls dress fairly well, why not? Have they not worked hard enough? It is not so much a question of spending money wisely as how to procure a living wage and have some to spend. When we think of the girls at piecework and the hard training how to make the most of the time, we may well trust them to spend the money wisely.[46]

There was an effort by 60 Russian Jewish milliners to organize in 1905. Mary van Kleeck reports their small group of organizers were often arrested for lack of the proper permit when speaking on the streets. They tried to lure members by setting up social events. "In the hope of appealing to their more frivolous fellow workers, they planned dances and gave entertainments. One of these, attended by the investigators, had a most delightful program of recitations and beautiful music rendered by some of the artistic foreigners of the East Side."[47]

The union effort collapsed when one of the leaders developed tuberculosis and had to move to Colorado for treatment.

One small segment of the women's hat industry did unionize. The American Federation of Labor (AFL) reported that straw sewers, whose work was rapidly being produced by a machine, had voted to become part of the Cap Makers union, who also used the sewing machine, in the winter of 1916–17. Milliners did not become part of Cloth Hat, Cap, and Millinery Workers International Union (CHCMW) until 1918.[48] But, the AFL's overwhelmingly male membership was unsympathetic to women workers. The hatters, who made men's hats, had their own union—the United Hatters of North America (UHNA) which did not unite with the CHCMW until 1934. The attitude against women in the workplace was rooted in the old philosophy of the women's sphere, which felt women should be in the home. "We stand for the principle that it is wrong to permit any of the female sex of our country to be forced to work, as we believe that the man should be provided with a fair wage in order to keep his female relatives from going to work,"[49] wrote one man in an AFL publication in 1905.

It would be sometime before another effort to unionize millinery workers would develop. Van Kleeck acknowledged: "It is exceedingly difficult to organize a trade in which the majority of the workers are together but half the year, especially when even that half is divided into two quarters and between these periods the milliners are no longer milliners, but salesgirls, artificial flower makers, operators on clothing or indeed, workers in whatever occupations they can find."[50]

Employers had many reasons why they couldn't improve conditions in their workrooms. They blamed the workers for being inefficient. One millinery worker pointed out the pressure in the workroom. "They pay by the week but they count the hats twice a day, and if you don't finish as many as they want, they scold you. They would like you to turn out 10 to 15 per day."[51] Employers also blamed their customers, who did not space out their buying evenly over the year. Finally, they blamed the fickle changes of fashion. One employer, who had been in the business for thirty-five years, complained: "I can tell you this is a treacherous business. You can never tell what is going to happen. Take this season: I had figured on fur hats and suddenly in December wool hats come in. I lost a thousand dollars in December."[52] Indeed, American millinery was completely dependent on Paris to set the style for each season. There were training schools for milliners but none in art and design. Parsons School of Design was founded in 1896, but did not have a fashion school until 1904. Even then, the new school was only focused on costume design for the stage.[53]

"Picturesque, bizarre, or otherwise conspicuous though its products may be, the millinery trade has not yet captured the imagination of the public as an industry of any significance in the labor movement."[54] That statement begins the final chapter of Van Kleeck's study. After all the reams of data, the graphs that showed employment rising and falling precipitously each season, the charts that aimed to detail every aspect of milliners' wages, the study was at a loss to report a plan to end the problems it had set out to study—problems that had existed since the nineteenth century when Emma Ann Foster struggled to find work. Van Kleeck knew it was a problem that went beyond the millinery trade but extended to most of the work available to women in the early twentieth century. New York State had studied the problem in depth too. Its Factory Investigating Commission recommended the establishment of a Wage Commission in 1915 with boards made up of employers, employees, and members of the public. Such a group would have the power to figure out a living wage for women and minors (child labor was still legal) and "recommend" that employers pay their workers enough to enable them to have a decent lifestyle.[55] Unfortunately, the bill proposed by the Commission did not include a way to enforce the Boards' decisions.[56] Melbourne, Australia had such a board and Van Kleeck analyzed its operations carefully, but didn't hold out much hope that such a board would be adopted "in a trade where present co-operation is meager, while its problems are quite beyond the power of individuals acting alone to solve."[57] Though Van Kleeck seemed to feel these boards would enable employers and employees to begin to work out the problems of short seasons, in the end, she felt it would be more realistic to educate the customers. Groups like the General Federation of Women's Clubs and the Consumers League were trying to reshape women's buying habits; she hoped they would pressure employers to provide new hats year-round, not just in the peak seasons of spring and fall. That "campaign" was the final hope for change in the industry Van Kleeck held out.

Earlier in the century, at least one woman tried to buck the trend. Mrs. AA Reiser was praised for her innovative business acumen in the male-dominated trade magazine, *The Illustrated Milliner*. She appeared in New York City in 1902 and established a shop at 240 Fifth Avenue in the heart of the fashionable district near the Madison Square Park. Like many women before her, Mrs. Reiser got into the millinery business when she was widowed in Erie, Pennsylvania, left with $30 and three children. She soon moved on to Pittsburgh, and then to Buffalo, where her store became the largest in the city.

Fourteen years later, Mrs. Reiser had an ambitious plan. She linked up with a Madame de Faure, a Parisian milliner. Through this partnership, she planned to produce "pattern hats." These were hats that were shipped to the United States specifically to be copied by American milliners so they would be able to sell the latest Parisian designs. She hoped to save fees usually paid to jobbers, importers, and commissioners, and sell her hats at half the usual New York prices. "Mrs. Reiser will be able, through her Paris store, to place, not a dozen or two, but hundreds of Imported and Pattern Hats in her New York store, where everybody can see them. She will not be afraid of any hats being copied, for she knows that as soon as they are seen they will be bought."[58] Indeed, she planned to make her hats so affordable that milliners would buy hats from her instead of bringing their trimmers to New York to copy them.[59]

Mrs. Reiser underwent a transformation! She became Madame Wallman. By February she reported she had 2,000 pattern hats on hand and planned to have 3,000 by March for her giant Easter opening. She maintained a "Style Service" via the transatlantic cable and established a workroom in London. In July 1902, Madame Wallman's store was featured in a photo spread in *The New York Tribune*. There were pictures of the beginning of milliner training, including cutting a hatband, making a frame, applying a facing, all the way to the correct way to hold and present a hat to a customer for a successful sale. Madame Wallman must have made a splash in the city to merit such a spread.[60]

Madame Wallman soon disappeared from the pages of *The Illustrated Milliner*. By 1909 it was all over. A brief article stated she had closed her New York store and gone back to Pittsburgh due to "Demands upon her time and the attention required for her three enterprises, overtaxed her strength . . . connected with heavy losses in affairs not connected with the millinery business cause her to go into bankruptcy."[61] She lowered her sights, selling hats at medium prices with smaller profit. Her last words of advice were "Judicious and liberal advertising is. . . the royal road to fortune."[62] With those words, Madame Wallman vanished into obscurity.

6

THE MEN OF *THE MILLINER*

Though the Progressive reformers, like Van Kleeck, struggled to deal with the problems of milliners in the early years of the twentieth century, the prevailing power in the millinery world was male. January 1900 marked the launch of the beginning of a new trade magazine, *The Illustrated Milliner*, a monthly with lofty goals that would express the views of the men who controlled the industry. Its editor decreed, "The pervading tone of *The Illustrated Milliner* will be one of cheerfulness. Its treatment of all matters will be vigorous and sprightly—but never flippant. It will not be a journal of personalities, a parcel of puffery, or a compendium of cut-and-dried data."[1]

Even though the magazine was aimed at creating fashions to appeal to women, the readership of *The Illustrated Milliner* was predominantly male. By the turn of the century, men controlled the millinery business in the United States. A business that had once been centered on custom-made work from small shops had succumbed to the demand for mass-produced ready-to-wear clothing sold in department stores. The millinery district in Manhattan stretched from Madison Square to Central Park—thirty-two blocks with twenty-nine millinery houses and more on the side streets.[2] A picture in the new magazine showed the workroom of John Wanamaker's New York store with 120 milliners working under the supervision of male managers.[3] Women were now working in large workrooms, producing hats for the wholesale market. Hats were big business. A woman in fashionable society was advised to have at least a dozen for every occasion.[4]

It was this competitive world the new magazine entered. The first edition addressed common concerns such as the question of whether a milliner should marry. This issue drew a mixed response from readers. There was still a strong feeling that after she married, a women's place was in the home coupled with uneasiness over what would happen to a women's business if a man was involved. As Mrs. H.S. Kidwell of Parkersburg, West Virginia, put it, "A successful

Figure 18 Making hats for the wholesale trade. Photography Collection, Miriam and Ira D. Wallach Division of Art, Prints and Photographs, The New York Public Library.

milliner should marry if she wishes, and also continue in business, but she had better invest her money in wax figures than in a man without means."[5] Another problem was the seasonal nature of the business. An article, titled "Why Are There no Millinery Millionaires?," summed up the problem in a nutshell: "Because of the short seasons that millinery is sold at a profit and the expensive work rooms where so many fine materials are carried over and prove of little value the following season. Most any other line is more stable than millinery."[6] Yet, the magazine offered its readers suggestions for sidelines to help tide the business over in slack times—hairdressing and accessories, needlework supplies, and ribbons. However, when a milliner from Ohio asked if an ice-cream parlor would be a good sideline in July and August, she was discouraged. "Ice cream and millinery have nothing in common, and your customers should be led to think of you as a milliner and a milliner only at all times,"[7] though the editors did suggest that she could offer space to a church group, which might lead to new customers in the fall.

Looming over the American millinery business was the influence of Paris. Customers considered Parisian fashion the finest, the center of all fashion inspiration. One letter commented, "It is not great exaggeration to say that millinery shops are as numerous in Paris as are saloons in New York City."[8] Hats were imported into the country to be copied. The trade was so important the magazine would devote an article to the millinery division of the Customhouse the next year. The article featured a picture of the United States Appraisers' Stores in New York City accompanied by pictures of the Examiner of Millinery Goods, Mr. George W. Scott and his assistant, Mr. L. B. Cathcart. New York was the primary port of entry for foreign goods, at a time when taxes and duties on imports produced nearly 90 percent of the nation's gross national revenue.[9] Twelve years before the enactment of the Sixteenth Amendment, which gave the nation an income tax, taxes on imported millinery goods were important. Indeed, the millinery division occupied the fourth floor of one of the largest government buildings in the city, levying duties as high as 60 percent on the trims and bodies that made up a fashionable hat.[10] Mr. Scott was the first to see the new Paris styles as they arrived in port. Each hat was packaged in its own specially made box anchored carefully so its fragile materials would arrive intact. If the hat broke free of its moorings, it was a loss of income to the national treasury:

> When one of these exquisite, but fragile, creations of filmy lace, delicately posed flowers, and beautifully dressed feathers breaks away from its original fastenings, and takes to itself a separate tumble every time the case is moved or the ship lurches, the millinery gem is certain to come out of its casket at the Appraisers' Stores a badly ruined mass—a millinery jumble, absolutely ruined, so far as its beauty of suggestiveness as a Paris pattern is concerned, and great dissatisfaction on the part of the Importer ensues.[11]

The "exquisite, but fragile creations" were just what the millinery industry wanted women to wear since they took hours of labor and mounds of trimmings like feathers, flowers, and ribbons that ensured a good profit. These hats were also what the editors thought women should wear—hats that emphasized their womanly nature. So, the first editorial in the magazine tackled the problem of "The Bare-Headed Summer Girl," the "the tendency of girls and young women to go riding, boating, walking, calling, etc., with nothing on their heads."[12] Women were engaged in sports more and more. The bicycle craze of the 1890s had led more and more women to wear "a durable hat made to stand dust, wind, rain, and sunshine—not a thing of beauty at any time."[13] These practical hats along with walking hats and sailor styles had cut into profits in the first half of the year. The editorial advised against protesting or claiming hatlessness was a danger to health and a lady's hair. "The only legitimate crusade you can conduct against the bareheaded habit is to make for your customers something that brings out so successfully her best points of beauty, that it makes her look so charming that she will be loath to miss the advantage which the hat gives her in the contest for compliments, prestige, attentions and personal popularity."[14] The crusade against hatlessness would be waged throughout the twentieth century. This was the first of many salvos against it.

One issue was not tackled in this first edition though there had been debates about it in the nineteenth century. Feathers were a huge and profitable business, but the concern was building about the ethics of slaughtering so many birds to satisfy fashion. The editors of *The Illustrated Milliner* fought hard against "the radical reformers who would banish all feather decorations from the head of beauty,"[15] and bring the ruin of many companies who advertised in its pages.

The debate over the man milliner surfaced. The question of what to do with such a creature in a workroom of young women was an issue that touched on the questions of propriety that hovered over life every day in the 1900s. A young man had appeared at a shop on New York's Fifth Avenue, asked for work, and to prove his worth produced a hat that sold on the spot. The shop compromised. The young man could not work with the other twenty-five young women in the workroom. He had to work behind a screen where he worked from 8 to 5 producing hats that always sold. The shop owner could not account for this "inscrutable genius" telling the magazine, "I always believed that hat trimming was an accomplishment in which women would never meet any masculine competition."[16] This was not the end of the issue. In January 1901, the magazine solicited the opinions of fifty milliners around the country and asked them if trimming ladies' hats was "a vocation in which a man can engage in with honor and a fair chance of success?"[17] The answers ranged from a flat no because "his dress is against him. To hold a hat properly he would have to put on an apron. If it were a plain one, he would look like a butcher; and if it were ruffled, he would look like a fool."[18] Furthermore, a man could not properly touch a woman and adjust the trimmings on her bonnet without upsetting the husband. "Or how many men do you think would allow their wives to loaf for half a day in a millinery shop if the milliner were a man? In a country town, the millinery shop to women is what the barbershop is to men—a loafing place."[19] Many felt there was not enough money for men in the business and men weren't qualified anyway since they did not have the right artistic temperament.

One man milliner in Fort Wayne, Indiana, spoke up and pointed out the large number of male dressmakers then working from Worth to Doucet, and Redfern.

I should like to impress upon the mind of any young man contemplating work of this kind he will experience much difficulty in securing entrée to most of the work rooms, and that after he has finished the trade he will ever be looked upon as a freak of nature, receiving almost as much marked attention as any of the paid specimens that pose in museums. As an offset to this line he can feel assured of a good position all the time, provided he is a skillful trimmer, and will receive 50% more salary that would a woman for the same work.[20]

In 1912, reaction against French fashion dominance set in. This was the same year suffragists in London raided millinery shops breaking the windows of

Liberty's and Harrod's to name a few. It was also a year *The Milliner* reported one of its numbers survived the sinking of the *Titanic*. Mr. George Rheims managed to swim to a rubber raft and cling there with twenty other people for six hours.[21]

Barely noticed in 1913 was a notice that appeared in April's edition that mentioned the growing sense that war was on the horizon in a way only a milliner could appreciate. "No doubt the Balkan situation and the threatening rumors of a great European war are responsible for the revived interest in military fashions. Helmet shapes and military shako, busby and cap effects were among the first novelties introduced this season: they are increasing in popularity in the same measure as military styles are popularized in gowns and outer apparel."[22]

The year 1914 started out with a focus on ongoing issues that could hurt sales and reduce hat wearing. There was the danger of hatpins. Women had been using the hatpin as a handy instrument to defend themselves against men in places like public transportation. Such aggression was deemed unladylike and dangerous to innocent men. Chicago had been the first of five cities to pass an anti-hatpin ordinance in 1910 even though women's clubs objected vigorously. As one Chicago clubwoman put it, "If the men of Chicago want to take the hatpins away from us, let them make the streets safe."[23] But no, "women wearing swords"[24] on their heads were a public danger.

A bigger threat to sales was in long-simmering controversy over wearing hats in the theater. Large hats blocked the view of the stage. Milliners had been urged to make low hats, but the problem had not gone away, especially when the craze for the huge Merry Widow hats took hold in 1908. Styles had changed, but the problem had not gone away. A very similar problem was the church hat. Minsters and rabbis had sermonized against fashionable hats for years, deeming them a symbol of unbecoming vanity that distracted for their services. A pastor in Pennsylvania had banned hats in his church in 1913. According to the local newspaper, "He practically admits his inability to compete with the headgear of the ladies. He admits that he has not the earnestness or eloquence, or other resource sufficient to compel the same attention to his sermon that the artistic bonnets secure from the audience."[25]

More trouble was brewing in Philadelphia where men were snipping feathers off women's hats when their faces were tickled on transit cars or on the streets.

"This is making war on women as usual," says an indignant milliner. "We make no objection to what men wear, and they have no business to object to what we wear, although they pattern and make everything that we do wear. It almost makes me a militant suffragette, with a desire to carry a hammer so that whenever a man puffs a cloud of smoke from a vile cigarette, a nasty pipe or a cheap cigar into my face, I can knock it from his mouth. It seems that all the laws are made for man with no defense for woman. You may smile, but you'll change your tune a few years hence when we begin to take a hand in the making of laws."[26]

Smoking in the workplace was another problem three years after the Triangle Shirtwaist Fire which killed 146 garment workers. The head of a company that dyed ostrich feathers was taken to court for smoking a pipe in his factory. Though *The Milliner* agreed such a practice was dangerous since millinery workplaces contained much flammable material, the editors still sided with the owner saying, "Isn't it stretching a point to interfere with a merchant smoking a cigar in his own office?"[27]

In April *The Milliner* commented on new labor laws that restricted the hours women could work in the wake of *Muller v. Oregon*, a landmark decision from the Supreme Court. The winning argument relied on "The Brandeis Brief," which cited the scientific evidence of the day to prove women deserved a shorter workday because they were weaker than men. The brief reinforced moral beliefs of the society with a special section that claimed to show long hours also had a bad effect on women's morals. It cited the testimony of one man who worked in a cotton mill:

> I have noticed that the hard, slavish overwork is driving those girls into the saloons, after they leave the mills evenings . . . good, respectable girls, but they come out so tired and so thirsty and so exhausted . . . from working along steadily from hour to hour and breathing the noxious effluvia from the grease and other ingredients used in the mill.
>
> Wherever you go . . . near the abodes of the people who are overworked, you will always find the sign of the rum-shop.[28]

The Milliner viewed the new decree dimly:

> It is all very well for the laws to restrict the hours of labor for female help to 54 hours weekly, but the law should restrict the male workers to the same number of hours. Those of us who employ female help exclusively are placed at a disadvantage, when competing with factories employing male help. Our orders are delayed because we are restricted as to time our employees shall labor, while male workers can work 24 hours a day, if they can stand it, making more money for themselves and their employers.[29]

The editors wanted "Equality of sexes," which meant "a woman should be able to labor as long as a man if she wants and be paid the same wages for good work."[30] They called the new labor laws extreme, adding that they went too far to protect the working man and woman "forgetting all about the employer whose capital is invested and who has to make a profit on his product so as to pay a living wage to his help."[31]

Everything changed on July 28 when Austro-Hungary declared war on Serbia. All the simmering tensions of Europe were soon to explode into a worldwide war. After Germany declared war on France, the American millinery world's first concern was the welfare of Paris since the ateliers were in the midst of preparing for their fall shows. A post dated August 5 indicated that the French modistes had already shipped their wares to the States at the end of July.[32] That meant the fall season was saved, but it was easy to see problems ahead. Shortages of dyes, straw braid, and raw silks were reported. Imports of ostrich feathers from South Africa were imperiled.[33] As to style inspiration, *The Milliner* predicted, "There will be a great deal of black worn—and not only in France—for mourning will be universal," but tempered the gloom with a perky prediction, "After peace is restored (and it may be soon!) we may expect to see a wonderful crop of styles suggesting military regalia."[34] October's edition had more alarming news, though shops had reopened when the threat of siege by the Germans had eased. The House of Paquin was making shirts for sailors. Couturier Paul Poiret was in the army. The American millinery world could only wonder what would happen next. "Will it be possible even for the volatile French nature to shake off the terrible depression bound to follow in the wake of this war, and once more give to the women of the civilized universe the exquisite touch that has been the delight in French fashions?"[35] Milliners labored on for, as one said, "What else is there to do? We all have to live and hats will be worn war or no war."[36] *The Milliner's* editors worried that American women would stop buying and sought to reassure its readers. "The U.S. is not at war, and thanks to the sensible stand taken by the government, will not go to war, and there is, therefore, no immediate need to prepare for the eventuality."[37]

In November, armies dug in east of Paris. Russia and Germany sparred on the Eastern Front. More nations were sucked into the war. *The Milliner* issued "A Plea for Paris" that expressed horror that European culture was a "colossus with clay feet" yet the editors expressed annoyance at the inconvenience war was causing to the world of fashion.

It is only natural that we should feel somewhat annoyed by this great upheaval of Europe, which robbed us of old reliable Paris, Paris with her Rue de la Paix, her boulevards, and her many smart shops, all of which have become so dear to the American heart. The embarrassment of finding that the great arbiter of Fashion suddenly has ceased turning out novelties at the usual rate and accustomed speed is really serious.[38]

American milliners were trying to fill the gap, but *The Milliner* found their effort wanting since "it has been extremely difficult for American designers to take upon themselves the responsibility of producing styles without any guidance."[39] In short, the American fashion industry still wanted the guidance of Paris, so in December buyers prepared to head across the Atlantic for the spring season.

When the buyers got to Paris, they discovered a different city:

New Fashion? None are to be seen in the streets. The Parisiennes, contrary to all contradictions, are wearing their last season's costumes, usually without even going to the trouble of having them altered. The style most frequently seen is the becoming costume of the voluntary nurses; white gown cape coat of blue military cloth and close bonnet with long, floating veil. And there is a great deal of black worn, though many are refraining from wearing mourning on account of the depressing effect it has on others.[40]

The *modistes* of Paris were focused on practical items.

The great demand is for woolen things, for waterproof garments, warm gloves and shawls, and for other articles that will bring a little comfort to the brave defenders of the Nation. Even the most fashionable modistes do not disdain to design comfortable wool or silk hoods that soldiers may wear under the helmet or the *kepi* and which will provide a wonderful protection in the event of a blizzard or a biting north wind.[41]

Later the year *The Milliner* complained about American designs—they were too simple—"and it has been anything but artistic or profitable to the milliner; these styles amplify the simplified millinery of past few seasons, which cannot be called the work of artistic designers, but rather the work of novices."[42] A month before the magazine had noted Lady Duff Gordon (the designer Lucile)'s approach to spring millinery which it warned, "May seem extreme to some." Lucile advocated simple hairstyles and urged women to "do away with false tresses . . . all the fuzz, fluff and puff must go."[43] Lucile also showed hats with a deep crown which was too much: "The day when the hat was worn deep over the coiffure, fitting close about the ears, has gone and is forgotten. To-day it is imperative that at least three-quarters of the head must show, be the hat large or small."[44]

Yet, Lucile's client Irene Castle showed up in June sporting her signature bob. *The Milliner* assured its readers the look could be achieved without cutting the hair, a radical step for most women.

If one does not wish to cut the hair off a "bobbed" transformation can be bought and the wearer hair tucked under. It is a rather serious matter to cut the hair off for a passing fad, and most women and girls prize their "crowning glory" too highly to part with it without urgent need. But for those who have had their hair ruined by bad Marcel waving the new style presents a chance to shear the hair off and start all over again.[45]

The Reform or Rational Dress Movement, which had its roots in the mid-nineteenth century, appeared again in 1916. A convention of women's clubs announced the formation of a style committee "to regulate styles in women's wear and prevent the rapid change in the make-up of almost everything from hats to spats."[46] *The Milliner* took a dim view of the movement especially since the editors felt an attempt to regulate dress could stop women from buying hats, but doubted their efforts would amount to much. "The club women might as well attempt to keep back the ocean tide with a broom as to attempt to regulate women's fashions without first taking Paris and the American milliner and dressmaker into consideration. Of course, they resolve to do this or that, and then go home and do as they please, wearing what they please."[47] The article concluded that "say so must come from Paris. If this is not true, why risk mines and bombs to get there?"[48]

But there were more pressing problems. The war with Germany had left the American millinery industry with a flower shortage. Imports from France and Germany had dried up and American women did not want the job, especially the low pay of the apprentice.

In past years young girls would gladly work for a few weeks without wages until they learned to do something, and then for small wages until they became proficient, many of them destroying more material than they earned in wages. Now the law limits the age and learners now demand almost as much as good workers earned in past years. We sent to the various charitable societies for young girls who want to learn the business and when they come down to see they turn up their noses at learners' wages.[49]

Later in the year, there was a sign that Americans knew the nation was on the verge of entering the war. A "Preparedness Parade" was held on May 13. One hundred forty thousand marched down New York's Fifth Avenue to show they believed in being ready for whatever war would bring them.

War was declared in April of 1917, and *The Milliner* put out a call for businesses to manufacture hats and caps for the army. In addition, the women workers were urged to use their time in the dull season to make hospital supplies for the Red Cross, adding that "millinery workrooms will be good places to train women in how to prepare the necessary supplies."[50]

Milliners continued to mine the military for style inspiration. In July pictures appeared of the designs of Lucy Hamar, described as a lover of small hats and toques. Her hats drew on French Army caps of three centuries. One piece of "horizon blue gabardine" had a brim that was "a small drooping cloche affair." But there were still frivolous creations like Gabrielle Chanel's "dressy sports hat" with "a bowl-crown of pansy velvet and a coolie brim faced with the same velvet and covered with circular tiers of chenille and wool braid in subdued tones of purple and jade green."[51]

As the war effort progressed, wholesale millinery houses closed the afternoon of June 5 to give their young men a chance to enlist. "There were no 'slackers' found among millinery men. All were willing to do their bit when it comes to protecting their homes against a foreign foe, as well as to battle for humanity and the right."[52]

September brought a harangue against waste. "Don't order goods you won't keep. Ask your customers to carry their packages home. Don't return goods. Don't send out goods 'on approval.' . . . Uncle Sam simply can't afford that."[53] Women were urged to keep knitting "on behalf of our soldiers and those of our allies, who will suffer in the frozen trenches."[54] Despite austerity brought on by wartime, *The Milliner* called for the production of trimmed hats, not simple sporty ones, reasoning that the fancy hats would keep more people working.

The theme continued in 1918. "If the advice of those advocating strict economy in all things pertaining to wearing apparel and the many items consumed in the home is taken seriously, our shops, mills and factories would be forced to shut down, lack of business is throwing thousands out of employment."[55] *The Milliner* opined, "consumers cannot be harangued into becoming dowdy dressers, or walking epistles of poverty by wearing their old clothes. They will wear what is fashionable, let the cost be what it may. No alarmist can influence them to do otherwise."[56]

The struggle against laws that would restrict manufacturing continued. This time it was a bill in the New York legislature that would prohibit manufacturing in tenement houses. From the merchant's perspective, this bill would be a disaster since it would "cut off a large part of the earnings of thousands of people. It would, moreover, very harmfully affect several important industries, such as the artificial flower industry, which industries could not be successfully carried on if restricted wholly to factory labor."[57] More legislation followed in May that would restrict employers from setting up shop in basements of their stores and set out rules for lunch and dinner meals.[58] Later in the year, the National Child Labor Law (Owen-Keating Act) would be declared unconstitutional by a 5–4 decision of the US Supreme Court on the grounds that it was an invasion of States' rights. The 1916 law had prohibited interstate commerce in goods produced by children younger than fourteen. Children from fourteen to sixteen could not work more than eight hours a day. *The Milliner* agreed that state laws were not adequate, but reasoned that millinery was not affected anyway since women and children in New York could not work more than fifty-four hours a week.[59]

The rigid rules of mourning were loosening, even though many were losing relatives in the war. Advertisements and articles on mourning wear had run almost every issue of *The Milliner* since the magazine was founded. In 1918, the magazine emphasized the beauty of the new millinery, not the duty of women to wear mourning gear.

> The mourning hat of former times, up to no more than a decade ago, were depressing things in their austere severity. Not only depressing to those that wore them, but spreading a feeling of sadness among all those who saw them. Since then rapid strides have been made toward developing mourning millinery along more generally becoming lines. Designers realized, that even though in mourning, a woman has the same, if not even greater, claim on a hat that is becoming.[60]

The worldwide influenza epidemic ended 1918 on a grim note. Schools and theaters were closed on the orders of the Health Department. Businesses already reeling from the war experienced a huge hit to their sales as people stayed home to keep the disease from spreading.[61] Epidemiologists estimate at least fifty million worldwide died of the rampaging virus. Scientists today believe the toll could have been as high as 100 million, half of them young people in their twenties and thirties. The disease killed more people in a year than the bubonic plague of the Middle Ages killed in a century.[62] *The Milliner* made little mention of this national tragedy only commenting in the November, the midst of the pandemic: "the closing of schools and the theatres, and orders from health boards to 'keep out crowds' has the effect of keeping people out of stores and within their homes."[63] In other words, the influenza was bad for business.

Despite all the changes in the world over the first two tumultuous decades of the twentieth century, it appeared not much had changed in the male-dominated world of millinery. The Millinery Travelling Men's National Association convention was held in Indianapolis in June of 1919. Planning included a complimentary lunch for the wives because

> No ladies were more to be praised than the good wives who stood with fortitude the lonesome days of separation while the husband was exerting himself to earn the money necessary for the support of the loved ones at home. The ladies were, after all, not only the better half, so far a millinery was concerned, they were the "whole thing."[64]

The postwar period was a time of anxiety. The patriotism of the war years morphed into fear of Bolshevism and anarchism, particularly after the Russian Revolution of 1917. Labor unrest and race riots swept the country. There were anarchist bombings in April and June. In December 1919, the anarchist Emma Goldman and 248 others deemed radical were deported to Russia. Fear of immigrants from Southern and Eastern Europe reached a high pitch. *The Milliner* was not immune to these pressures. In January it published a rather confused editorial, blaming the unrest on the "newly rich" who spent money freely after the war and flaunted their wealth in public "creating envy and jealousy and a spirit of unrest that began to manifest itself not only among the working classes, but among those in the middle walks of life."[65] *The Milliner* viewed the strikes as "demands for more pay and less work, naturally lessening production and adding materially to the high cost of living."[66] Though the government had stepped in and many had finally returned to work, the editors called for more stringent measures. "There is still a cankerous growth on the body politic that needs the surgeon's knife. Deportation, however, is the only operation that will prevent a recurrence of the past year's experience."[67]

The next month an article addressed the problem of the many disabled veterans now back from the war. "The enlightened employer knows that it is his duty to give any job under his control to a cripple, if that cripple has the qualifications for it."[68] Since "there were a number of jobs a seated man could do just as well as a normal man could,"[69] one firm had a double amputee cutting out celluloid patterns. "He is well satisfied with the pay envelope he takes home each week. His hands are just as nimble as this any other man in the place and knowing his difficulty in securing employment he is more apt to be a steady worker than the average man."[70]

Disabled veterans could not fill the growing need for workers. A labor shortage developed. By July, the draconian mood against immigration at *The Milliner* evaporated. There was a National Immigration Conference in New York. The magazine issued a plea for more protections for immigrants.

> As an immigrant be may be of great value to the country as an unskilled laborer, regardless of his inability to read. . . . Our present labor shortage is estimated at between 4,000,000 and 5,000,000, and this would be relieved by a policy of admitting immigrants without book learning, but of good character, sound body and mind and the Old World habits of frugality and industry.[71]

But, the magazine ended the year on a bright note with an unusual humorous feature on how to wear a hat.[72] Miss Carroll McComas an actress starring in the popular play *Because of Helen* at the Punch and Judy Theater demonstrated the right way and the many, many wrong ways. The tilt of the hat would give you away. One style was too "Thoid Avenue."[73] Another style was too "country." Ladies were cautioned against showing too much individuality. "Since the cooks are getting wages equal to or superior to those of prima donnas, they can patronize the highest priced shops. But what are they going to do with what they buy after they get it, if they can't wear it the way they like? The picture shows individuality expressed till it hurts—others."[74] A "demure school teacher" could not wear a hat in a "rakish way" to teach a Sunday school class.[75] Finally, the article warned women not to look like the new figure who was turning up around the country. "She is a 'flapper,' and she always did adore her little terrier with its eyes gleaming out from under its forelock—so she had to wear her hat to match."[76] *The Milliner* would learn this new woman and her attitudes about millinery was a figure it would have to contend with.

7
1920s

When Americans look back at the 1920s we seem to see the decade after one of the nation's most destructive wars through a hazy, gauzy lens as if the whole decade was like an evening garden party pictured in a movie of *The Great Gatsby*. There were flappers dancing the Charleston and drinking gin, but there was also a dark side to the decade.

One of the most important events of the 1920s actually took place at the end of the previous decade, the result of a movement that began in Ohio on Christmas Eve 1873 and grew to become a nationwide crusade—Congress passed the 18th Amendment to the Constitution in December 1917 and sent it to the states for ratification. The final push toward prohibition had begun. The nation was about to begin a social experiment that would change it forever. At the time hopes were high that the nation was on the path to virtue. Earlier in the long march toward the amendment, one congressman equated passage of a nationwide ban of liquor with the survival of the moral fiber to the nation. "If a family or a nation is sober, nature in its normal course will cause them to rise to a higher civilization. If a family or a nation, on the other hand, is debauched by liquor, it must decline and ultimately perish."[1]

Ratification was completed by January 1919. Nine months later Congress passed the Volstead Act, a law that specified how the new amendment would be enforced. By January 17, 1920, the new law went into effect and the nation was officially dry.[2]

Less than six months after the 19th Amendment went into effect, another new amendment was ratified on June 4, 1919. Nearly a century after the movement for women's rights began in 1848, Congress voted to grant women the right to vote. It had taken more than a year to get required two-thirds of the states to ratify the new amendment. It went into effect on August 26, 1920, in time for women to vote for the first time in the November elections.[3] *The Illustrated Milliner*'s editorial congratulated them and urged them to "vote for business men and women who will enact laws to benefit the many, not the few."[4]

Figure 19 When women vote. What will happen if the polling place is in a millinery shop? *c*. 1909. Library of Congress.

The two amendments were linked by more than timing. Neither would probably have been possible with the other. Women in the anti-liquor or temperance movement developed political organizing skills in the movement that would help the suffrage movement expand its reach. In 1876, the formidable head of the leading temperance organization, Frances Willard, decided to throw the support of her thousands of members behind the ballot for women. She promoted the belief that giving women the right to vote would ensure morality in politics and ensure the end of evil drink.

Men, who had to vote state by state to approve the amendment, were won over to this reasoning. A notable example is the writer Jack London, who wrote a memoir about his drinking life. In *John Barleycorn: Alcoholic Memoirs*, London describes riding to vote on women's suffrage, something he had opposed for years. "Because of the warmth of the day I had had several drinks before casting my ballot, and divers drinks after casting it,"[5] he writes. When he gets home and before he has another drink, he tells his wife Charmain, he voted to ratify. Why? He claims this is the only way to close the saloons because women would use the ballot to vote for prohibition. For London, that would end the problem of alcohol since the new generation would know nothing about the lure of drink. "Not having access to alcohol, not being predisposed toward alcohol, it will never miss alcohol. It will mean life more abundant for the manhood of young boys born and growing up—ay, and life more abundant for the young girls born and growing up to share the lives of the young men."[6]

London felt his drinking was not due to any problems he had with alcohol, but as a part of male life that inevitably included the saloon.

A newsboy on the streets, a sailor, a miner, a wander in far lands, always where men came together to exchange ideas, to laugh and boost and dare to relax, to forget the dull toil of tiresome nights and days, always they came together over alcohol. The saloon was a place of congregation. Men gathered to it as primitive men gathered around the fire of the squatting place or the fire at the mouth of the cave.[7]

When both amendments went into effect, it became clear the results of each law were not what their supporters intended.

The effects of Prohibition were exactly the opposite of the dreams of its supporters. Saloons did close, but in their place, illegal speakeasies opened hidden behind storefronts, hair salons, and restaurants. To the surprise of the reformers, women flocked to these speakeasies to drink alongside men. The very group dry crusaders had promised would lead the way to a more virtuous nation, were now enthusiastically flouting the new law and smoking and dancing shocking dances to boot. Times had changed. The patriotism that dominated national opinion when the amendment was passed had dissipated. People were tired of intense progressive politics. They wanted to relax and have fun.

As the first year of the new decade ended, the labor shortage continued. Young women were not taking jobs in factories anymore, preferring more prestigious office jobs even if they paid less. *The Milliner* felt the shortage was also due to the shutdown of immigration during the war and again urged the ban to be lifted: "The only remedy for such shortage is the opening of our gates to immigrants to the right sort, who will not be too proud to work in a factory at a good wage."[8]

An optimistic story appeared in *The Illustrated Milliner* in 1922 titled "Hatting Newly Arrived Immigrants." It described a millinery training course at a public school in the Midwest. The teacher, Miss Lillian Wulfeck, was enthusiastic about her students' prospects:

The emigrant woman, who has never had a hat on her head before reaching us, is by far the most fascinating pupil, I should say. All her life this woman has rested content with a head-scarf, tied under the chin, and enclosing the entire head. Now this woman is in the United States, where women wear hats, and not head-scarves. She has put her house in order; she wants to learn millinery, that she may open shop and sell hats to other emigrant women in the tenements and, incidentally, that she may produce hats, real-up-to-the-moment American hats for herself![9]

The reality was quite different. Discrimination against the few immigrant milliners continued.

But, the tide of public opinion was turning against immigration. The Ku Klux Klan revived in 1915. By the 1920s the group had spread across the nation and had four million adherents by 1924—white Protestants who feared they were being eclipsed by the newer immigrants from Southern and Eastern Europe. Unlike the Klan of the post-Civil War, most of the Klan's members were in the North. The Klan members felt threatened by the changes in society. This meant they were against African Americans, many of whom had moved north to escape racism in the South, but had added Jews, Catholics, and Asians to the list of groups they hated. Tolerance for immigrants was in short supply especially since the native-born white Protestants feared the immigrants' higher birth rate would overwhelm the nation.[10]

Fear of an immigrant flood lead to the passage of the Native Origins (Johnson-Reed) Act of 1924, which restricted total immigration by 80 percent and established restrictive quotas for all immigrants based on their percentage of the population according to the 1890 census, when white Protestants were still in the majority. Proponents based the restrictions on the false science of eugenics, which had been promoted for decades by elite "intellectuals" that included powerful figures like the H. Fairfield Osborn, head of the American Museum of Natural History in New York City and longtime Senator Henry Cabot Lodge of Massachusetts. The law remained in effect until 1965.

But though the change in immigration laws was aimed at turning back the tide of change in the country, the world had changed for women already and there was no turning back. Women during the war had taken on jobs, sometimes wearing uniforms, to support the war effort. But even before the war, women's silhouette had changed from the full-bosomed figure made famous by Charles Dana Gibson's famous drawings of the Gibson Girl. Even though women had been pictured participating in sports like bicycling which required less confining clothing in the 1890s, the lines of dress began to change drastically in the 1910s when influential designers like Paul Poiret changed the silhouette to a tubular draped line. Poiret's trips to the United States before the war opened Americans' eyes to the possibilities of the new silhouette. There were other forces at work. The nation was swept by a dance craze in 1912 when Irene and Vernon Castle returned to New York from Paris where they were dance sensations. Soon, Americans were dancing the tango, the Grizzly Bear, the Bunny Hug, and the Cakewalk, to the tunes of ragtime, music whose rhythms came from African American culture. America was ready for change, as fashion arbiter Cecil Beaton pointed out: "when we take up the 'new' it is only because we have a secret need of it and have unconsciously prepared for its coming."[11] Irene Castle's appearance was indeed unique. "the primary effect she created was one of exquisite grace combined with an extraordinary boyish youthfulness. There was something terrifically healthy and clean about her."[12] The boyish look was emphasized by the shorter dresses she wore and her short-cut hair which was a radical change from the long styles women had worn for centuries. Beaton points to the Castles as the opening wave of modernity.

> Not only were the Castles the precursors of modern ballroom dancing, but by their grace and distinguished example they opened up the hearts of millions and sped "modernish" on its way. The dance craze that they popularized promoted a freer, less restricted social exchange between men and women. It was only a step in the revolt that would bring in the shingle and knee-short skirts.[13]

By the 1920s, a new female ideal emerged—the flapper. *The Illustrated Milliner* made fun of her at the beginning of the decade, but women did not take the style advice of these men or of the churches and legislatures who tried to regulate women's dress. Clothing had changed already during the war years and there was no going back. Skirts had been shortened due to rationing in the war years and went back to the ankle from 1919 to 1923. The hemline began to rise again reaching just below the knee in 1925.[14] Some so-called Bright Young Things eliminated the corset, but most women opted for a new type of undergirding—a long elastic corselette with heavy boning and lacing which flattened the bust and attempted to contain the hips, so the wearer could have the fashionable girlish silhouette.[15]

The State of Utah tried to fine and imprison women who wore skirts that were more than three inches above the ankle. In Ohio, a law was introduced that would forbid a woman older than fourteen from wearing a skirt that did not fall to the top of the foot. The YWCA had a nationwide campaign against the new dress.[16] But the die was cast.

The changes in dress were a symbol of the changes in social norms. Women did not only go to speakeasies with men; they smoked openly, wore makeup, and rode with men in automobiles without a chaperone—all signs of looser sexual norms. One of the characters in F. Scott Fitzgerald's *This Side of Paradise* announces brightly, "I've kissed dozens of men. I suppose I'll kiss dozens more!"[17]

The new icon was promoted by the newly powerful advertising media. The suffragists had wanted women to have the vote as a route to have more control over their lives. Historian Nancy Cott points out that advertising and increased consumer merchandising translated desire for individuality to increased consumption and gives an ad from *The Chicago Tribune* as an example: "'Today's woman gets what she wants. The vote, slim sheaths of silk to replace voluminous petticoats. Glassware in sapphire blue or glowing amber. The right to a career. Soap to match her bathroom's color scheme.'"[18]

The flapper's image was all pervasive in the 1920s epitomized by women like Zelda Fitzgerald, wife of F. Scott Fitzgerald, and "Lipstick," pseudonym of *New Yorker* writer Lois Long, who prowled the nightspots of New York's for her column "Tables for Two." Long described nights full of booze, jazz, madcap dancing, and, even, a police raid of one of the clubs she frequented between 42nd and 60th Street: "It was one of these movie affairs, where burly cops kick down the doors, and women fall fainting on the tables, and strong men crawl under them, and waiters shriek and start throwing bottles out of the windows."[19] Antics like these lead another *New Yorker* writer to call Long "Miss Jazz Age."[20] However, fashion historian Emmanuelle Dirix cautions not to apply the term to all women of the period:

> I consciously refer to the flapper as a type of modern woman because contemporary ideas about this creature have been shaped by her popular representation during the period rather than a perception of her as a living breathing human being. . . . Which is not to say she was an invention of the commercial industry but she was its tool; she was thus both the literal and metaphorical illustration of an ideal—an idea linked to a debate very much alive in the 1920s popular culture; the debate about the rise of the New Woman.[21]

It is important to note that uptown in Harlem was the vortex of 1920s culture. Its nightlife fueled by jazz came out of the African American culture. Long, like many other whites, went "slumming" in Harlem. In one of her trips, Long denigrated Harlem's entertainers, even claiming whites were better dancers. She observed "most of the Negro girls entertaining along Lenox would do well, either to take Charleston lessons from one of the thousand flowers of American womanhood adorning our [downtown] choruses, or to invent a new dance."[22] She described one dancer there as "one of the most vigorous animals I have ever seen turned loose in public."[23] This racist sterotyping was common at the time. Historian Joshua Zeitz points out that for Long, as for most Americans: "Flappers weren't supposed to look only slim; they were supposed to look white."[24]

This dynamic was in play in 1924 when Parisian couturier Jean Patou, known for his fashionable sportswear, placed an ad in the *New York Times* seeking "three ideal types of young American women who seriously desire careers as mannequins in his Paris atelier. Must be smart, slender, with well-shaped feet ankles and refined of manner."[25] The turnout was overwhelming. Five hundred applicants auditioned. Patou ended up picking six models, all of them young white women who conformed to his vision of Americans as women who were taller, slimmer, and more athletic than French women. These were women he felt would show his clothes off to the best advantage. Though the African American dancer Josephine Baker would take Paris by storm in 1925, in the fashion world, the ideal American woman would continue to be white long after the image of the flapper faded.

The "New Woman" would also become known for a new hairstyle, a short cut originally worn by children known as the "bob." Dance star Irene Castle (1893–1969) is considered the one to introduce the style to the United States in 1914, though designer Coco Chanel (1893–1971) also cut her hair short around the same time. Avant-garde women were cutting their hair short by 1917. By 1920 most women had accepted the style which became a symbol for the "flapper." It was very controversial. Women were warned that shorter hair could weaken the scalp and increase hair loss. They were also told men would not want to marry women who sported the bob. Movie stars like Louise Brooks, known for a "Dutch Boy" cut with full bangs, Clara Bow, and Colleen Moore appeared on screen in the bob. African American dancer Josephine Baker wore the most extreme version, the Eton crop, a very short cut slicked down with brilliantine. Screen star Mary Pickford, known for her long golden curls, agonized over the decision to cut her hair. She finally succumbed at the end of the decade.[26]

Women's hairdressers were not prepared for the new style. They had been trained to arrange the hair and pile it high on the head, often using hairpieces to augment the arrangement. They also knew how to decorate the hair with combs and other ornaments and to color, curl, and wave the hair. But few had been trained to style hair by cutting it, which was precisely what the new style demanded. So, women flooded to men's barbers to get the look they wanted. They invaded a space traditionally reserved for men like the saloons Jack London had written about nostalgically. The famous American trial lawyer Clarence Darrow wrote about this "invasion" of his hometown barbershop in an article to *Vanity Fair* in 1926:

> I had, of course, realized that in many ways the world was changing; that new machinery and a modified social life were making their inroads everywhere. With all the rest I knew that the Nineteenth Amendment, bobbed hair and women's clubs were "ladysizing" the world. I have never realized that the barber shops too, were suffering from the blighting touch of new ideas and social customs.[27]

Darrow finds change has come to his small town when he stops by for a shave. Gone are the copies of *Police Gazette* with pictures of chorus girls. They are replaced with *Women's Home Companion*. Also missing are the cuspidors for used cigarettes and the rack of shaving mugs, replaced with a cupboard of powder, lipsticks, and rouge. The barber has changed too: "His voice was modulated to a lower key. He was not talking. He was a solemn, quiet and respectful man. He did not even look like a barber. He looked and dressed like the secretary of the Y.M. C. A."[28]

As Darrow meekly waits his turn, the young woman in the barber chair gives directions: "'Cut the ends just a little bit at a time so we can tell when we strike the outline that I want. Don't go too deep at the back of my head, where it's flat, you know.'

'Yes, yes—I remember,' answered the obliging young man; 'you'd look good with a swell new wind-blown touzle.'"[29]

After her cut, the young woman

patted the whisk-broom effect bristling over her ears, chummily asking, "Would you have a hot oil shampoo, if you were me, or would you wait until I have my next marcel?" The barber hesitated, thoughtfully, before replying, "Well—for your style of coiffure I'd advise only water-waves. We have just got in a Ritzie line of water-wave combs, in the big show case next to those 'Vanity Razors.'"[30]

More women enter the shop. Darrow flees. "As I went away I pondered over the long steady invasion of women into what was once men's domain and what this invasion means to both. Is not the so-called 'Women's Awakening' taking the colour and freedom from the world?"[31]

The new bob had long-term effects. The short hair needed to be cut much more frequently than hair in the past. Since women of all ages and classes had embraced the new shorter styles, there was an opportunity for hair salons where women could go and receive other beauty services as well—coloring, permanent waves, facials, and manicures with the newest beauty aid, nail color.[32]

The new hairstyle demanded a new style hat. The signature hat of the 1920s was the cloche, a close-fitting bell with virtually no brim that was worn straight on the head almost hiding the eyes. Debate rages over who actually invented the cloche style. Some give the credit to Parisian milliner Caroline Reboux, who is said to have produced a deep-crowned hat with a brim that was not as wide as the huge "Merry Widow" hats heavy with trims that were the rage in 1908.[33] Fashion historian Madeline Ginsburg gives the credit to Gabrielle Chanel, who began her career as a milliner before the war,[34] while historian Susie Hopkins claims another French milliner Lucy Harmar introduced the cloche in the pages of *Vogue* in 1917.[35] Whoever was the first, it is clear that the changing times had a strong influence. Women working for the war effort needed simpler, less cumbersome designs, and the wartime shortage of material meant there was less material available for hats. Another cause of the shift in millinery fashion was the automobile. In 1916 Lorinda Perry pointed out that "the vogue of small automobile hats"[36] was one reason women were not buying as many in the summer.

By 1911 hats had gone from being horizontal with huge brims to vertical with hats that had helmet-shaped crowns that rose high often decorated with ribbons or even, wings of birds.

The huge hats of the past did not have to fit the head exactly. They perched on top of the woman's pile of hair secured with hatpins. Women could also buy a Pullastic, an adjustable inner band that could be adjusted with a drawstring for a tight fit. But, the short, shingled hair of the 1920s meant a hat had to be blocked to fit the head exactly. Gone were the wire frames that gave shape to the hats. The cloches were softer with little buckram or other interior construction.

This simplicity worried many milliners who were afraid the new style would mean they would lose business. Caroline Reboux herself was afraid the cloche would mean the end of millinery.[37]

But the new hats were simply too popular. *Harper's Bazaar* commented in October 1923 that "the cloche (like the chemise dress) is so youthful that women simply will not relinquish it."[38]

Despite these worries, the allure of the Parisian milliner was still strong, American retailers imported them, copied them, and sold their designs under their own labels. Indeed, fake labels could be purchased by the bolt. It was all legal since the country had no laws against it.[39] There was plenty of demand for new hats; American retailers loved to display them. Chicago flagship department store Marshall Field set up a special salon that catered to young women aged sixteen to twenty-two. It was decorated in the "French" style with a dressing table covered in lace, hand mirrors, and cosmetics boxes imported from France along with miniature French dolls. *The Illustrated Milliner* approved:

> The deb and sub-deb are a mere step removed from the grown woman of to-morrow. Their patronage is most important, for not only have they more time to shop (and having their minds burdened with less responsibility they shop much more critically that their elders) but the hat's becomingness is all-important to them. When pleased, they will bring a host of friends to the store and department showing themselves eager to please them.[40]

They will also spend money in a decade devoted to relentless consumerism. "They pay more for their hats, buy hats oftener, and once their friendship is gained life-long patrons for the establishment are made."[41]

More cosmetics became acceptable because the cloche was worn pulled down low to the eyebrows. *Vogue* editor Edna Woolman Chase declared "chic started at the eyebrows."[42] Cosmetics to emphasize the face became acceptable spurred by the images of Hollywood stars whose makeup was devised by Max Factor, a Polish Jewish immigrant who created their looks to counteract the strong lighting used in the films of the day. Factor established his own makeup company which competed with Helena Rubinstein and Elizabeth Arden for the customer's dollar.[43]

Sales of cosmetics rose sharply from $17 million in 1914 when wearing cosmetics was scandalous to $141 million in 1925. By the end of the decade, consumers were spending $700 million annually on cosmetics and beauty services.[44]

Across the country there was an increased interest in fashion due to increased purchasing power and easier access to credit after the war. Department stores transformed themselves focusing on making the shopping experience a grand source of entertainment featuring dramatic displays of goods in huge windows and on the retail floor. "Sell them their dreams," a speaker told a convention of display artists in 1923.

> Sell them what they longed for and hoped for and almost despaired of having. Sell them hats by splashing sunlight across them. Sell them dreams—dreams of country clubs and proms and visions of what might happen if only. After all, people don't buy things to have things. They buy things to work for them. They buy hope—hope of what your merchandise will do for them. Sell them this hope and you won't have to worry about selling them goods.[45]

Across the country department stores expanded. In New York City's Fifth Avenue underwent a metamorphosis from a residential street where the wealthy had their mansions to a shopping district. The area between Thirty-fourth and Fifty-ninth Streets was rezoned by 1929 while just a block away on Madison Avenue advertising firms set up shop.[46]

Another specialized area was set up for garment industries. Before the war, a portion of Seventh Avenue was zoned to keep these businesses downtown, so garment workers would not flood the sidewalks of Fifth Avenue at lunchtime. Between 1921 and 1929 the ready-to-wear garment industry and its ancillary suppliers, showrooms, and studios moved to Seventh Avenue between West Fortieth Street and in the 1930s down to almost Twenty-third Street anchored by three large buildings between West Thirty-sixth and West Thirty-eight streets.[47] Five of the largest millinery houses followed the rest of the industry and moved to Seventh Ave at 36th, 37th, and 38th Streets.[48] By the end of the decade, "Seventh Avenue" meant fashion and cemented New York City's place as its leader.

The milliners themselves were still restricted by the society's view of working women from the past. The passage to the Nineteenth Amendment gave women the right to vote, but many other elements of their citizenship remained to be settled. Oddly enough, the image of the flapper worked against them. Historian Alice Kessler-Harris points out: "In return for limited economic and sexual freedom women were encouraged to adopt a flighty, apolitical, and irresponsible stance. The image was intended to guarantee only peripheral involvement in the male world without the threat of competition."[49] Women were to know their place in the work world and it was to be subservient to their male bosses.

It was still assumed that women's natural place was in the home. Reformers in the early twentieth century felt what they called women's special traits—

compassion, morality, and sympathy for others—would be crushed in the workplace. If women had to enter the work world, the thinking went, special laws needed to be enacted to preserve these qualities. Many of the protective labor laws were grounded on the assumption that women were weaker physically. The findings of the "Brandies Brief," written before the war, would restrict women's progress in the world of work since it encased assumptions about women's weaker physical condition in law with "scientific" data, such as "Physicians are agreed that women are fundamentally weaker than women in all that makes for endurance: in muscular strength, in nervous energy, in the powers of persistent attention and application."[50] Enshrining these beliefs in law lead to prohibiting women from working in many jobs just as the labor market was opening up after the war. Many of the gains women had made during the war by filling formerly male jobs like trolley conductor, heavy manufacturing, and welding evaporated as men returned from the front. In 1926 Republican Secretary of Labor James Davis reaffirmed his backing for this protective labor legislation proclaiming "the place fixed for women by God and Nature is a great place" and "whenever we see women at work we must see them in terms of motherhood."[51]

Davis seemed to feel the "New Woman" of the 1920s was a danger and expressed concern about "the increasing loss of the distinction between manliness and true femininity."[52]

A logical place for women to gain better working conditions would have been membership in a labor union, but by 1920 the number of organized women was miniscule. Twenty percent of the workforce was made up of women, but less than 8 percent[53] were in a union despite the labor strikes and organizing of the previous decades.

Unions themselves were not welcoming to women workers. The men who ran them believed with the Secretary of Labor that women should be in the home. They had the additional fear of being undercut on wages since women were paid less than men. "Every woman employed displaces a man and adds one more to the idle contingent that are fixing wages at the lowest limit,"[54] thundered an editorial in the *American Federationalist*, the house organ of the American Federation of Labor (AFL). Those words were written in 1896, but the attitudes persisted. AFL president Samuel Gompers frequently wrote articles in *The Federationalist* with titles like "Should the Wife Help Support the Family?"[55]

By the end of the decade, women were working in a wider variety of jobs, such as office work, nursing, teaching, retail sales, as well as the garment trades. These were all jobs that were fixed in the public mind and policy as jobs women could handle. Men and women were segregated in different job categories, partly due to protective labor legislation and societal and educational norms that directed women into what was deemed appropriate. Class played a role as well. Married and poor women were expected to stay at home, while white, native-born unmarried women had more opportunities. There were fewer immigrant and black women in the workforce and fewer jobs for them.[56] For milliners, there was another problem. The new hat styles required them to learn new skills. Milliners had been trained to cover wire frames with shirred material and embellish the hats copiously with feathers, flowers, and ribbon trims. The new cloche eliminated the inner wire structure and had to be blocked over a form to give it the proper shape—a hot, steamy job that required upper arm strength. Few women had been trained in this work, so men or blockers were hired and paid more for this work.[57] As millinery historian Wendy Gamber tells us,

> Male and female coworkers were not equal. On the contrary, the modern millinery manufacturer instituted a division of labor that recalled the distinction between (male) finishers and (female) trimmers in the men's hatting industry, a distinction that carried weighty if nonsensical connotations about masculine and feminine capabilities. Blockers claimer the exclusive right to perform "the heavy machine processes' and thus 'earned' the designation as the most skilled of millinery workers, relegating trimmers—once the aristocracy of the trade—to second class citizenship."[58]

To add to the problems of the milliners, the hat industry moved to mass production in the mid-1920s. Machines were invented that blocked hats. Production increased. The new hats were cheaper. Customers could buy a new hat each season rather than keep a custom-made hat and retrim and clean it over the years.[59] The new machines were another drawback for women millinery workers since men controlled this work as well.

They were still relegated to monotonous jobs behind the scenes. Opportunities to open a shop were much more limited. There were a few exceptions for women with exceptional drive. Peggy Hoyt was one. She apprenticed herself to a milliner when she was a teenager and was able to save $300 to open her own shop on upper Fifth Avenue. She later moved to the Fifty-fourth Street, which was becoming the center for custom millinery. Her shop had hundreds of employees selling hats on one floor and clothes on another. Her success was largely due to her actress clientele which meant her creations would be seen and coveted by other fashionable women.[60]

Lilly Daché was another success story. She arrived in New York in 1924 from France where she had been trained by Caroline Reboux. She worked at Macy's for a short time but was able to find a partner in a shop on the Upper East Side. Daché was very good at promoting her French taste and style. After several moves she was to establish herself on Madison Avenue where, like Hoyt, she catered to movie stars. She would continue to influence millinery styles into the 1960s.[61]

Custom shops with expensive hats and accessories still survived. At the other end of the scale were shops that appealed to local trade, usually

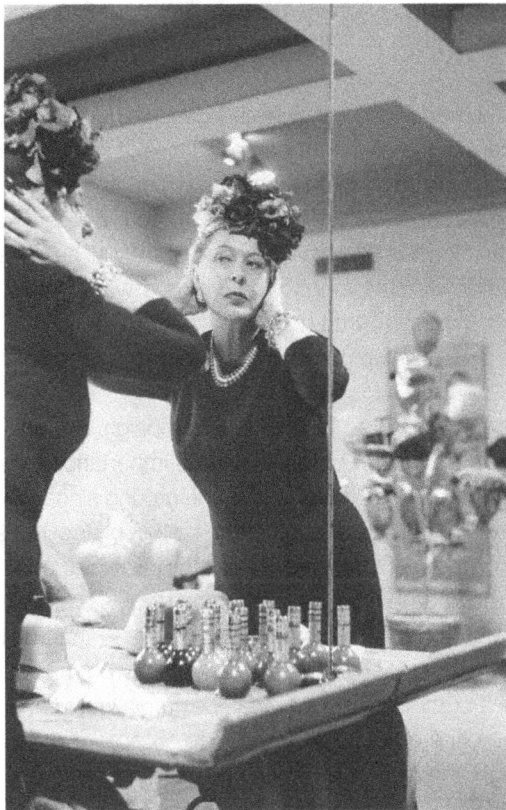

Figure 20 Hat designer Lily Daché checking out a new design, 1956. Photo by Leonard McCombe/The LIFE Picture Collection via Getty Images.

working-class women who were not at ease in department stores. Neither of these was the majority of the millinery world. The intimacy of the smaller shop was largely replaced by the department store and the wholesale factory where women worked for men. The sales clerks who staffed the millinery departments replaced the milliners as the prime contact for customers, but they had no connection to the production of the goods they sold. The emphasis of the factories was to produce as many hats as possible. Women had no real choice in what was produced since men decided what styles to turn out each season. They were the ones who went to Paris each season to see the newest models.[62]

Despite all the frenzied production, government statistics show that "millinery and millinery dealers" declined from 121,446 in 1914 to 69,598 in 1920, a decrease of more than 40 percent.[63] There was a brief scare in the middle of the decade, something milliners feared most—hatlessness. Delegates to the United

Hatters, Cap Makers, and Millinery Workers Union's 1929 convention worried about this phenomenon:

> In addition to the trade evils mentioned above, we have lately been faced with the development of the vogue for bareheadness. It first appeared about three years ago and it was considered a passing whim of the public. It kept gaining favor however and now we find the youth in the colleges, high schools, and even elementary schools to have discarded entirely all headwear. Even during the severe winter, we find young men who are warmly clad in good winter coats and even in furs wearing no head coverings whatsoever. If this fashion should continue to develop, it may destroy our trade entirely[64]

The union tried to launch a nationwide campaign on the importance of wearing a hat "as a protection of health and its importance for a well-groomed appearance."[65] The campaign never got off the ground since few manufacturers were interested. Union officials scorned "this indifferent, irresponsible and short-sighted attitude of the manufacturers make the task of the Union to maintain some stability in the trade even more difficult than would ordinarily be the case."[66] Still, as the end of the decade approached, it seemed the public's appetite for fashion and love of shopping would never end and even more prosperous days were ahead. It was commonly thought that the nation would only continue to get richer and more prosperous.

In 1928, though, the *New York Times* called the end to the era of the flapper asking, "Who has seen in recent days this creature? . . . Her hair was famously frizzled. Her smoking was overenthusiastic. Her chewing gum was too loud and too large. Her vocabulary was imported directly from the trenches. She was startlingly picturesque—and now she is no more."[67]

Whether that editorial was a prediction or not, it all came crashing down on October 29, 1929, when the stock market crashed.

> The crash of 1929 was the end of a dream. The lush days were gone. The rich layers of fat that cushioned the American economy melted away. For all business the months immediately after the stock market crash were perforce a period of stocktaking. In the millinery industry, the impact of the terrific wastes inherent in its anarchic and chaotic structure made itself felt almost overnight.[68]

The next decade would be a time for retrenchment and reevaluation in the millinery world. For all, the era of the Flapper was truly over.

8
1930s

Black Tuesday (October 29, 1929) created waves that reverberated through the fashion world throughout the 1930s. American buyers for department stores and garment manufacturers did not show up at all for the presentation of spring collections in Paris the following January. Paris had relied for decades on American customers who bought the licensed copies of the new fashions.[1] The relationship between Paris and New York had been strong with New York relying on Paris for design inspiration while Americans manufactured versions of those designs at all levels to be sold through the nation's strong network of retail outlets. Now, there were patriotic advertising campaigns that urged Americans to buy American goods to stimulate the economy. The government added to the pressure by raising import taxes that could go as high as 90 percent.[2]

The silhouette of women's clothing had begun to change toward the end of the 1920s. The natural waistline emerged again, hemlines were lowered and a more "ladylike" style emphasized the figure instead of the flattened chest of the "garconne." After the reign of the simple cloche hat in the 1920s, the decade began with a fedora-style hat to top the more structured suits and dresses of the time. Women quickly realized they could change their look by changing their hats and save some money on dresses. Millinery styles began to change every season and with each change came controversy. In 1931 a style called the "Empress Eugénie," swept the country. It was inspired by a hat worn by Greta Garbo for her role as an Italian soprano in the 1930 movie *Romance*, a nineteenth-century period drama. Designed by Adrian[3] and named for the wife of Emperor Napoleon III of France, it was small, "low-crowned, point-brimmed, fitting the head like a piece of orange peel with curled edges. It flourished a provocative ostrich feather"[4] and was worn angled over one eye. Fashion journalist Ernestine Carter recalled that the hat "was copied widely at all price levels, its original ostrich plumes dwindling to a single feather, and as it plummeted to bargain basements, often plucked from lesser fowls. As we now know you can be too successful, and by 1932 the Eugénie hat had become a joke."[5] Garbo was an enormous influence on fashion in the 1930s, an example of the growing influence

Figure 21 Homesteaders' daughters are employed in the millinery department of the cooperative garment factory at Jersey Highlands, Hightstown, New Jersey. Photography Collection, Miriam and Ira D. Wallach Division of Art, Prints and Photographs, The New York Public Library.

of Hollywood. Her style off-screen was equally influential. She preferred slouch hats and berets worn with man-tailored styles. The clothes of other film stars like Rosalind Russell, Jean Harlow, and Joan Crawford were promoted by the Hollywood publicity machine. Women could buy copies and find out more about the fashions of the stars through the many movie magazines that appeared during the decade.

Another hat appeared in 1930 that set a new direction for women's hats. This was Elsa Shiaparelli's Mad Cap, a tiny knitted tube that could be shaped any way the women who wore it wanted.[6] That hat was so successful it was copied by the American designer Clare McCardell while working for the powerful retailer and wholesaler Hattie Carnegie. A section of McCardell's notebooks from that time opens with a section titled "Hats for Hattie." One (which McCardell was pictured wearing in 1939)[7] is definitely her version of the "Mad Cap."

The Eugénie style was quickly replaced. Milliners were determined that fashion would not dictate one style as in the 1920s, so they mined history, the native headgear of exotic foreign countries, art movements, such as surrealism, and everyday items like peach baskets, lampshades, and milk cans for hat designs.[8] *Contemporary Mode*, a millinery trade magazine, editorialized in 1936:

The nude hats[9] must not come back—the pea in a pod kind—all alike. It means monopoly of business, controlled buying, the complete crushing of the creative art of hat making. This brings us to the need of constant changes in millinery fashions. Individualized interpretations, more colors, better designed shapes and the necessity of developing and accepting American designers . . . and, creating an appreciation for the importance of the correct hat for the correct occasion, and the right hat for the wearer.[10]

In order to realize the optimistic view of the future of millinery fashion, the industry would have to overcome chaos spurred by the Depression. Twenty percent of the millinery businesses in the country failed every year.[11] A special report for the National Industrial Recovery Board chaired by the future New York governor W. Averell Harriman stated: "The Millinery Industry was completely unable to deal with the chaotic labor and trade problems with which it was faced. The facts . . . show a completely disorganized industry scattered over the country, using every competitive method known and many engaged in vicious exploitation of labor."[12]

The union that eventually came to represent the milliners had a hard struggle to exist in the early decades of the twentieth century, which put it at a disadvantage when the Depression hit. Originally, the union represented only cap makers, mostly men who cut out and sewed cloth caps commonly worn by the working

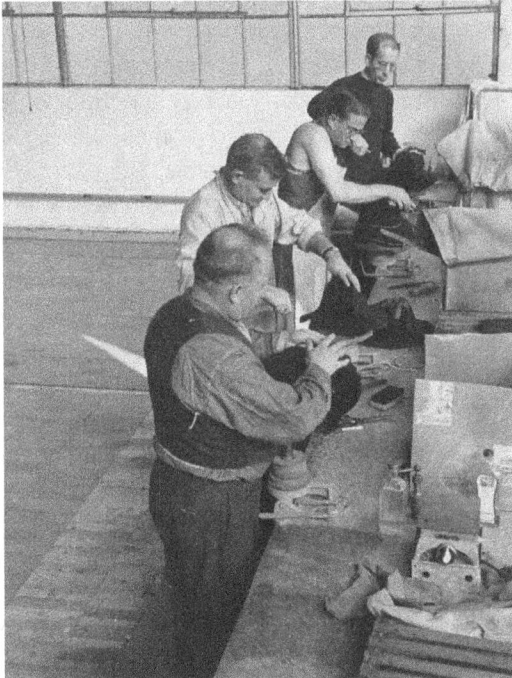

Figure 22 Hat makers blocking and finishing hats in a cooperative garment factory in Hightstown, New Jersey, 1936. Photography Collection, Miriam and Ira D. Wallach Division of Art, Prints and Photographs, The New York Public Library.

class. It became clear the union would have to organize millinery workers too since milliners were also making fabric hats. This was difficult due to the seasonality of the employment of the workforce. The milliners were suspicious of the men who were trying to organize them. Sixty percent of the milliners were native-born, who considered their work a "highly refined occupation to which 'nice' girls could go and still not be considered run-of-the-mill factory workers."[13] The cap makers' union was largely an immigrant work force, so their male organizers had to overcome the milliners' suspicions and prejudice.

The organization proceeded in fits and starts. The workforce was fragmented, due to the way workers were organized at the time. The Cap Makers were part of the AFL which organized its workers by the particular trade or skill, a system called "craft unionism."[14] This made it difficult for the Cap Makers to expand since the skills needed for fashionable hats varied often from season to season. The entire history of the union is replete with mergers as different locals representing different skills were blended into a larger union. Often, the Cap Makers would find themselves in conflict with another union that claimed the same group of workers. This made it difficult to confront the challenges they would face from outside groups who would try to take control.

In New York City, the center of the millinery industry, the union appealed to workers downtown in the area of sweatshops, while the milliners who worked uptown in more exclusive shops resisted organization. The men in the downtown businesses scorned the uptown women calling them "lipstick girls."[15] Employers fanned the prejudices of their workers, sometimes claiming that the men in the union wanted to drive women out altogether. There was some truth to this claim since women knew the AFL had often blocked women from membership, viewing them as strikebreakers and as workers who kept wages low. Bitter strikes and lockouts characterized the years between 1910 and 1919. The union made some progress but hit a wall when the postwar depression hit in 1921, just when the union's contract expired. Manufacturers stonewalled all the union's demands. When the contract expired in 1922, the union would not see another for ten years. But, there would be even greater challenges from the outside that would threaten the union throughout the 1920s.

Earlier in the century, a number of young immigrant Jewish women, including Rose Schneiderman of the Cap Makers turned to socialism. The Socialists established a school to educate workers. Their learning often led them to union activity. None of these women were milliners, but their energy and organizational ability would lay a foundation for other female workers to follow. Many of the leaders of the union were also Socialists or sympathetic to their outlook.[16] But, shortly after the Russian Revolution in 1917 a challenge to the Socialists and the entire union movement emerged. Communists set out to take over the union through the formation of another educational organization, the Trade Union Educational League.

Initially, the union tolerated the Communists since they were often good organizers, but problems developed quickly. The Communists groups began to try to tear the union apart from the inside. An organizer in the Chicago local, Anna David, was hired in 1929 on the condition that she would not use her position to push her politics, but union leaders discovered she was trying to take over the Board of the local and then went to a Communist conference in Pittsburgh in 1928. Participants in the conference tried to form a union to oppose the United Mineworkers, a union the Cap and Millinery Workers had been allied with for some time. David was immediately fired, but bitterness remained. Soon there were pitched battles on the streets of New York between knife-wielding furriers sympathetic to Communism and the hat makers.[17] The Communists were finally ousted in the UCHCMWE Convention of 1929, but an even bigger challenge had already surfaced in 1927.

The enactment of the Eighteenth Amendment had another consequence its backers did not foresee. Racketeers quickly began smuggling liquor into the country to satisfy the nation's insatiable thirst. The enormous profits that resulted made it easy for the mobsters to extend their power. Labor unions were a prime target.

The Mob operated on four fronts. They pressured employers to hire them to "protect" their business from unions. Of course, there was a substantial fee involved. They also were hired by unions to "protect" the group from gangsters hired by the employers. Phony unions were another tactic. These fronts were used to extract money in the form of union dues from the workers and extort fees from their employers to keep the business operating. Finally, the mobsters sought to take over a union completely to control the union's resources and maintain power over workers and employers.[18]

The hatwear industry was targeted by "Little Augie" Orgen, an East Side gangster who had a squad of gunman to back him up. Augie appeared in the offices of Local 24, the key union for milliners in New York. He was backed up by a gun-toting bodyguard named Legs Diamond.[19] Augie told Alex Rose, the local's secretary-treasurer, he was supplying protection to thirty-five of the largest manufacturers uptown. For the fee of $100,000, Augie guaranteed no strikes and lower wages for the workers than the union was demanding. Rose refused to call off the strike, but the threat remained.

At the same time, the head of the Chelsea Hat Company in Lower Manhattan was approached and told Augie could keep his workers from unionizing for a $2,000 payment. Before the payment could be made Little Augie was shot and killed on the streets of the Loser East Side. Legs Diamond was severely injured.

This was not the end. Jacob Kurzman or "Tough Jake" took over Augie's district and continued to infiltrate the garment trades. New York City was awash in booze and corruption with 5,000 speakeasies in Manhattan alone.[20] So, when the union went to local law enforcement in 1930 for help in expelling the racketeers, the district attorney hauled the union leaders before a grand jury on the strength of a corrupt manufacturer's complaint.[21]

Finally, in September 1931, the union president Max Zaritsky asked New York's lieutenant governor Herbert Lehman for help to expel the Mob from his ranks. Lehman set up a committee of 700 volunteers who overran the millinery district downtown and called workers out on strike in the shops "protected" by the mobsters. The police commissioner of New York assigned uniformed officers and detectives to the office of Local 24 to keep those who worked there from being assaulted.

Lehman also directed the union and the manufacturers to begin bargaining for a contract, which they reached in 1932. The new agreement achieved major improvements in their members' working conditions and wages. This was at a time when the industry was contracting and the workforce had dropped from a high of 33.000 in 1927 to 27,000 in 1931.

The union then called a general strike for March 17 in an effort to organize all of New York and eliminate the gangsters. Targeted strikes and considerable union pressure brought results. Five hundred shops were organized, bringing 3,000 new members to the union. Ninety percent of the trimmers in the uptown shops joined. The Mob and its phony unions were eliminated; however, there remained a problem with male blockers who had resisted the strike and worked through it. That fight would drag on until 1933 when the two groups agreed to unite.[22] Still, unionization was barely respectable in most of the country and the union braced for more battles ahead.

That would change in March 1933 when Franklin Delano Roosevelt became the thirty-second President of the United States. Roosevelt's approach to the grinding economic crisis was a complete change from his predecessor, Herbert Hoover, who had opposed involving the federal government in relief efforts. Roosevelt launched the New Deal, which saved banks (which were almost out of funds), launched infrastructure projects to put people back to work, and established relief programs for farmers—part of a series of thirteen major bills he pushed through Congress in his first hundred days. The last of these bills was the National Recovery Act (NRA) whose goal was industrial recovery. The first part of the bill established codes for each industry to ensure fair competition, set up standards for the workplace, and ensured the trade unions' right to exist. The second part of the bill launched the Public Works Administration. For the unions, the most important section of the new bill was Section 7(a) which gave unions the right to collective bargaining. The new act adopted the "Blue Eagle" as its symbol. Industries that complied with the new wage and work codes displayed the symbol and consumers were encouraged to support those industries.[23] There was even a pledge for school children: "I promise as a good American citizen to do my part for the NRA. I will buy only where the Blue Eagle flies. I will ask my family to buy in September and buy American-made goods. I will help President Roosevelt bring back good times."[24]

The unions rushed to organize. Even though the president backed them, it was still a dangerous time. Historian William Manchester points out that the President's Commission on Violence looked back on the history of American labor in 1969 and declared the United States "has had the bloodiest and most violent labor history of any industrial nation in the world."[25] This comment was aimed specifically at the 1930s when organizers were often murdered; companies hired private detective agencies to battle their workers and stocked weapons to keep workers under control. The violence was not limited to the heavy industrial unions like mining where one company bombed miners' homes and burned crosses on the hills near their company towns. When women in the garment trades began to agitate for better conditions, a manufacturer's trade journal editorialized, "A few hundred funerals will have a quieting influence."[26]

The Millinery Workers were no strangers to violence, but the men who headed the union were determined to avoid it and use the new provisions in the NRA to achieve reforms they had been advocating for years and bring an end to price gouging and cutthroat competition that kept the industry in chaos. As President Max Zaritsky and his Secretary-Treasurer Alex Rose began to negotiate with the companies, they discovered the business leaders were in favor of the fair trade practices called for in the Code. But, they were not enthusiastic about instituting fair labor practices the Code called for. Nonunion companies were opposed to minimum wage brackets which would mean companies could not try to get more of the market by paying lower wages, giving them an advantage over the unionized companies who had negotiated higher wages for their workers. The union also wanted a thirty-hour workweek, which all companies resisted.[27]

The new rules worked best in markets where the union was strong like New York City. Manufacturers in the South resisted. There were thousands of violations issued. On the whole, the NRA helped the industry. Millinery output went from $77,347,000 in 1933 to $88,988,909 in 1935. Workers' wages went from an hourly average of 36.2 cents in 1931 to 62 cents an hour in 1934. The union compromised on the workweek hours fixing it at thirty-seven and half hours per week. This was a huge change from the ten-hour days demanded by employers at the beginning of the century.[28]

NRA officials went all out to publicize the Blue Eagle label and educate consumers to look for it. In February 1935 Edward Fries, the Label Review Compliance officer, in Los Angeles, gave a radio address titled "Sale-ing with the Good Ship 'Label'" [29] Fries emphasized the humanitarian need for consumers to back the new Code:

Your new dress has come from the store. It is your most becoming color and it fits you like a dream. You try it on to see again how nice it looks. If your mirror could tell you the story of your dress, over your shoulder you would see the faces of those who had made it for you. Are they healthy, contented, intelligent? Or are they hungry, weary, perhaps diseased? You can't see the people who made your dress, but you can find out something about them, because if your dress has the Blue Eagle in it, you can tell that it was made under acceptable working conditions by people who were paid a fair wage and whose working hours were not too long. If your dress has no such label, you can be pretty sure that the opposite is true, that sweatshops, child labor, low wages, long hours and unsanitary working conditions were the experience of those who made it for you. . . . Above all, look for the label in everything you wear [original emphasis].[30]

Another label review officer set up a group of shoppers to check for labels in their area and educate retailers and consumers. Because no paid advertising could be used, churches, civic groups like the YMCA and YWCA, the National Consumers' League, and other women's groups were contacted. As Easter approached the slogan, "Don't Be a Dumb Bunny!," appeared urging women to look for the label when they purchased their Easter finery, since Blue Eagle-labeled clothing were "the only clothes fit for the Easter Parade."[31]

The Code Authority had big plans to reform the millinery industry and proposed an ambitious "Planning and Education Program." The first section was aimed at educating manufacturers since 20 percent of them went out of business every year. Again, "cutthroat competition" was blamed for ruining the market for millinery. "It may be said that millinery had literally been placed on the 'auction block.' Millinery has been removed from its style setting and placed in a bargain basement level."[32]

One practical suggestion was to encourage manufacturers to "Know Thy Costs" since many manufacturers did not keep any accounting records and did not know how to calculate their costs before going into production. The report urged the Code to assume this role since the millinery manufacturers did not have a national organization to coordinate such a push for improved business practices. "The manufacturer must be made to realize that his very existence depends on the maintenance of an accurate cost system, yet the methods employed to convince him of this all-important fact must pursue a course which will not arouse antagonism."[33] Monthly mailings were suggested along with semi-annual conventions for the manufacturers where they could learn about the new economic challenges they would face.

But, the recommendations went further. Seasonal sales had been a problem in the industry for decades, so the report proposed a push for "Four Seasons Instead of Two." The year would be divided up into short selling seasons—spring season would run from February to April, summer from May to July, fall from August to October, and winter from November to January. The goal, just as the goal of Mary van Kleeck's study earlier in the century, was to keep milliners working year-round and to end competitive price slashing that destroyed the market in the middle of the previous two seasons. The report cited as evidence the introduction of a new "Summer Millinery" season that had recently been introduced in 300 cities across the country and increased sales in May and June. One buyer for a large San Francisco department store agreed with the plan, saying it would increase stability into the market.

> If buyers would depend on these dates [the new seasons], they would have a longer season in which to do a profitable business; they would have less reductions to take and faster movement of reduced merchandise, because all these reductions would occur simultaneously, and the consumer would not feel she could get reduced merchandise at any time as she does now.[34]

Retailers were encouraged to form associations and hold fashion exhibitions to grab the interest of the consumer in millinery. This would have the added benefit of fighting any trends to hatlessness, which had been a worry in the industry since the 1920s.

To increase sales even more and enhance the special nature of millinery for a woman, the report proposed another campaign called "A Hat for Every Occasion." [35] The idea behind this was women should be encouraged to buy a new hat to coordinate with the rest of their dress for each special day. Apparently, fashion writers had been contacted about this idea and were enthusiastic. The Code Authority proposed augmenting the message by distributing radio scripts to push the new idea.

Finally, the report urged that retailers be encouraged to make their millinery departments special again with increased advertising, plenty of window displays to show off the latest styles, and sales staff that understood millinery and were trained to sell it. Restoring millinery to a prestigious position in stores would hopefully counteract a slide that began when the Depression hit and women began to demand cheaper hats.

Millinery departments in many stores had been taken over and leased by syndicates, who controlled buying and distribution for much of the millinery market. That meant the buyer was more concerned with cheap prices than with style, according to testimony in 1938 by a representative of the Millinery Stabilization Commission before Assistant Attorney General Thurman Arnold, head of the Antitrust Division. The testimony went on to claim that the large firms stifled competition by receiving excessive credit from suppliers and employing sweatshop work to keep overhead as low as possible.[36] "The industry lives on style. For prosperity in the industry, there must be a morale conducive to the inspiration of new designs."[37] This testimony urged the adoption of legislation that would allow the smaller manufacturers to band together to fight the strength of the large buying syndicates.[38]

It should be noted here that all the key players in the millinery world—labor, management, and government—were men even though the workforce was largely female, making a product that was to be worn exclusively by women. After the enactment of the Nineteenth Amendment, women's political power ebbed. Historian Susan Ware points out that "Politicians had discovered they had little fear from female voters: women tended to vote just like their husbands, if they voted at all."[39] Even though there was a Department of Women in the federal Department of Labor, the basic assumption undergirding labor laws on women was much the same as it had been in the nineteenth century—women should be encouraged to marry and have healthy families. An indication of the attitudes toward women workers appears in *Designing Women*, a guide to dressing published in 1938. Writing about what to wear in public, author Margaretta Byers cautioned women to wear a wrap even in the summer: "True, times have changed and long sleeves are no longer *de rigueur* on the street. But, you must have some sort of sleeve even in summer, . . . If you don't care for frank comment from unknown admirers, you'll want to make assurance doubly sure with a jacket or cape; obviously capes are coolest."[40] Byers also gave advice for dress in the workplace. "Receptionists are taken for their face—and figure—value. All you need to be a receptionist is a reasonable amount of looks, perfect grooming, and an impressive wardrobe."[41] A woman executive is told: "Your boss, who can't understand why his wife spends so much on clothes, is not likely to reckon with your wardrobe when paying your salary, yet, if you don't dress superlatively, someone else will get your job."[42]

The common attitude to women workers shows up in the conversation of the officials of Local 24 as well. They debated what to do about organizing in New England where a young woman named Feigel Levine was having trouble getting men to cooperate with her, even though the men of the union felt she was an "able organizer." Union president Max Zaritsky even says Levine "has the determination of a bull-dog when she gets hold of a manufacturer."[43] However, the men cannot decide what to do, since appointing a man to help her would be awkward. They naturally assumed the new man would have to be Levine's superior and be paid $50 more a week![44]

Local 24 in New York City continued to try to organize custom milliners uptown in the area near Fifth Avenue and 57th Street. This was "the most aristocratic part of town, where people go out shopping with dogs,"[45] as Alex Rose told his Executive Committee. Workers here made one hat a day, which sells for $25, a huge extravagance in 1934 equal to $475 today. Alex Rose told Local 24's Executive Board these milliners did not think of themselves as workers but considered themselves designers and artists.

The union hatched an ingenious publicity stunt to bring attention to their organizing drive. As Rose told it,

> We realized that the only way to impress that part of the city was to picket in their own way, and we had already hired little dogs and were going to have our pickets walk up and down with signs, holding the dog on a leash and we were going to have photographers snap pictures and we expected to be the talk of the town.[46]

Before the picketing could begin, the president had intervened, pressuring the company to settle. Rose sounded regretful. Local 24 did manage to organize Milgrim Hat Company, a major firm that had been in business serving a wealthy clientele since the 1920s, even distributing its hats nationally.

The next target was Lilly Daché on Madison Avenue. Organizing began in April of 1935. Daché claimed to be compliant with the NRA, but her prominence made her an important target.

The union's dreams hit a roadblock in June 1935 when the Supreme Court unanimously declared the NRA unconstitutional. Labor and management continued to spar bitterly getting to the brink of a lockout in November when New York mayor Fiorella LaGuardia stepped in and called both sides to City Hall. Out of this meeting came the Millinery Stabilization Commission, an independent agency that could audit the books of the manufacturers and monitor the trade. It was headed by Max Meyers, a highly respected figure who had negotiated the "Protocol of Peace" that ended crippling nine-week strike of cloak makers in 1910. Meyers had also headed the NRA's Millinery Code authority, part of his long experience with the garment industries. He managed to keep the industry engaged in many of the ideas for reform proposed under the NRA including training manufacturers in cost accounting, promoting the long seasons, and fighting cost cutting. The commission also continued a crusade against "ash-can hats," hats that were actually pulled from the trash and resold without being cleaned.[47]

The commission also conducted campaigns to encourage new designs. "It has gotten Hollywood Stars to wear these new creations in films; it has introduced them in dramatic fashion shows; it has plugged them in newspapers and magazines, all in hopes that new modes would be launched and American Women would start rushing toward the nearest hat shop."[48]

The industry and the union would have to respond to drastic swings in hat styles from the middle of the decade on. The comparatively simple "mannish" fedora-style hats that had evolved as a reaction to the cloche would not be the only styles available. Indeed, by the end of the 1930s, there were almost too many styles to keep track of. *Life* magazine observed:

> Since the dictionary definition of a hat is "shaped covering for the head"; women can go completely haywire by wearing what they will and still call it

a hat, if it covers the head. Why the coverings take the strange shapes they do, is an unfathomable mystery. . . . Milliners say that all hat styles seem strange until they are a year old. Then they are accepted as normal. But by that time no chic woman would wear them. She must go on to new lines, new trimmings, new gadgets to make herself look different.[49]

To prove this point, the article was accompanied by photographs taken on the streets of Manhattan of women wearing hats, including the writer Dorothy Parker.

"None is a trick hat, made as a gag and posed on models for a laugh. In each case the wearer thinks hers is smart or flattering or serviceable or something."[50] *Vogue* spoke up for the extreme swings of style, saying: "Say what you like, there are certain moments, certain moods, when a Sound Hat simply will not do; when a mad hat, a fey hat, a sheer flight of fancy, is the only course."[51]

Women's hats got more and more extreme due to the influence of the Surrealist movement in art. *Life*, a weekly magazine that was the leading chronicler of current events and trends, covered the ups and downs of hat fashion, often in a cover story feature.

In 1937, it was veils.

This year, while the women of the Near East are still rejoicing in the fairly recently acquired freedom of showing their faces, more women of the West will cover their features with veils. No one knows why, but manufacturers in the U. S. are running their factories overtime to supply a demand for veils 19 times greater than last year's.[52]

Then, in 1938, couturière Elsa Schiaparelli introduced the doll hat, a miniature hat worn precariously forward on the head. It took the world of fashion by storm. A storm of ridicule erupted. In its article on the subject, "Now the Fad is Dolls' Hats/Did the Comics Inspire These Pee-Wees?," *Life* writers compared the hats to those worn by cartoon characters. "*Life* hereby calls attention to the fact that these 1938 apologies for hats are adaptations of two American classics: at left, Mlle. Minnie Mouse in her piquant chapeaux designed in 1928 by Walt Disney and at right, Happy Hooligan in his original stovepipe designed in 1900 by the late Fred Opper."[53] A picture accompanying the article showed a doll hat with dotted lines around it so it could be cut out. The caption read: "Here is a pee-wee leghorn, reproduced actual size so that fashion-conscious readers may cut it out along the dotted lines and see for themselves how they would look in a Schiaparelli stovepipe. This one sells at Bonwit Teller for $17.50."[54]

Along with the fashion for doll hats came snoods, which encased the hair and balanced the front tilt of the doll hat. It too was met with controversy. Milliners thought snoods would contribute to hatlessness. The Millinery Stabilization

Commission ran a "Hats vs. Snoods" ad campaign against the style; Hairdressers hated them. *Time* reported that

The 1939 snood, balancing front-tipped hats, almost completely encased the hair in fabric—jersey, velvet, grosgrain—nullifying the hairdressers' art.

U. S. hairdressers were hopping mad. When Mab Wilson, beauty editor of *Vogue*, addressed the New York State Hairdressers and Cosmetologists' Convention last week on coiffure trends, her audience was fit to be tied. Miss Wilson actually appeared in a vivid green pillbox, her hair lushly snooded.

Honorary President Emile Martin glared at Miss Wilson's snood and leaped to his feet after her talk to present a resolution damning snoods. Even the fluttered Miss Wilson voted aye.[55]

Covering the hair continued in 1939 as designers went back to the Middle Ages, the wimple, which completely covered the hair and neck, was introduced. *Life* attributed the style to the problems of keeping the doll hat on the head.

Since the introduction of the pee-wee hat last summer, milliners have been experimenting with devices for anchoring all types of small hats to the head. Bits of ribbon and elastic, net snoods, and even hatpins were used. Winter presented a further problem of preventing small-hat devotees from getting colds in the head. Discarding as too simple the obvious solution of making hats bigger, milliners revived a style which medieval duchesses and nuns of all times have found flattering.[56]

In the next edition, several readers complained about the new style. One man from Washington, DC, wrote, "Sirs: Now you've found a name (wimple) for the rag around your head, the women who used to wear these things at housecleaning time, and refused to answer the doorbell, will come out of hiding and wear them in public. W.M. Temple, Washington DC."[57] Another letter writer called the wimple "freakish"[58] and said the model wearing it could "celebrate the recent Pan American Convention by representing a Peruvian Indian belle,"[59] ending with the question: "Why don't Schiaparellli and her ilk take up basket weaving or retire into a convent and quit goading American women into abnormalities of dress? Peevishly yours, Robert Ridgeway Jr, LA."[60]

The turban style also emerged, inspired by the Directoire Ball in Paris in the spring of 1937.[61] By 1939, turbans and other styles were swathed in veiling, *Vogue* enthused: "And now—hairnets! Nets cut in new shapes for the new hairdos. Nets that are part of your hat. Nets that tie with a bow. It was inevitable—this revival. But don't think any old net will do the trick. It is the new versions that make these nets head-liners in the new mode."[62]

Looking back on this prewar period, the artist Marcel Vertès felt the search for novelty went too far, as he wrote in his book, *Art and Fashion*: "On the heads of the couture's feminine clients they were going to put shoes, mutton chops, setting hens, all disguised as hats. Objects less tragic in their implications than Neville Chamberlain's umbrella but nevertheless marking the end of an epoch."[63]

New York City itself was changing by the end of the 1930s, emerging from the Great Depression determined to challenge the great capitals of Europe. Skyscrapers loomed creating an imposing urban landscape. In 1932, Lord and Taylor executive Dorothy Shaver made a radical move, showcasing American designers by name in the store's windows and on the fashion floor. Before this, American designers and milliners were not featured by name since the department stores felt the mention of their names detracted from the store's brand.[64] *Vogue* responded to the new interest in the work of American designers with its first "Americana" edition in February of 1938, but the magazine did not mention milliners by name, only manufacturers and retailers, especially textile manufacturers. However, there had been a breakthrough for American milliners the month before. In the first issue of 1938, the magazine featured the first editorial pictures of fifteen American hats.

This new confidence in American style from New York had a dramatic setting at the end of the decade. The 1939 World's Fair was intended to showcase all that was new and advanced in the city. The fair, which *Vogue* called "the Coney island of the intelligentsia," covered 1,200 acres in Flushing Meadows dominated by the fair's symbols, the Trylon which rose 700 feet over the Perisphere which contained a diorama/movie called the World of Tomorrow.[65]

The "Americana" issue that February had a cover that showed Lady Liberty crowned with the Trylon and Perisphere. Inside an article showed futuristic fashion created by scientists, artists, and architects. A *Vogue* feature shot on the site of the fair shows models dressed in day suits, each with a hat to complete the look. The accompanying copy crowed:

> *Vogue* gives you Spring 1939, editions of these unquenchable fashions— fashion of a type that will conceivably go on till the end of time. Like as not, the fabulous creatures of To-morrow will take off for Mars in a neat little suit, stroll the parapeted ramps in prints, and play comet golf in clothes not unlike the ones that we show on these and the next 4 pages.[66]

Thus, it was a great honor when Lilly Daché, one of the most prominent American milliners, was chosen to place one of her hats in the World's Fair time capsule. She responded with her best and predicted: "When scientists dig up this time capsule, in 6938, they will know that women were chic, even five thousand years ago."[67]

But, for all the optimism displayed in *Vogue* and at the fair, the millinery industry was still plagued by the same problems. In 1939, the Department of Labor headed by the first female secretary Frances Perkins produced its own report on the millinery. Despite a decade of legislation, negotiating, and government intervention, the problems described in the 136-page report replete with many charts and graphs bear a striking similarity to the problems cited at the beginning of the Depression.

For Local 24, the 1930s ended with one advance. They managed to organize uptown fashion house Hattie Carnegie. "It is an aristocratic shop, selling hats wholesale a $23 each and retail for about $40 each. It has always been non-union. It was never in competition with the cheaper grade shops, yet it was a matter of prestige for the Union to show it can also organize the higher, and even the highest priced makers."[68] They were helped in this drive by the International Ladies' Garment Workers (ILGWU) whose 400 members closed down the company, staged a sit-in, and refused to cross the milliners' picket line until the company settled.[69]

By September of 1939 war loomed over Europe. In the United States, there was a hot political debate over getting involved in another conflict. The American fashion industry began to wonder what it would do if it was cut off from Paris's inspiration.

American milliners were ready to exercise their creativity, believing that they had to feed their customers new styles constantly or they would stop buying. Sally Victor expressed the feeling widespread in the industry—a fear of returning to the hated 1920s, the time of the cloche:

Let us go back to that time which still must be fresh in the memories of the majority of the industry, to the time when fashion inspiration was stifled and everyone wore a cloche. Organizations of fabric manufacturers, trimming houses, milliners, tried every means of propaganda to bring back millinery that was millinery. The time when nothing but the felt cloche made a uniform head covering did more to wreck the millinery business than anything before or since.[70]

The mayor of New York, Fiorello LaGuardia, felt New York could become one of the world's great fashion capitals. He threw the weight of his administration behind the promotion of one of his city's largest industries. While the world waited to see what would happen to Paris, he told a gathering of fashion professionals in March 1940: "New York is the center of fashion of the entire world . . . I don't see why we have to take our fashion from any other country . . . and I hope to see a time when people will be copying New York models."[71]

LaGuardia's confidence stemmed from the widely held belief that American women had a special "look" that distinguished them from Europeans. It was described by *Vogue* in 1938 in an article titled "The Best Dressed Women—and Why." The copy stated flatly that American women were special because of the American system of government:

> Even God and Democracy are in cahoots. Well, maybe not God, but that polyglot blood in our veins gives us, to help carry off that dress—long legs, thin ankles, narrow hips, bright eyes, a passion for youth, a hopeful attitude. And thanks to our political, up-by-the bootstraps system, every little girl has her chance to keep up with the glamour girls.[72]

Some fashion editors were not sure American women were ready to be fashion leaders, among them *Harper's Bazaar*'s editor-in-chief Carmel Snow, who told the Fashion Group she thought American women were too casual in their approach to fashion:

> On the whole the American women have too little personal point of view about their clothes. They grab a new dress and go out to dinner. They never have a dress rehearsal. They want to look like everyone else. They won't take chances. Yet they want to look well dressed. Often they don't deserve to look well-dressed. They haven't done enough about it. They care passionately, but ignorantly.[73]

Several years later, two young *Vogue* staffers, Eileen Ford and Carol Philips learned firsthand how strongly Snow felt about dressing correctly at all times when they ran into her on a train platform in Penn Station. "Both women had taken off their hats and gloves, a huge no-no at the time. 'We had put them in our pockets and Mrs. Snow really chewed us out,' Ford recalled. I remember she said, 'Where's your hat, young lady? Carol almost died.'"[74]

But more and more young women were beginning to go without hats. A youth culture emerged in the late 1930s with a style that was more casual than those seen on the fashion pages. "Girls' daytime wear . . . prescribed twin sweater sets (cashmere or angora for the affluent), mid-calf plaid dirndl skirts, ankle socks (later to be known as bobby sox), and babushkas."[75] The babushka—a simple triangle of cloth tied under chin traditionally worn by Eastern European peasants—was definitely not a style American milliners wanted to encourage.

Harper's Bazaar ridiculed these young women calling them "half decapitated creatures."[76] *Contemporary Modes* enlisted men in the fashion industry to extol women in hats. One of them invoked aesthetic reasons: "As a photographer, I'm concerned aesthetically with the contours, line, expression, bone structure and shadows which heighten interest in a feminine face. When a woman appears on the street without a hat, the entire composition is unbalanced and the absence of shadows means the removal of charms which compensate mechanized backgrounds."[77] Another ridiculed hatless woman, saying, "You have hit on one of my pet peeves—the hatless dame. The one girl I don't want to meet—and I'm sure most men will agree—is the one who walks down the avenue hatless, with a cigarette in the side of her face. She must be about as uninteresting as she looks."[78]

Vogue aimed to stamp out the problem with a feature called "Half a Hat Is Better Than None," which showed two leading debutantes, celebrities who were known for going hatless in the new "half-hat" style, "A mere excuse for a hat. A half-hat invented for bare-headed young rebels."[79] This was quite a coup since one of the debutantes was Brenda Frazier, a media sensation. For milliners, the photograph of Frazier was worth a thousand hat sales. The caption breathlessly described the hat on her famous pageboy: "No longer bare-headed as usual, but with a hat. It's a mere cluster of grapes and leaves, which doesn't hide her long black hair."[80] Since debutantes were considered fashion leaders among the young, who were the most likely group to go hatless, milliners thought Frazier's new hat would solve the problem. It did not. Hatlessness was a problem that would continue to obsess American milliners throughout the war years.

However, the war seemed far away from American shores in 1940. American milliners were focused on using whatever time they had without Paris to get the recognition they felt was long overdue. They felt that with the right imagination and style they could convince women to wear their hats. A hatless future was unimaginable. So, as American women entered a new, dangerous decade, fashion dictated that they would enter it with spirit. "With more seriousness, deeper realization—American Woman are turning their eyes forward, turning their hands to directing airplane controls, gathering relief funds, campaigning for domestic issues . . . hands no less helpful for being well-gloved, eyes no less perceptive for being shaded by a becoming hat."[81]

9
WAR AND STYLE

Great Britain and France declared war on Germany on September 3, 1939. That month *Vogue* editor-in-chief Edna Woolman Chase told the Fashion Group that the war would not kill their industry:

> Today here in America we are prepared to give a much better account of ourselves as designers today than we were a quarter of a century ago, so I do not think we need fear for fashion's future. Besides, there is always something about the psychology of war that seems immensely stimulating to love and to fashion. Men in uniform always stir up the feminine emotions, and women in love always want to look their loveliest—so naturally, the beauty parlors flourish and the dressmakers prosper.[1]

Despite the tension, it still seemed possible Paris fashion would be able to continue as it had during the First World War.[2] The mood in Paris was tense since no one knew what to expect. Bettina Ballard later wrote of the strange suspended mood of the city.

> Life was at a standstill in France with the morale being sapped from our veins, with no compensating demands for our help or for our courage. It was as if all France had been wound up like a clock and never allowed to strike. . . . Everyone was corroded with boredom, and the abnormal tension of waiting for something, you couldn't imagine what, had a numbing effect.[3]

Then, in June 1940, German troops marched into Paris. The "phony war" had ended—the Occupation had begun. Across America, fashion observers wondered what would happen. During the last great conflict, Paris designers had still managed to maintain their salons and export their styles. This war was different. Many ateliers had closed as their designers fled the country. In July, German authorities raided the offices of the couturiers' association, Chambre Syndicale de la Haute Couture, and removed its files, concentrating on those that dealt with overseas markets. A month later, Lucien Lelong, the president of the Chambre Syndicale, was informed that the Third Reich had decided the new headquarters of couture would be Berlin or Vienna. Parisian couturiers and their highly trained workforce would be required to move to these two cities. The future of French haute couture was in peril.[4]

Since the full effect of the Occupation was unknown, Americans in the fashion industry sensed an opportunity. It was a new world for American designers, who eagerly prepared to take advantage of the opportunity with no real idea of what the future held. Morris DeCamp Crawford, editor of *Women's Wear Daily* and astute observer of the American fashion scene, echoed the fears that accompanied the new challenge, "After the natural sympathy and the real sense of loss had abated in New York, a curious reaction took place. What would we do without Paris styles? Would our factories close down, and our stores become arid deserts? Could America create its own styles?"[5]

Promoting and supporting American fashion became associated with patriotism; money spent on clothing and accessories would help the economy and provide money for keeping the American economy afloat at a time when most of the country's trading partners were shut down.

By August of 1940, it was clear that there would be no Paris fashions that fall. News from Paris was blacked out. *Time* magazine reported on August 19:

> Last week, for the first time in more than two decades, some 300 U. S. dress manufacturers, designers, buyers and fashion editors failed to spend early August in Paris, France. . . . For the first time since they began publication *Vogue* and *Harper's Bazaar* sent to press their all-important autumn issues without a single last-minute Paris model to rave about.[6]

On August 22, Mayor LaGuardia held a meeting with twelve leading fashion writers to learn more about the city's fashion industry. Despite his earlier pronouncements of confidence in the ability of New York's fashion industry to succeed, and possibly, surpass Paris, it was clear he was confused about the world of fashion. At the beginning of the meeting, he told the writers: "I'm interviewing you today; you are not interviewing me. I want to learn about the fashion business."[7] As the conversation went on in the stifling August heat, it was clear the mayor was becoming frustrated: "The Mayor listened in rapt attention as the conversation flew rapidly around the circle in this informal gathering. From time to time he mussed his hair as first one then another editor talked of the former leadership of Paris, explaining how it furnished this market with models."[8] None of the writers were able to tell him how to harness the creativity of New York designers to make them a world leader that set the trends in fashion.

When one fashion writer told him that fashion spread from the top of society that "snobbery of style gave it its élan,"[9] the mayor exclaimed, "Snobbery can't be the controlling power anymore; times are changing."[10] He then told the writers he had a plan for the industry but was not ready to tell them what it was. Then he expressed the competition in terms he understood.

> When the question of the possibility of turning out as good clothes in this country as Paris produced was brought up, the Mayor reminded his listeners that we had gone through the same period of uncertainty in trying to produce good beer, cheese, and spaghetti. "And now we make better spaghetti here than they do anywhere else because we have the wheat and machinery."[11]

On September 8, the *New York Times* began to credit American designers by name in its Sunday fashion pages.[12] This was an important step to change public opinion. If Americans were going to respect the skills of the American garment industry and its designers, they would have to learn more about who these designers were and see their fashions covered regularly.[13]

The fashion magazines turned to New York designers to fill their pages. *Vogue* announced in a full-page advertisement in the *New York Times* on September 5, 1940, that it would cover the American collections like the magazine covered Paris.[14] The magazine's two September editions were dubbed "American 'Openings'- Issues."[15] The advertisement's copy posed the question foremost in the minds of the fashion world:

> For the first time in fashion history, American is on its own—without the direct inspiration of Paris. . . . The first completely American Collections are now ready. They settle, once and for all, the question agitated in the headlines of every newspaper. "Can America Design?" For the American Openings have given us clothes that are wearable, charming, original. American women will keep their reputations as the best dressed women in the world![16]

Vogue promised its coverage of the American styles would be "reported with the same authority, the same critical judgment, the same brilliant picturing of the mode by top-flight artists and photographers, that *Vogue* has brought to the reporting of the Paris openings during the past fifty years."[17] This was a major change in editorial policy since before this time *Vogue* had not gone to the showrooms of American ready-to-wear manufacturers to see their samples.

The exiled designer Elsa Schiaparelli did not feel New York could replace Paris as a fashion capital. She told an audience at Lord and Taylor's in late September that the two cities had fashion industries that were very different. She pointed out that Parisian couture had developed over 300 years into an industry that produced models "with an emphasis on beauty and on creations designed for the individual."[18] By contrast, Schiaparelli claimed American designers were hampered by the emphasis in the United States on mass production and the

American women's lack of appreciation of "fine workmanship and high quality materials."[19] She told the group that the United States could not replace the taste and elegance of Parisian couturiers, asserting: "France and its industry have not been smothered . . . there may be ashes on the fire, but the flames are still there. This industry struggles to thrive and produce once more. Be assured it will rise again to its place as the center of artistic creation in fashion."[20]

As Paris millinery struggled to survive, in New York the fashion industry was preparing for its biggest showing of fashion ever. The "Fashion Futures" show staged in December 1940 was given high priority by the Mayor's Office. The head of City Hall's business advisory committee told the *New York Times* the industries affected were worth more than ten billion dollars to the city economy.[21] The Fashion Group and the Fashion Originators Guild worked with the six uptown stores that had participated in the show and 150 manufacturers in all facets of the industry including millinery.[22]

More publicity came from Mayor LaGuardia who appeared at the International Dress Company in late December to "inspect" the work being done for the show. On his tour he studied the hem lengths, the cut of lapels, and posed for pictures with the company's models.[23] Then, the mayor "picked up a tape measure and with deft hands measured the bust and then the waist of a dummy."[24] He pronounced the new styles "pretty, practical and trim."[25] However, when he was informed the new dresses would retail for between $18.25 and $25 (equal to $281.08 and $379.83 respectively), he paused, since these were not garments his working-class constituents could afford. Finally, he finished his tour with the promise of a polished politician, saying: "If they are to be worn by secretaries and young professional women we'll have to see to it that their salaries are raised."[26]

After the *Fashion Futures* show, the *Times* declared New York was the unquestioned Fashion Center of the World with 70 percent of the American women's market and "enough talented milliners here, turning out 55 percent of the hats manufactured in the whole country, to keep the men of the country talking the year around."[27]

But, as the year 1940 ended, it was far from clear that the new styles were successful. In December, *Time* magazine reported that hatlessness was still a problem for the millinery industry. There was a $6,000,000 business slump that began in the summer.[28]

Three milliners emerged as leaders in the American fashion world, "uptown" designers whose work would set the pace for the industry and be copied endlessly by the Seventh Avenue merchants downtown.

It is true to say that if the fashion hegemony of Paris was ever seriously challenged it was challenged through millinery. Despite the great modistes of the City of Fashion, a convincing case can be made for New York as the leading millinery city from the late 1930s up to the 1950s, with designers such as Lilly Daché and Mr. John often outstripping the Parisians in wit and style.[29]

Designing the hat for the time capsule was the capstone of a very successful decade for Lilly Daché, one of the best-known fashion personalities of the day. Born near Bordeaux, France, she learned millinery from her aunt, moving on to Paris around 1915. She apprenticed with leading milliners Caroline Reboux, Suzanne Talbot, and Georgette. She came to the United States after the First World War and worked her way up from a millinery job in Philadelphia to ownership of a small shop on New York's Upper East Side. By 1937, her business had flourished so much she was able to commission her own nine-story building at 78 East 56th Street where she would base her business until the late 1960s.[30] Her influence was so strong that she would go on to be featured in ads for cigarettes and cars.

Since she was based in New York throughout her career, Daché is considered an American milliner. However, she always emphasized her French roots, attributing her flair for design to this background. She traveled frequently to Paris to acquire materials for her creations and keep up on the latest French styles.

Her clients included Hollywood stars and society leaders as well as stylish women from around the country who came to her salon for just the right hat. Daché believed fervently in the ability of a hat to illuminate a women's personality, to bring out what might be hidden under the simple lines of the dresses and suits. As she wrote in her autobiography, "A woman's hat is close to her heart, though she wears it on her head. It is her way of saying to the world: 'See, this is what I am like!' Or—'This is how I should like to be.'"[31]

Just as famous as Daché was Mr. John, who was part of the team of John Frederics in the 1930s.[32] Nicknamed "The Mad Hatter" and "The Emperor of Fashion," he was famous for his outrageous designs and flamboyant personal style. In her autobiography *Talking Through My Hats*, Lilly Daché commented that her competitor's designs were not for everyone, because "the madder his hats, the better he likes them. His customers like them too, so all is well."[33] Details about his early life are difficult to find because he embellished his tales considerably and changed his name at least four times. But, it seems clear he was born in Munich with the name Hans Piocelle Harberger and came to the United States as a child. Both his mother and grandmother were milliners, but John had to overcome his father's opposition before he was able to become a milliner himself.[34]

He was noted for his wizardry with materials. Years later, Fay Hammond, the *New York Times'* fashion editor, described Mr. John as "like Napoleon incarnate but when he manoeuvres a silk scarf into a hat before your eyes, he commands the dexterity of a magician and the sensitivity of a fine artist."[35]

He also created iconic hats for Hollywood, such as Marlene Dietrich's hats in 1932's *Shanghai Express*. He formed a close association with Adrian, Metro-Goldwyn-Mayer's head of costume for sixteen years, and also designed many

Figure 23 Mr. John demonstrating a spring hat in New York City. 1962. Photo by Yale Joel/The LIFE Picture Collection via Getty Images.

hats for Paramount's costume designer Travis Blanton. However, Mr. John never joined the union and he never received on-screen credit,[36] so we will never know just how many hats he actually designed for films.

The hats he designed for the actress Vivien Leigh to wear in *Gone with the Wind* are some of the most famous in movie history. They include a "Parisian" bonnet presented to Leigh's character, Scarlett O'Hara. John claimed he was paid $20,000 for this hat alone. Metro-Goldwyn-Mayer's press release called him "America's most outstanding designer of feminine headgear."[37]

Behind all the posturing was a craftsman who was proud of his work. Stanley Marcus in an important 1940 article on the state of the American fashion industry pointed out the firm's unusual emphasis on its American roots. "John-Frederics, one of the country's leading millinery creators, was the first and only American designer, to boast 'Made in America' on its hat labels."[38] The press release for the new salon confirms this, proclaiming: "Americanism is the mood of all John

Frederics' hats. From the tricorne of George Washington to the monkey hat of the moment, the manner and the making are all-American."[39]

By the end of the 1930s, he was reaching the peak of his powers. In 1940, *Vogue* commented: "He is famous for his firework flow of imagination, the maddening, but becoming whimsy of his hats (people say he laughs and laughs as he fits a woman into coal-scuttle and makes her like it). The son of a milliner, he has great feeling for beautiful detail, for timelessness, and for drama."[40]

The final member of the triumvirate was Sally Victor, an American product through and through. Born in Scranton, Pennsylvania, she began her career as a saleswoman at Macy's in New York and went on to become the head millinery buyer at Bamberger's Department Store in Newark, New Jersey. She married Serge Victor, a ready-to-wear millinery manufacturer, and had a son, but soon went back to work. After Victor established her own label, she, and she alone, was the public face of her company. In 1934, Victor opened her own exclusive shop in Manhattan's Upper East Side and her work was featured by Dorothy Shaver in Lord and Taylor's advertisements and windows on New York's Fifth Avenue. She was immediately identified as a designer to be reckoned with. "Sally Victor, though she may not originate, picks up a trend and enlarges it with uncanny judgment and speed. . . . Hats are things that either make or mar. Sally Victor has been making the 'right' kind for about three years now."[41] She was extremely productive, able to make thirty hats a day when under pressure—a

Figure 24 Milliner Sally Victor designing a hat, 1948. Photo by George Silk/The LIFE Picture Collection via Getty Images.

total of 2,000 designs a year.[42] She spoke often about drawing her inspiration from the art in American museums, but she was able to create hats inspired by vegetables, kitchen bowls, and the traditional sunbonnets of the American West. She firmly believed that women should wear hats that made them look pretty, an idea somewhat at odds with the prevailing style of the 1930s when the ideal was to look as chic and sophisticated as possible. In a 1932 interview, Victor credited her work in department stores for giving her insight into what her customers wanted: "My experience as a buyer in a department store," resumes Mrs. Victor, "has given me a very definite appreciation of the retail customer's slant. . . . Of course, I take trips abroad, but my designs are my own."

Unlike Daché and Mr. John, Victor aimed for the middle-class customer and didn't mind if her work was copied, though she too, counted Hollywood stars and socialites as her customers. Her strength as a designer came from her firm belief in the power of a woman's hat. As she told a millinery class at New York University in 1941, "Hats tell stories and they tell stories on you. The right hat for the right woman tells a flattering story. People talk a great deal nonsense about hats, but the choice of your hat is a serious matter. I have seen the choice of a hat change a woman's destiny. Hats give or take away a women's sex appeal."[43] That philosophy would guide a career that would last into the 1960s.

As 1941 began, an article in the *New York Herald Tribune* pointed out that even the leading designers were having difficulty getting materials imported from Europe: "Lilly Daché has had to forego the metal trimmings and plastics which she reserved for her most exotic bonnets. She is replacing them with fur, wool, feathers, and ribbons."[44] There were also problems getting millinery felt, so the industry began to experiment with substitutes.

Women were also encouraged to make hats themselves. Building on a nationwide craze for knitting and crocheting clothes during the Depression, magazines published articles equating knitting with patriotism. Knitting made the cover of *Life* magazine in November 1941 with the picture of a young college student straining over her first knitting project. Inside, the article asked the great question for American women, "What can I do to help the war effort?" and answered it with one word, "Knit!"[45] There were three pages of pictures showing how to knit, two more with advice from European knitters on finishing knitted pieces, and a picture of a hat and gauntlet gloves one could make with a pattern available by mail from *Life*. The picture's caption made it clear that knitted hats were for the young, stylish, and frugal: "Hats and matching gauntlets are a popular young fashion. This set is made with hanks of knitting worsted in contrasting colors. Their spiral effect is achieved by shifting colors. This type of yarn costs about 65c a hank. Set can be knit for $1.30."[46]

The mainstream millinery business viewed the handcraft trend with trepidation, feeling that more casual hats could lead to no hats at all. Maud Moody, longtime millinery writer for *Women's Wear Daily*, addressed the question in her spring talk to the Fashion Group on hats for the upcoming spring:

> The crocheted business, which has been a definite trend, I think, is going to go right along, and I personally want to go on record as saying that there is only one thing I think is important for the millinery industry, and that is to have something on the head other than a flower or a bow, I don't think it matters one bit whether it is a crocheted or woven or sewn, or what it is, or draped, as long as it is something on the head other than nothing.[47]

Hatlessness was on the rise again; despite the fact that milliners had persuaded Brenda Frazier to appear in a hat in a *Vogue* feature in 1940, debutantes, that is, young style leaders, were perceived as the root of the problem. *Hats* editorialized that if milliners didn't begin to attract them, the hatless "plague" would spread to all women. The editors advised some soul-searching:

> Perhaps we're not giving the "Young Thing" the type of hat she wants. When we gave her the porkpie hat two years ago more young heads were covered than had been for some time. Check your stock right now and see how many of your hats you yourself would accept and wear if you were sixteen or thereabout. Then cater to the needs of the "Young Thing" real seriously, if you would combat the plague of hatlessness before it spreads to all three groups.[48]

The magazine enlisted Damon Runyon, the well-known chronicler of New York life, to weigh in on hatlessness. His opinion—the human head looks much better with a hat on it, so both sexes should wear a hat on the streets of the city. He conceded that women's heads looked better than men's because they had more hair, but argued that without a hat to prevent the hair from blowing around "long hair is more likely to gather germs flying about in the air, and then as a result we have hay fever, influenza and similar maladies."[49]

Then he cinched his argument in a truly novel way:

> Not too many female heads look well without a hat, especially a head with blonde hair. The zephyrs ruffle the hair down to the roots exposing the dye. Loose hairs are carried away by the breezes to land on an innocent male gabardine and get a guy in trouble at home, if his ever-loving is a brunette. Can you imagine a bloke saying, "It must have blown on me?"[50]

Sally Victor fought hatlessness at every turn. *Women's Wear Daily* reported in horror that when Victor went to speak to a group of high-school girls on careers in millinery, she found them hatless:

LESS THAN 50 OF THE 1200 WORE A HAT! [original emphasis] But they were all dressed up otherwise. So Mrs. Victor changed the topic of her subject and proceeded to tell the girls how really alike and uninteresting they looked. At the conclusion of her talk she asked the girls to try on hats and requested comments on the results. One girl said: "Her friend looked strange in a hat— another that she looked so dressed-up."[51]

The *Women's Wear Daily* reporter had no solutions but worried about the implications for the future of American millinery style. "This is just another example of how the younger generation feels about hats—and makes us wonder what REALLY, IF ANYTHING [orginal emphasis], is being done to combat hatlessness among the generation that will soon be taking over the reins of buying all over the country."[52]

Hatlessness may have been the greatest scourge the American millinery industry could think of, but public attention was consumed by the war. By the end of the year, the United States was in the war on two fronts. Americans were afraid they would face blackouts like the British. Sales of flashlights were brisk.[53] Always attuned to the mood of the time Sally Victor designed the first American blackout hats harking back to a phosphorescent circlet of orange-blossoms designed by Suzanne Talbot in 1940.[54] Victor's hats were less romantic and more practical, featuring a small flashlight that could be attached or removed at will. One was of sporty white asbestos or glass and the other was "a pouf of pleated Val lace,"[55] for cocktails and dinner. "All of the hats are white to show in the dark, and the materials have been specially fire-proofed."[56] She followed up with an air-raid helmet that was more utilitarian: "A helmet with a back built down to protect the nape of the neck. The crown has a false top and an inner headband-supported so that if some missile should hit it, there is space and give to prevent striking the skull."[57] America was going to war and its milliners were determined they would be part of the war effort.

Two days after the country entered the war President Franklin D. Roosevelt told the nation in one of his radio broadcasts: "We're in it—all the way. Every single man, woman and child is a partner in the most tremendous undertaking of our American history."[58] Sixteen million men entered the military, while the civilian population mobilized for the war effort. The goal was to finance the war effort, to conserve natural resources for wartime use, and to ensure an endless flow of material to our military and those of our allies. Six million women (including the designer Elizabeth Hawes) went to work in factories to keep the war machine running, while many more volunteered for the war effort, organizing efforts for war relief and taking office jobs formerly held by men.[59] Women were also mobilized by the military as nurses and uniformed units, such as the WAACS (Army) and the WAVES (Navy).[60]

Women's clothing did not escape government regulation. Stanley Marcus, head of the prominent Dallas department store Neiman-Marcus, became head of the War Production Board's textile division, charged with making sure enough raw materials were available for the war effort. Following the lead of the British who had introduced rationing of textiles and promoted design regulations called "Utility Clothing" and "Austerity Directives,"[61] Marcus aimed to freeze fashion as it was in 1942, "thus forestalling any radical change in fashion making existing clothes obsolete."[62] The new regulations restricted fabric use and regulated every detail of ready-to-wear dress manufacture from the depth of hems to the number of pockets. Shoes were also subject to restriction since leather was needed for the military. However, hats escaped regulation.

> The gentlemen in Washington don't care about your hat . . . officially, at any rate. The width of your skirt, the length of your jacket, the lining of your coat, the question of pockets, cuffs, lapels . . . these are matters of concern to the WPB. Your hat, though, is different. It's still up to you. No decree says that it shall be large or small, heaped with flora or fauna or void of ornament, limited in size or shape. No laws are being laid down to deprive it of brim or band, veil or ribbon, quill or pin.[63]

Therefore, milliners were freer to innovate than the rest of the designers in the fashion field. However, they had to appeal to the new mood. It was no longer sufficient to appeal to patriotism; millinery designs could not look too frivolous. Thus, the article describing the new regulations was careful to point out that "Hats are voluntarily simple . . . decorative. undecorated."[64]

Vogue started out the year by emphasizing out how important millinery was to the nation:

> Many a woman with the best intentions in the world thinks she is doing her bit, making a noble sacrifice, by refusing to buy any new clothes during the duration. But so complex is our economic life that this very act of self-denial may work injury to the delicately adjusted gears which must continue to mesh if that great machine is to continue to function, if that great machine is to swing through the "mightiest armaments' production efforts of all time."
>
> Arms and munitions, boats and planes are made by workers, who are paid in the money that comes from Defense Bonds and taxes. A sizeable part of these taxes comes from the clothing industry—in peacetime, the second largest of our country.[65]

Even though women were filling new roles, *Vogue* told them there was a hat to fit the job.

> Hats for your hours on duty—Many of us will work in uniform, with uniform caps on our heads. But many of us will work in the self-chosen uniforms

of women with business to attend: the tailored dress, the ever-dependable suit. Your hat must be neat, unobtrusive, comfortable . . . but it needn't look as though it had been stamped out of boilerplate. It can have your most becoming color, most becoming lines, and it can be new. If one of your jobs is driving a car, there are soft little hats with ears to tie under your chin, or to tie back of your head.[66]

Hollywood star Veronica Lake, known for her long peekaboo hairstyle, was shown in a newsreel getting her hair rolled into a pompadour style, so she could face the world "with both eyes in the clear."[67] The film also buttressed its point by showing shots of women on an assembly line brushing their hair out of their eyes: a gesture the narrator intoned was "as futile as it is dangerous,"[68] adding that "the rhythm of precision work can be upset, resulting in faulty work."[69]

The film went on to show an even better solution—safety nets for hair. There were pictures of women covering their hair with stretchy caps that had a vaguely military look intended to "shield the hair from grease, dust and soot."[70] Over a picture of the same women working productively on an assembly line, the film ended with the words, "Industrial fashions are the new note, setting the style for a new way of life."[71]

The fashion magazines wrote women could still look stylish, even in work gear. In an article titled appropriately "More Beauty, More Work," *Vogue* commented brightly, "Today's war factory girl has replaced yesterday's night-club beauty as national glamour girl."[72] and described the efforts to make these new workers happy and productive.

> Directors of defense factories, struggling with the problems of replacing men with green young girls, are seeing, by actual trial and error, that women, allowed to look pretty, work harder. And so, for the solemn job of their enormous war output, factories all over the country are catering to female pride. They offer becoming uniforms; make-up bars; factory house-mothers, who absorb as many tears on their shoulders about boy-friends as they do about the mean old foreman; and plant managers are ponderously changing the names on doors from "washroom" to "powder room."[73]

Designing the "becoming uniforms" was a patriotic gesture. Milliners rushed to design becoming safety nets to cover the hair. Lilly Daché created a simple blue toque with an attached snood for the Sperry Gyroscope factory on Long Island to go with their Vera Maxwell uniforms.[74] However, the hard-working Sally Victor seems to have designed the widest variety of chic safety headgear. One featured in the *New York Times* was made of washable blue-and-white cotton ticking. A drawstring in the snood made it adjustable.[75] Another designed to complement a blue denim jumpsuit by Helen Cookman was of blue wool jersey "with a flattering coronet front and a full snood back. A bright cherry-red ribbon ties it securely."[76] The same design was also made in red bandanna material to match a work blouse.[77] But, the pièce de resistance was a welder's helmet covered in blue cloth with a red "V" for victory on the crown for the workers at General Electric.[78] It was so successful General Electric featured it on the cover of its brochure for Arc Welding Supplies complemented with chartreuse leather work gloves.[79] Both Daché and Victor also designed hats for women in the service. Victor's beret for the Army's Cadet Nurse Corps made the cover of *Harper's Bazaar* in 1943.[80]

If wartime budgets didn't stretch far enough to buy a hat, women were told they could easily make them. In March, *Life* showed how one of their staffers purportedly made thirteen hats in three days for $10.[81] The article cautioned that the editors were aware that "the strategy of hatmaking has as many pitfalls as the strategy of invasion,"[82] but claimed to have put each creation through a "public-appearance test,"[83] which included wearing one of the homemade hats while riding the subway, shopping, and, even, lunching at the Ritz! Each hat was pictured with the time it took to make and its price. As it did with the knitting instructions the year before, *Life* offered free instructions.

Woman's Home Companion featured Sally Victor who demonstrated how to make the all-important Easter hat—three different styles with detailed pictures of the process for each;[84] while for the woman looking for a chic turban, Marcel Vertès designed scarves for Wesley Simpson that could be folded easily without losing the printed design. *Harper's Bazaar* claimed that manipulating the squares of silk would be simple for the wartime woman: "It's a cinch for anyone who has mastered the bandage chapters in the first aid manual."[85]

Even with all the attention focused on hats, the industry still worried endlessly about hatlessness. So, when Maud Moody, well-known millinery editor for *Women's Wear Daily*, went before the Fashion Group in April 1942, the questions from her audience were not about the new styles, but about whether people would continue to wear them. Moody assured her anxious audience, made up mainly of millinery buyers, that wartime conditions would be good for business: "Because women will do more walking, they will be more particular about their appearance. . . . Good grooming will be reflected in millinery and other articles of clothing."[86] She was equally reassuring that women would spend money on hats.

Women represent an audience for economy, but seldom practice it. Show a woman a good hat and, nine times out of ten, price is no object in her buying bracket. She may plan to spend less than she did before the war (providing she is not one of the new money class, who spend more), but once she finds what she wants, she changes her mind about letting price stop her.[87]

Figure 25 Millinery was viewed as a necessity on both sides of the Atlantic despite wartime restrictions. Here, a British milliner creates 1940s Easter fashion. Tim Gidal *Picture Post* via Getty Images.

Sally Victor had no patience for wartime hatlessness. When asked to design a simple hat many women would wear to work, Victor vowed to get them back in proper hats.

> No one ever took a challenge with more fire-in-the-eye than Sally Victor when the fashion world asked her to do something about the peasant scarves of Government girls, from Clare Luce on down:
>
> "They asked me to design a typical Washington kerchief or some sort of frilly dilly the gals could cover over their heads to go to work," Sally said with a snappy gleam in her pretty dark brown eyes. "I said nothing doing. I'll convert government girls to hats with creations so beautiful they can't help themselves."[88]

Another tack was the formation of the Millinery Fashion Inspiration group, a joint designing team made up of Lilly Daché, John Frederics, and Sally Victor.[89] The wholesale millinery industry pushed this collaborative effort hoping to get more women across the country into the stores by providing them with high-style hats at moderate prices. The designers were supposed to meet and set the millinery trend of the season, then each produce twenty styles to be manufactured for the wholesale market. Getting the three designers to agree on anything was a tall order, as Daché remembered:

> Our conferences over the new hat silhouette of the season were most lively sessions. John would say we must have "more hat" and Sally would say bonnets should be the rage, and I would perhaps vote for turbans. Sometimes we all talked at once, and then we would at last agree and each of us would go back to our own salon and design exactly what we wanted to, anyway. The result was that the public was just as bewildered as ever—but they did get some good designs.[90]

The confusion stemmed from the fact that the hats were sold with the label "Millinery Fashion Inspiration" only. There was no mention of the designers themselves.

The Millinery Fashion Inspiration team unraveled after only a few seasons due to the fact that it proved to be more work than any of the milliners involved had anticipated. However, the publicity their hats received was a big help in making each designer a household name. How much the joint venture contributed to combating hatlessness was questionable.

As New Year 1943 began, the war in Italy was raging. General George Patton and Field Marshal Bernard Montgomery raced up opposite sides of the island of Sicily. In the Soviet Union, Hitler's troops were still battling on the Eastern Front, while in Great Britain, American and British generals debated the merits of invading France. Such news meant those on the home front knew the war was far from over. *Vogue* began the year by warning women:

> The one way not to look this spring is—helpless. Frail clothes, like frail spirits, are ante-bellum. The Woman of the Year, this year, walks, works, and waits, fetches and carries, markets and manages . . . and expects her clothes to be as capable as she is herself. Clothes that don't go out of commission, that are unfazed by rush and pressure, that make her look her best while she does her best. . . . Hats that stay on—Hats that stay put in the jostling crowd or a high wind; hats that don't need your busy, package-carrying hands for a ballast.[91]

Later that year a *Vogue* cover simply said, "Take a Job!,"[92] while the high society magazine *Town and Country* had two covers featuring war workers, one in March for Red Cross Month and another in September with a war worker from the Douglass Aircraft plant in El Segundo, California, as the cover girls.

Americans were not the only ones influencing the nation's fashion scene. After Paris was invaded in June 1940, refugees poured out of the city.[93] Many of them went to Vichy France, while others migrated to Spain and Portugal. Some managed to come to the United States. By 1943, *the New York Times* reported: "an overwhelming majority of the 253,000 newcomers of all creeds who have found a haven in this country were helped in adjusting to the American way of life and making their full contribution to the democratic war effort through the program of the National Refugee Service."[94]

Many of the émigrés added their talents to the American garment industry. Three of the most notable were milliners—Tatiana du Plessix Liberman, known professionally as "Tatiana of Saks," Roger Vivier, and Suzanne Rémy, who formed the design team "Suzanne et Roger."

Tatiana du Plessix, the widow of a French military officer, arrived in New York in 1941 with her daughter Francine and her lover and future husband, Alexander Liberman, who became art director of *Vogue* and, later, editorial director of Condé Nast. A powerful personality who had already emigrated once, from the Soviet Union to France, and who had studied sculpture in Paris, Tatiana trained in millinery at the École de Couture and in the atelier of Fat'ma Hanoum.[95] Tatiana was able to find work quickly at Henri Bendel. Her talent was quickly recognized. In 1942, Albert Gimbel of Saks Fifth Avenue hired her to design hats to complement custom-made clothing designed by his wife, Sophie, for the store's couture salon. The collaboration was a great success. Tatiana's work was a perfect counterpoint to Sophie of Saks's more traditional elegant style. The *New York Times* commented that her hats demanded "a proud carriage of the women who intend to wear them"[96] since they were "destined to dominate any costume with which they were ensembled."[97]

She would continue to design for Saks, producing sixty hats a year,[98] until her dismissal in 1965,[99] an American fashion leader who always remained true to her European roots.

Roger Vivier was already well known as a shoe designer when he arrived in New York in 1940. Like Tatiana, he was trained as a sculptor but began work in a shoe factory when he was seventeen. By 1937, he had opened his own private shop on the Rue Royale, one of the most prestigious streets in Paris, and had an exclusive contract with Delman, an American shoe company known for the well-made elegance of its footwear.[100] He spent two years in the United States, arriving back in Paris just in time to be called to military service. He headed for New York as soon as his service ended, managing to sail from Lisbon on one of the last liners to cross the Atlantic before the war closed the port. While on the ship he met Suzanne Rémy, a senior millinery designer for the great modiste Agnès and former milliner in the House of Schiaparelli, who was to become his partner.[101]

Vivier opened a shop for fine footwear on East 55th Street when he arrived but had to find other work when the United States entered the war in 1941 since wartime regulations restricted the use of leather. Under the tutelage of Mme. Rémy, he learned the exacting craft of millinery in less than a year.[102] They opened a shop at East 64th Street in 1943 under the name Suzanne et Roger.[103] Their hats were lauded in the *New York Times* for their feminine style. Virginia Pope of the *Times* wrote: "Finesse is the outstanding characteristic of their chapeaux—they are spirited and full of coquetry."[104] Vivier was proud of his millinery training. In later years after he returned to France and became famous as the shoe designer for the House of Dior, Vivier pointed out a black satin shoe trimmed in white organdie and asked, "Can't you see the milliner in that?"[105] He is remembered today as one of the greatest shoe designers of the twentieth century.

Suzanne Rémy remained in New York, continuing to run her shop. She later worked at Bergdorf Goodman, creating hats for famous clients like Greta Garbo and Marlene Dietrich. She died in New York in 2001.[106]

Because the L-85 regulations limited innovation in women's clothing, women were encouraged to vary their look with accessory sets. As an article in *The Binghamton (NY) Press* pointed out,

> The first designers to shift their point of view were the milliners. There is hardly a custom-made hat designed today that does not have an accompanying something—gloves, bag, muff, scarf, vest, gilet, sleeves, etc. The list is endless and the young woman who wants to give an ensemble look to her wardrobe will be quick to adopt the idea. It is not difficult to choose a becoming accessory to make it more important.[107]

By 1944, milliners adopted a voluntary code on the use of materials. These government-approved regulations show the types of shortages milliners were wrestling with even though they were not hampered with rules like L-85.

1. The maximum circumference of hat brims on felt bodies (this means hats of one piece) shall not exceed 48 inches. No limitations on crowns.

2. Berets are not to exceed 38 inches in circumference when made out of felt bodies or any other materials.

3. Hats made of fabric shall not consume more than 6 yards of fabric, 36 to 39 inches wide (or its equivalent) for one dozen hats.

4. The maximum use of (fur) felt skirtings (yardage) shall not exceed 8 strips per dozen of 15 to 18 inches wide and 45 inches long (or its equivalent).

5. The (wool) felt yardage, 72 inches wide, shall not exceed 3 yards per dozen hats.

6. The maximum amount of ribbon to be used is 1 and a half yards per hat, not including the head-size band.

7. Veiling of 19-inch width shall not exceed 1 yard per hat or its equivalent.[108]

Vogue assured its readers that the new regulations would not cramp milliners' style. Its fashion spread that month contained "hats that conform to these regulations—hats that are pretty, flattering, and do not violate either the spirit or the letter of this self-imposed law."[109]

But there was more intrigue that month. While the Americans were working within new regulations, new photographs surfaced of the strange Parisian styles via a Swiss magazine mysteriously sent to a long list of American stores. American fashion observers were horrified. This was not the Paris they remembered. Articles about the hats appeared across the country with comments similar to those of Eve Keelher in the *Cleveland News*:

> Please do not jump to conclusions when the eye falls on these pictures. They do not comprise a new comic strip, nor were they taken at a costume ball.
>
> They are reproductions from a Swiss fashion magazine, showing what Paris is wearing this springtime.
>
> These hats are said to be creations of Parisian hatters, who, in days not harried by war, created perfectly divine numbers that were the envy of every woman who did not own one.[110]

There were many rumors of conspiracy. Dorothy Roe, fashion editor of the Associated Press, wrote, "The story behind the presentation of these hats seems to be that they are part of Nazi propaganda to create a demand for German-controlled French fashions."[111]

The horror Americans felt when they saw the fashions of the Occupation is understandable. Americans did not understand that for those living in Occupied France the outlandish hats were a way to show their defiance of the enemy. Army Sergeant Mickey Thurgood arrived in Paris as part of a secret mission to discover how close Germany was to producing an atomic bomb. Though his mission was deadly serious, he noticed the Occupation Hats and wrote home about them on April 9, 1945: "They [Parisian women] are well dressed and groomed despite what we've heard. The madamoselles [*sic*] still bravely try to maintain Paris's prestige as a fashion center by wearing the cockeyedist hats the world ever saw. Under the present strain they have over-compensated a bit, I think."[112]

On August 29, the Occupation of Paris ended. American soldiers marched through the streets of Paris and found that even though "ration coupons are issued for the commonest articles,"[113] food was in short supply and "three cigarettes a day are all anyone ever gets,"[114] the public had not been subjected to the same kind of clothing restrictions as Americans.

> Paris disturbed some Americans. It didn't look like an enslaved capital. Compared to London, it was prospering. Ed Murrow[115] was surprised by the number of well-dressed women in the streets . . . all the famous couturiers

were in business—Molyneux, Lanvin, Schiaparelli[116]—and their French customers were wearing full skirts and mutton-legged sleeves, which had been out of the question for American and British women limited by clothes rationing.[117]

Whether or not Paris could actually be the force it was before the war was still an open question, but war had brought another change stateside—the "bobby soxers," a name given to high-school students who had grown up during the war. *Life* reported on them as if they were a species found on a remote island, saying, "They live in wonderful world of their own—a lovely, gay, enthusiastic, funny society almost untouched by the war."[118] These girls, flush with allowances they received from their working mothers or earned themselves, had their own style.[119] "By their energy, originality and good looks they have brought public attention down from debutantes and college girls to themselves. It is a world of sweater and skirts and bobby sox and loafers, of hair worn long, of eye-glass rims painted red with nail polish, of high-school boys not yet gone to war."[120]

Most alarming to milliners was a photograph that accompanied the article showing a large group of bobby soxers pushing a Model T in some public square. None of them were wearing hats.

Ever alert to new trends that might affect business, the Fashion Group held a session on the bobby soxers and their habits. Evelyn Green, *Vogue*'s beauty editor, told them that the young girls had a different way of working with their hair. "One of the most important influences on the new hair fashions is just the beautiful, plain unadorned hair of teenagers. . . . The very young girl doesn't give a snap of her fingers for hair-fashions. What she is looking for is pretty hair."[121]

Miss Green went on to describe a beauty routine that included frequent brushing, do-it-yourself "cool waves" and styles set with bobby pins or rags—a contrast to the pompadours of the older generation. There was an interest in showing off the hair itself without a hat.

But for American designers, the thought that these young girls could signal a future without hats was far-fetched, especially at a time of record profits. The president of the Fashion Group had Mr. John speak to the group and introduced him by remarking on the industry's profits: "Mr. John is the man who told me the other day, to my extreme excitement, that the hat industry last year did $125,000,000 worth of business last year. That seems to be an awful lot of hay."[122]

Lilly Daché stated flatly, "The uncovered head seems obviously in the past. It's not chic and a woman is not well-dressed without a hat. It's impossible to achieve a clean-cut look without a hat."[123]

Daché was taking no chances though. The March 15 issue of *Vogue* contained a large back cover ad for her newest creation—the inexpensive "Dachétte," a small colored hair net that contained the hair but did not hide it. The ad told potential customers "Lilly Daché says it's chic to be neat."[124] It seemed to be the perfect thing to complement the new "page boys" of the younger set. However, it was not without its critics. Jessie Mize Ingram reported in the *Atlanta Journal*, "Lilly had all New York aghast when she introduced the Daché net for the hair. Her premier show featured 16 models with different hair styles, all with the net—from breakfast-in-bed to wedding." She ended with a dire warning, "The Daché net bids fair to be a good reason for all America to go hatless this summer. Watch this prediction!"

In 1941, Morris de Camp Crawford, textile expert and editor of *Women's Wear Daily*, looked back at the end of the previous war and attempted to analyze what had happened to the fashion world he knew so well, a world he knew would profoundly change after the war he could see already raging in Europe. He knew that during the First World War, women's clothing had developed simpler, straighter lines, and women's hats had shrunk from their elephantine proportions of the prewar years. But, he couldn't have foreseen the turn fashion would take in 1947, a change quite different from the trend toward simpler lines after the earlier war.

On October 24, 1945, more than a year after V-J Day, the hated L-85 regulations came to an end. But it was far from clear which direction fashion would go in the future. What was clear was the fact that America, undamaged by the war, was a leading world power, and New York, its leading city, was its crown jewel.

American fashion leaders hoped their wartime experience in the fashion spotlight would enable them to continue their leadership. One store executive told the press: "American women are more independent, more active, more important in business and political circles than their sisters overseas. Too, they are more democratic, expecting and receiving, even at low prices, the same high standards of design and fashion that were produced in pre-war Europe for only a limited fashion aristocracy."[125]

On February 12, 1947, Christian Dior showed his first collection. The new clothes were the opposite of the austere, pared-down look American and British women had become used to during the war—a look Dior abhorred. He was determined to bring women's clothes back to the days of elegance he remembered from his childhood, even though France was still struggling with the war's aftereffects.

In the United States, the New Look was controversial. It would require women to completely overhaul their wardrobes after years of being told about the virtues of austerity. Leading fashion editors like Mary Morris of the *Detroit News* faced a dilemma. She had spent the war years tirelessly promoting American fashions. Two years before she had devoted her entire Sunday section to "Designers who Make the 'American Look'" and had urged her readers to support them. Morris felt strongly that the fashionable woman had a duty to "accept the responsibility of bringing to life the 'American Look.'"[126]

On February 16, 1947, Morris told her readers everything had changed. Usually, her Sunday column was short, brief copy to accompany a pictorial spread, but on that Sunday, the article was bluntly titled "Off with the Old—On with the New." Morris did not mince words.

In Fashion as in all phases of life there comes a time when a vital decision must be made; one must go right, go left or stand still. Hesitating at the intersection actually constitutes a definite decision-to go no place.

Nineteen Forty-Seven is the most important clothes crossroads to which a woman of this generation has come. She must wholeheartedly accept the new; tenaciously cling to the old or shilly shally in between.

The first course is the wisest. It's progress. The second is understandable for the diehards who cannot bring themselves to accept change. The third, that of trying to straddle the old and the new, is as futile as it is cowardly.[127]

Morris had covered longer skirts already in her visits to New York, but these skirts were much longer than any she'd seen there. She cautioned readers not to try to adapt last year's look.

Everything about the new silouet [sic], from the top of the head to the tip of the toe, is new in actuality, not merely in the fashion writer's blurb. . . . Most common, and most horrible example of the defeatism of compromise is the 1947 suit jacket length, but with its skirt cut back to 1946 length—proportion is completely cut off.[128]

The new proportions would also mean women would have to invest in an entire new wardrobe of hats and cut their hair.

The headline, molded by hat or coiffure is small and neat. Hats hug the bony structure, from well back of the forehead to well down on the nape of the neck. If there is trimming, it juts to the side and back. This is the opposite of last year's hat silouet [sic], which perched flatly forward with trimming bulging.

Coiffures do the same sort of skull molding. Gone are the pompadours, tortured topknots and overcurled bangs. The sophisticated hair-do has a Madonna-like simplicity, parted smoothly and swept away at the temples. Hair ends are curled ever so slightly or smoothed in a moderate-sized chignon.[129]

Reader reaction was swift and surprising. On Thursday the 20th, Morris wrote, "We had expected last Sunday's fashion page to be controversial—but not in the way which it was. Instead of resenting longer skirts or the idea of giving up fancy platform shoes, all the cash customers seemed perturbed about was the millinery news."[130] One woman called the new hat styles "skullduggery" and complained, "A small hat makes me look like a peeled onion."[131] Another wanted to know how to give an outfit the right "importance" without a big hat. "Others objected simply on the grounds that the stark lines of the cloche or casque aren't pretty or Eastery enough."[132]

Detroiters weren't the only ones upset about the new fashions. *Time* magazine reported that sales of Easter clothing were off that year. This slump was partly due to high prices, which were up 10 percent from 1946,[133] making a salesgirl at Hattie Carnegie's exclusive shop complain: "A woman who bought six hats last year will only buy four this year."[134]

By the end of 1947, American milliners knew they faced a future of stiff competition from France since Dior had brought Paris back to the forefront of the fashion world. Now that the wartime restrictions on clothing were off, hats were not the only novelty women could purchase to vary their look. One thing seemed certain. The "New Look" meant a future full of beautiful hats.

On December 15, Kay Sullivan, president of the Fashion Group, told the group that spring 1948 was hat season, predicting flatly: "None of these clothes are clothes for hatless people. Their effect is too good to be tossed away lightly by a tossing coiffure."[135] It seemed clear to those in the fashion world that hatlessness was permanently out of fashion in the postwar world.

American milliners realized they would be looking across the Atlantic again to see what Paris decreed and be pressed to keep pace with what was shown in the Paris collections each spring and fall. But, the work they had done in the war years meant that their work was now taken seriously. In the future, women would buy American millinery, not just copies of Paris originals.

One thing fashion experts on both sides of the Atlantic agreed on—hatlessness was defeated. In 1948, Bettina Ballard told the Fashion Group that hats were the "most seen, most copied, and most worn Paris importations."[136]

10
RISE OF THE HAIRSTYLE

America emerged from the Second World War, a power with new challenges its citizens didn't entirely understand. As its soldiers returned to civilian life and began to pick up their lives again, a new type of war, a "Cold War," began. The fear of the Communist world pervaded everything.

It was the Cold War in its purest form, a show of global threats and feints, brinksmanship brought to a terrifying, but casualty-free climax in the Cuban Missile Crisis of 1962. The vast Communist world and the embattled capitalist nations somehow agreed to avoid a third world war, while in America, consumerism and industrial production struck a balance that produced, for the masses, a greater ease of living.[1]

That "greater ease of living" was astounding to a generation that had weathered the Depression and a devastating war. Americans wanted their lives to be normal again. They moved to the suburbs, started families, and began to taste the fruits of the new abundance brought on by the war. "Never has a whole people spent so much money on so many expensive things in such an easy way as Americans are doing today," an article in *Fortune* crowed in 1956.

Life in America, it appeared, was in all ways going to get better: A new car could replace an old one, and a larger, more modern refrigerator would take the place of one bought three years earlier, just as a new car replaced an old one. Thus, the greatest fear of manufacturers, as they watched their markets reach saturation points, was that their sales would decline, this proved to be false. So, did another of the retailer's fears—that people might save too much.[2]

The postwar message to women came early. An article in the January 1946 issue of *Vogue* showed how attitudes toward the independent women of wartime were changing. Bluntly titled "Back on the Pedestal, Ladies!" author Barbara Heggie told readers it was time to let men take the lead again: "So now, we should stop making the decisions, stop being aggressively punctual, stop driving the car like Eisenhower's WAC, develop a sudden inability to balance our checkbooks, say what do you think, stop making lists of things and carrying them around with us."[3] According to Heggie, one of the first steps to this new postwar attitude was a change in wardrobe: "Fashions are here to help women re-remember their sex. Hats are sheer nonsense and necklines hark back to the Restoration—a period in which women were notably appreciated."[4]

Americans, in short, were proud of their country and proud of the industries that were driving it to become the most modern nation on earth. There was one area where the influence of another country dominated—fashion. Even though American designers had made their mark during the war years, the success of Dior's New Look brought French fashion back to the forefront. Every year women across the country awaited the news from Paris to learn what the couturiers there decreed. After the war, American manufacturers flocked to Paris, drawn by the instinct that American women still loved French fashion, as they had for much of the century.

In 1894, Thorstein Veblen wrote that fashion was based on the idea that "nothing can be worn that is out of date. A new wasteful trinket or garment must constantly supersede the old one."[5] This belief was based on observations of the American mass market and its ability to push change. As one businessman

Figure 26 Milliners create hats and wedding veils for the Neiman-Marcus department store, Dallas, Texas, 1946. Photo by PhotoQuest/Getty Images.

wrote in 1903, "the wearing of last year's hat or coat or costume is an evidence of inability to buy—an inability which every American man or woman hesitates to admit. This is the fact that should be recognized by all connected with the trade, nor should any fail to make use of the powerful lever thus put into their hands."[6] In a country where men and women were judged by their ability to buy, this was a powerful tool. A vast industry grew up to feed this desire for fashion aimed at bringing French fashion to the American consumer at all levels.

After the Second World War, Americans were almost the only people with the capital to spend on French luxury goods. Few Americans were actually buying couture, but the French couture business became a powerful marketing tool for American department stores and manufacturers.

The news of buying trips to Paris was gobbled up by an American woman who had a new definition of femininity. Even though women did continue to work during the 1950s, those working women were virtually invisible in the popular imagination. Advertising copy was pitched to the woman who did not work, stayed at home, aimed for the perfect home, and supported her husband above all. Her position in life and society's view of her was described in ads that pushed Americans to buy new and better products, like one called "This Is Your Wife" a full-page ad run by Bell Telephone in 1957. At the top of the page were five pictures of the same attractive women wearing five different hats with the following copy,

> This is the pretty girl you married.
> She's the family chef and the nurse and the chauffeur and the maid.
> When she's all dressed up for an evening out—doesn't she look wonderful! How does she do it?
> Of course, she's smart and it keeps her busy, but she never could manage it without the telephone.
> When the chef needs groceries, she telephones. Supplies from the drugstore? The "nurse" places her order.
> A train to be met? The telephone tells the "chauffeur" which one. A beauty shop appointment? A call from the "glamour girl" makes it easily and quickly.
> Handy ever-ready telephones—in living room, bedroom, kitchen, and hobby room—mean more comfort, convenience and security for everyone.[7]

Anne Fogarty, an American designer of ready-to-wear dress whose full skirts and tight bodices echoed the Dior's New Look, published a guide to dressing well titled *Wifedressing: The Fine Art of Being a Well-Dressed Wife* full of advice such as "Never underestimate the power of a man, for he who pays the bills deserves consideration in the way you look as wife, hostess, helpmate, community participant, or working homemaker."[8] Ironically, Fogarty was a businesswoman, head of a company that distributed her clothing across the nation. Yet, she decreed flatly: "I have been married for sixteen years and, despite having worked at a career all that time, I still think of myself first and foremost as a wife."[9] Her attitude was by no means uncommon at the time.

Many of the 1950s women lived in new suburbs, which isolated them from the old neighborhoods where they grew up. So, they depended on women's magazines for direction as never before. Magazines like *Ladies Home Journal*, *McCall's*, *Redbook*, and *Good Housekeeping* constantly told women how to do their job—with the aid of the latest gadgets that were being pushed in each magazine's advertising.[10] This message to buy was reinforced in a powerful way by television, a brand-new medium, where new products were pushed relentlessly.

> By the mid-fifties a new and powerful media, the television, portrayed a wonderfully antiseptic world of idealized homes in an idealized, unflawed America in both its advertising and programming. There were no economic crises, few if any hyphenated Americans, few if any minority characters. . . . These families were optimistic. There was a conviction, unstated, but always there, that life was good and was going to get better.[11]

Fashion decrees came from the top as well. "This was a time when American ladies of style willingly followed the dictates of lively, yet dogmatic fashion reports. In the 50s women composed their wardrobes according to the style and etiquette devised by fashion editors who, for the last time in history, were almost exclusively influenced by Paris couture."[12]

Hats were an important part of the postwar style. The directive came from Christian Dior himself would not dream of showing his clothing without them. He and his assistant Mitzah Bricard would spend hours picking the right hat for each ensemble. For him, this was an essential step in creating a collection.[13] He was emphatic about this:

> It may seem odd that we should go to all this trouble over hats when women are wearing them less and less. In my opinion, this regrettable departure is due to a reaction against those miserable pieces of headgear, in straw, bedizened with plumes and flowers, with which women disguised the poverty of their wardrobe during the war. As for me, I consider a woman without a hat to be not completely dressed. . . . It would be out of the question to show a collection without hats.[14]

Dior emphasized this attitude in his *Little Dictionary of Fashion*. The entry titled "Hats" reads: "I think that in town you cannot be really dressed without a hat. . . . A hat is the quintessence of femininity with all the frivolity this word contains! Women would be very silly not to take advantage of such an efficient weapon of coquetry."[15]

Historian of the 1950s Karal Ann Marling points out that a series of fashion movies in the mid-1950s that were set in the exclusive fashion world gave American women a glamourized look inside. The most famous of these films is *Funny Face* (1956), which featured Audrey Hepburn who danced with Fred Astaire dressed Givenchy gowns. The most dominant character though was Maggie Prescott, the fashion editor played by Kay Thompson, whose musical number "Think Pink" supposedly gave the audience a look at how fashion movements were launched. Marling notes that the fashion business is a women's world in these movies: "The hat is a badge of membership in the sisterhood of the empowered: fashion commentators and editors, poker-faced mannequins, salesgirls, brisk premieres, designers, and knowing customers all wear outrageous concoctions on their carefully coiffed heads."[16]

One of the most enthusiastic customers for the new hats of the 1950s was Mamie Eisenhower, who was exposed to Paris fashions when her husband General Dwight D. Eisenhower was stationed in Paris after the war. But, though she loved fashion, the prices of Paris hats were too much for a thrifty military wife from Iowa. Mamie quickly became the most famous client of milliner Sally Victor. Later an article in *The Milwaukee Sentinel* would point out: "When Mrs. Eisenhower lived in Paris, Sally would send her hats to her, despite the fact that her eminent customer was living in the heart of Parisian couture."[17] When Eisenhower became president, Mamie wore a Victor creation called "The Airwave" to his first inaugural in 1953.[18] The gray hat with four layers which were slashed to show a green lining hat was an enormous hit. Macy's sold hundreds of copies. The White House was swamped with letters from women asking where they could get the hat. Mamie wrote to Sally: "An attractive, flattering hat always helps me feel my best and look my most confident, so you can see your selections were so important in boosting my morale."[19] Mrs. Eisenhower was such a fan of Victor's hats she gave four of them to Queen Elizabeth II when the queen visited in 1957 and another to Nina Khrushchev, wife of the Soviet premier, on their state visit in 1959.[20]

Like Mamie, most women were careful to accessorize every outfit with the right shoes, bag, scarf, gloves, and hat plus plenty of costume jewelry, buying habits that stemmed from the war years when consumer items were often in short supply. Milliners stretched out into less expansive lines that could be distributed quickly across the country. Lilly Daché had already featured the Dachette, Sally Victor had the "Sally V" line while Mr. John (no longer partnered with Fred Hirst) came up with Mr. John Juniors.[21]

One thing hadn't changed—the seasonality of the millinery business. Bill Cunningham, who had a millinery shop called "William J" in the 1950s, recalled: "Each year, after the millinery collection opened in the first week of July . . . there would be those horrible two months of midsummer when there is absolutely no business. These were penniless days, and all the money made on the spring collection was spent on creating the fall collection."[22]

The specter of hatlessness still loomed. An article in July 1953 blamed "Lack of Newness" for a downturn in business. New hairstyles presented a challenge. In 1953, the Italian cut, a short layered style seen in new neorealist Italian films, became popular. Women did not like covering this style with a hat, so milliners were urged to work with hairdressers to get the right hat for the new hair.

Twelve years after the New Look debuted, in 1959, *Time* magazine lauded Sally Victor on its business pages as the milliner who helped end drooping sales in the hat business and led the industry to sales of $300,000,000 in 1958.[23]

> The hat industry, long in a slump, is now on the way back. From a total of $400 million in the '20s, hat sales dropped to a low of $250 million in 1953. Part of the trouble was a shift in fashion; the longtime dictum that every woman had to wear a hat to be well dressed almost died in the flight to the suburbs and the new, casual living.[24]

The article had a simple reason for the earlier decline in hat sales:

> But, fault also lay with the hatmakers; hats became too silly even for women to wear. Says Designer Victor: "We forgot one thing—to make the hats pretty. All you have to do is show a woman that she looks prettier with a hat on than off, and money doesn't mean a thing." As hats became pretty again (Designer Victor scored with her flowered hats), sales rose, are expected this year to reach a postwar high.[25]

Victor was still holding fast to her theory that pretty hats would keep the industry going into the next decade. She had reason to be optimistic. The 1950s had been good to her. Her business was bringing in $500,000 a year.[26] Her clients included Hollywood stars Joan Crawford, Irene Dunne, Merle Oberon, and, most important, First Lady Mamie Eisenhower, whose hats were covered in the press every spring and fall. However, Victor's stars were all older that year. Joan Crawford, who had made her name a style icon, was now fifty-four, Irene Dunne sixty-one, with Merle Oberon the youngest at forty-eight.[27] Mamie Eisenhower was sixty-three and was still on the Best Dressed List by virtue of her visibility as First Lady. Victor herself was fifty-four[28] and her leading competitors were of the same generation, Lilly Daché was sixty-one and Mr. John was approximately fifty-seven.[29] A new generation was coming of age, born after the war. They weren't going to take their style cues from women in their fifties.

Beauty standards were changing. Women didn't want to simply be pretty anymore, they wanted to be glamorous and sexy. The leading movie star of the decade was Marilyn Monroe, known for her short, tousled, curly platinum blonde hair. Marilyn was never seen in a hat.

There were other forces at work too strong for pretty hats to overcome.

The cosmetics industry was already a major part of the economy. By 1940, companies tied their new offerings to the fashion seasons.[30] Advertising told women to lift their spirits with new beauty products, just as milliners had urged them to buy a new hat. One fashion writer commented that Sally Victor's hats "do more to flatter a face than a triple dose of pancake makeup,"[31] but most women weren't listening.

"Following World War II, the beauty industry entered a rococo period and, like other consumer industries, began to produce a limitless array of goods, colors, and styles. By 1948, 80 to 90 per cent of American women used lipstick, about two-thirds used rouge, and one in four used eye makeup."[32] Along with this hunger for new goods was an increased faith in science as the way American society could advance.[33] The chemical industry turned its vast research facilities to developing consumer products like cosmetics along with components for the defense industry. *Time* magazine heralded the chemists of the Dupont Chemical Company as "The Wizards of Wilmington"[34] in 1951, and quoted its president's belief that "there are 90-odd chemical elements and that only a tiny fraction of their possible combinations has been put to commercial use. Says he: 'The greatest discoveries are yet to come.'"[35] Many of these new products would be developed by the cosmetics industry.

After the war, the cosmetics industry exploded with the most successful companies investing millions in new product research and spectacular advertising campaigns. In 1952, Charles Revson, who employed more than seventy chemists to develop product lines,[36] launched the "Fire and Ice" campaign for a new shade of lipstick and nail polish. The advertisement reeked of glamour—the elegant model Dorian Leigh dressed in a sheath covered with silver sequins with a billowing red wrap loosely draped around her shoulders set the standard of glamour. On her lips were the new scarlet lipstick and her perfectly manicured hands were painted with the same shade. Her dark hair was perfectly coiffed—with no hat to top it off. The Revlon Company brought out new shades every six months, making its cosmetics part of the fashion world.[37] By 1956, *Time* reported the company had a 54 percent sales increase to $51,600,000 for the year, counted record profits of $3,500,000 compared to $1,200,000 in 1954.[38] The new makeup created a strong face that did not need a hat to set it off.

Americans spent 4 billion dollars on beauty products and services in 1957, double the amount they had spent in 1947,[39] much more than the $300,000,000 reported by the millinery industry in 1958.[40] The difference in their profits margins was striking. Milliners needed large stocks of expensive materials to create beautiful hats while a tube of lipstick could be manufactured for 4 to 6 cents and sold for $6,[41] equal to $45.34 today.[42] More women were likely to buy a tube of expensive lipstick than spend $55 to $90 for a Sally Victor hat[43] (equal to $401.90 and $657.66 in 2008).[44]

Similar innovations were going on in hair care. The Toni Company introduced a home permanent wave woman could give themselves in the late 1940s. Its success led to a line of related products such as Toni Cream Shampoo, White Rain Shampoo, and even "Tonette." a home permanent wave just for little girls. Other companies like Richard Hudnut and Permalette quickly followed Toni's lead.[45]

Women were also able to improve the color of their hair themselves, thanks to innovations in the chemical process. At the beginning of the decade, *Life* reported on the change:

> Thanks to improved processes, dyed hair no longer looks as artificial as it did years ago, and thanks to changed social ideas, it no longer automatically labels a woman as "fast." But until recently the time and money involved have kept most women from getting their hair dyed. Their latest encouragement to try is a new product called Tintair. Selling for two dollars, it enables a woman to change the color of her hair at home simply by painting the dye on. The danger of streaking, which has always made home bleaching a risky venture, is averted by a catalyst in the dye which stops color oxidation when it has reached a maximum intensity—about fifteen minutes.[46]

The article was illustrated with a picture of a young woman applying the dye. *Life* predicted the future looked bright for this product, "On the basis of beauty parlor statistics, Tintair thinks there are 10 million women in the U.S. who would like their hair dyed, and it expects its product to color American hair almost as universally as the home Toni Wave curled it."[47]

On the next page of the article under the headline, "A Dye for Salons," another new company was mentioned, one that would become far more lucrative than Tintair:

> Since last March, U.S. beauty shops have had a quick hair-dying process which they think is sure to stand up against the competition of home hair dye. It is called Miss Clairol and, like Tintair, it bleaches, dyes, and shampoos in one operation. In the nine months since it was introduced, three million Miss Clairol dye and retouch treatments have been sold at $3 to $5 a head, and Clairol is busy training 1,000 operators a month in the new technique.[48]

For $3 to $5 (equal to $26.55 to $44.25 in 2008[49]), a woman could have a new look for a fraction of what she paid for a new hat.

It wasn't long before Clairol moved into the home hair coloring market. Its advertising campaigns like the one launched in 1956 helped make hair coloring respectable since it featured pictures of clean-cut, young women, not the sirens of the Revlon advertisements. The slogan, "Does she . . . or doesn't she? Only her hairdresser knows for sure,"[50] became a part of the culture. The campaign was so successful that within six years, 70 percent of all adult women were coloring their hair, and Clairol's sales increased 413 percent.[51] Other competitors such as L'Oréal quickly joined the market; even Lilly Daché produced her own line.

Life magazine, the barometer of popular taste, began to report on hairstyles in earnest. A cover story in 1952 compared the ponytail and the new, short "poodle cut."[52] Neither of these styles was shown with a hat. By 1956, the chemical industry invented aerosol containers to make the application of cosmetics easier. The new containers were especially good containers for hair spray, a product that could fix a hairstyle for an extended period of time. Women could now fix their carefully constructed hairstyles in place for several days. Hair was set on large rollers, then, carefully "teased," backcombed, and sprayed into ever-larger styles. The resulting "bouffant" style was huge. One pictured in *Life* that year measured fourteen inches wide.[53] In the summer of 1956, *Life* told the country the new styles eliminated the need for a hat:

> More exaggerated than anything seen since women hid rats in their hair at the turn of the century, this new style is a completely smooth hairdo evolved by cross breeding last year's page-boy hairdo with this spring's outsize hat. The bouffant look is basically a thick page-boy hairdo, 8 to 10 inches long, which has been puffed out at the sides and lacquered in place. . . . The new hair style rules out any possibility of hats; but wearers can decorate their widespread tresses with giant hair bows, jewels, of feathers.[54]

All the new products available meant women were spending more than ever before on their hair and faces. As *Time* reported in 1959,

> Beauty aids, once considered a luxury, are now a necessity—especially to the 20 million women who have jobs. Young girls now battle parents to wear cosmetics in grammar school, and women's magazines are full of frightening stories about older women who let themselves go—and wake up to find their husbands gone. "A woman who doesn't wear lipstick," says Max Factor, president of one of the top five U.S. cosmetics firms, "feels undressed in public. Unless she works on a farm." The result: 95% of all women over the age of twelve now use at least one of the products manufactured by the U.S. beauty industry.[55]

A woman who spent her money and time on the perfect hairdo would not want the effect covered and probably squashed, by a hat, no matter how pretty it was.[56]

The fashion silhouette was changing too. By the spring of 1957, the New Look silhouette would become history. Christian Dior introduced the "Fuseau" or "Spindle" line, a slim, waistless shift that was a direct opposite of his wasp-waisted New Look of 1947. The new silhouette set off a media whirlwind. Dior was not the first to introduce this look. Others, most notably Balenciaga, had shown waistless dresses earlier in the decade. However, Dior's influence was so strong that the chemise was news across the country. Many women swore they would never wear one, but by the spring of 1958 *Mademoiselle* magazine was featuring the same silhouette for summer for its younger readers.[57] The chemise style was not one that called for a hat, but young women were less likely to wear hats anyway—just like the bobby soxers of the previous generation.

Milliner Bill Cunningham combed the obituaries every day to see if any of his customers had died: "After all, my millinery business was made up of mostly elderly matrons, as the young people weren't wearing hats, and there were few enough of my customers left."[58] He could see change coming to the millinery world: "The years 1956, 1957, and 1958 were excellent for millinery, but I knew there was a very dark cloud on the horizon. The wearing of hats was soon to be unfashionable. . . . Like all milliners, I put my head in the proverbial ostrich hole, trying not to see the coming threat of bareheaded women."[59]

By the end of the decade, the young had taken the lead in fashion. They were not interested in wearing their mother's hats. An election was looming in 1960. Mamie Eisenhower's days on the Best Dressed List were numbered. A new, younger First Lady whose style was in tune with the new generation would soon eclipse her.

The milliners simply could not battle change, which is the essence of fashion. In the middle of the decade, Cecil Beaton, longtime observer of the fashion world, wrote what could have been the epitaph for the industry: "Sooner or later, all fashion artists, whatever their medium, learn that the odds are against their survival. At most, they can successfully express their era for ten or twenty years; even the most famous dressmakers do not hold the throne longer. There is a curious paradox emerging from all this:

FASHIONS ARE EPHEMERAL BUT FASHION IS ENDURING. [original emphasis]"[60]

American milliners had played an important role in the development of what came to be called "American Style" in the twentieth century, supplying women with hats that challenged the imagination with their wit and beauty. The years from 1937 to 1947 could be called "The Golden Age of American Millinery," since their ingenious creations defied the adversity and drabness of the war years. That creativity was not enough to stop the trend toward hatlessness, which that had been building in society for decades, but the hats of those ten years defined fashion in that decade. Their inventiveness and beauty inspire us still.

But, Fashion is a capricious goddess. The best-informed experts are often proved wrong when they attempt to predict the future. Longtime observer of fashion Cecil Beaton expressed this well when he wrote: "Fashion and style are like some alien, complicated watch whose springs and wheels often defy even the jeweler's attempts to discover the motivation of the work."[61]

11

FRENCH-FRIED CURLS

In 1960 actress Jane Fonda appeared on the cover of *Vogue* hatless, her hair long and loose. It was just one sign of the many changes that would take place in the world in the upcoming decade. A new generation was coming of age—the "baby boom," the group born after the Second World War. Their purchasing power and taste would transform the fashion world and upend the millinery world completely. This change did not occur abruptly with the ringing in of the New Year. The fashion industry had "teenage" styles in the late 1950s, but they were not a major influence on the fashion world. The leaders of the fashion world, profiled in the influential fashion magazines, were leaders of society. Couture was the standard. Seventh Avenue in the United States would take note of what was shown in Paris. Wholesalers could use a variety of strategies to adapt the new couture to the taste of the American customer with the permission of the couture house for a fee. Garments were advertised as "inspired by" or an "original" copy. Thousands of these copies at all price points were produced every spring and fall.[1]

Rudi Gernreich, who would become one of the most avant-garde designers of the 1960s, was beginning his career at George Carmel, a coat and suit manufacturer in New York, in the early 1950s. He found the atmosphere on Seventh Avenue stifling:

> Everyone with a degree of talent—designer, retailer, editor—was motivated by a level of high taste and unquestioned loyalty to Paris. Christian Dior, Jacques Fath, Christobal Balenciaga were gods. You could not deviate from their look. Once they'd decided on a dropped shoulder line, an American designer simply could not use a set-in sleeve. Once they'd established a hemline you couldn't depart from it by an inch. Seventh Avenue fed on their designs. I was bursting with original ideas, but they were always rejected because they did not fit into the French idiom.[2]

Young women basically had few choices, as an English designer remembered, "There weren't clothes for young people at all. One just looked like one's mother."[3]

Fashion historian Marnie Fogg describes the experience well: "I can remember being made to wear white gloves and carry a handbag like a miniature middle-aged woman."[4] One must assume this ensemble also included the proper hat.

The new energy in fashion came from what initially seemed an unlikely place—London, which had been a backwater of the fashion world in the 1950s. Young designers, many of them graduates of art schools, emerged. They set up shops that came to be known as "boutiques" in off-beat parts of the city where the rents were cheaper. They manufactured their own stock and manned the shops themselves. Shopping changed. Customers developed the habit of dropping by the boutiques to see what was new: "Shopping, therefore, involved not only the purchasing of clothes and their accessories but became a means of self-expression and identification with the burgeoning subcultures of the time. It ceased to be a peripheral activity and became central to the experience of being young, attractive, and cool."[5] The new subculture acquired a new name, which would define the decade—Youthquake.

Preeminent among the new British wave of designers was Mary Quant, who actually opened her boutique Bazaar in 1955 on King's Road. Quant had attended Goldsmiths College where she met her future husband Alexander Plunket Greene and later Archie McNair who became their business partner in the new shop.

Quant had no training in the fashion world. Her first job was as a junior apprentice for a milliner, Erik. Quant never became an experienced milliner, but she learned a lot of basic skills in Erik's workroom. Patricia Stacey, who worked with her, remembered that the young apprentice was not inspired by creating hats for an already shrinking market: "She was young, and wanted to enable people like herself to enjoy fun, affordable fashion. I would like to think . . . she learned more than hat-making skills. Things like the importance of a good window display, a simple but memorable logo, or a well-executed fashion show."[6]

Initially, Quant functioned as a buyer in her shop, but she began to turn out clothes on her own, adapting Butterick patterns and working in her apartment. She would turn out a day's inventory, run them up on the machine, and sell them in the afternoon. The sales would allow her to buy more fabric and start the cycle all over again.[7] The dresses were short shifts with simple lines in bright unusual colors, just what her growing group of customers wanted to wear. Quant is often credited with the invention of what came to be called the miniskirt, the short style that began to dominate fashion in the mid-1960s. A controversy arose over who showed the miniskirt first. Parisian designer Andre Courrèges claimed his 1964 couture collection introduced very short skirts and that Quant only "commercialized the idea."[8] Quant dismisses this, adding, "It wasn't me or Courrèges who invented the miniskirts anyway—it was the girls in the streets who did it."[9]

Quant was joined by a bevy of other talented designers who established their own boutiques—Barbara Hulanicki of Biba, Sally Tuffin, Marion Foale, and Ossie

Clark. There was even a milliner in the group, James Wedge, a partner in Top Gear, who created helmet-style hats. Wedge eventually opened his own shop, so he could reach young customers. As he remembers, "I was trying to sell younger hats, and young people didn't go into the millinery department of the stores, and there was no other outlet."[10] Hats were not important to Quant, Hulanicki, and the other young designers. They were too associated with the past.

In 1965 Quant's style came to the United States in force. She toured the nation coast to coast promoting her line for J. C. Penney, a retailer from the early twentieth century that was aiming to adopt a fresh new image to appeal to the youth market.

The American fashion industry was still influenced by Hollywood stars and society leaders like Babe Paley, wife of the head of the CBS Network, who regularly appeared on the International Best Dressed List, which was introduced in 1940 by publicist Eleanor Lambert to promote American fashion. These women were influenced by the Paris couture and were loyal to American department stores and their buyers. Even though Penney's sales of Quant's designs were profitable, the other department stores had trouble fitting the new British clothing into their system. The American fashion editors, who were older than the baby boom market themselves, viewed a new wave from Britain as clothes for teenagers.[11] Most of them still worked at their desks in a hat and gloves. Geraldine Stutz, head of Henri Bendel, told a fashion writer she thought the Youthquake trend was over in 1966, saying: "If you mean 'mod' then I do think that that kind of cheap English fashion has had it."[12]

Stutz was missing a change in fashion distribution similar to new retail patterns in Great Britain. By 1966 boutiques were sprouting up on the East Side and down in Greenwich Village. One of the earliest and most famous was Paraphernalia on Madison Avenue between 66th and 67th Streets. Its metallic interior glittered invitingly while models danced on a raised platform. The shop sold a plentiful range of British designers and hired college graduate Betsey Johnson, a *Mademoiselle* magazine guest editor, to be its in-house designer.[13] Soon, Paraphernalia boutiques dotted the nation. Department stores established their own in-house boutiques for special new youthful designers. Stutz herself redesigned Bendel's first floor as a "Street of Shops," a series of fashionable boutiques under one roof.

Under the leadership of Editor-in-Chief Diana Vreeland, *Vogue* magazine devoted pages of editorial space to the ever-changing boutique scene. Vreeland urged her readers to "invent yourself. Improvise—underplay, overplay, create. Modern fashion isn't a setpiece, it changes every day."[14]

The new clothes expressed a desire by the young for informality and comfort, a world away from the carefully constructed look of the 1950s which was undergirded by a girdle. Dior's ideal had been a woman between thirty-five and forty. "I rarely design anything but wedding gowns for young girls,"[15] he told the

Collier's interviewer in 1955. He left the stage in 1957 before those young girls and their taste took over the fashion world and pushed fashion to places he could not have imagined.

In this new fashion world hats were less and less relevant. Young women did not want to dress like their mothers. In 1964, Fashion Editor Eugenia Shepherd addressed the problem, one she claimed the industry had ignored too long: "For a long time it was considered crude and unkind to tell the truth—that there are many women in the world who never wear hats. There are some who have never worn a hat. But to write about it was bad for the whole industry and, besides, everybody likes the milliners. They're such lively, creative people."

Sally Victor claimed her shipping was up in 1966 and that her business was better than ever, though she did concede there were fewer hats seen on the streets.[16]

Bill Cunningham knew better:

> By 1960, I knew the millinery business was finished as a fashion force. I still could make a living with the older women who wore hats, but I felt that was no life for my ambitious spirit. Besides, the matrons and I were in constant conflict—they wanted dull, uninteresting hats, and I was continually creating new shapes. We were like fire and water.[17]

Politics would play a part. In 1960 the United States had a new First Lady who was a radical change from Sally Victor's top client Mamie Eisenhower. A new generation took over the White House. Jacqueline Kennedy was thirty-one, while Mamie was sixty-four when her husband left office. Kennedy immediately became a fashion icon for the entire country. Diana Vreeland put it well: "Jacqueline Kennedy put a little style into the White House and being First Lady of the land, and suddenly 'good taste' became good taste. Before the Kennedys, good taste was never the point of modern America at all."[18] Everybody wanted to dress like Jackie Kennedy. *Ladies' Home Journal* noted that "Jackie's slightest fashion whim triggers seismic tremors up and down Seventh Avenue."[19]

The new First Lady was not a hat lover. When she was married in 1953, she did not wear the hat that went with her going-away outfit, but carried it with her instead, even though etiquette demanded a hat with such an important outfit. However, the Milliners' Union was an important early supporter of her husband. Union President Alex Rose lobbied her to wear hats to support his American workers. The union was still powerful. Rose and David Dubinsky, the equally powerful head of the International Ladies' Garment Workers, had contributed nearly $300,000 to her husband's presidential campaign, so Mrs. Kennedy had to concede to their power and wear hats in public. It wasn't easy as she told her saleswoman in Bergdorf Goodman's millinery department, "Oh dear it was so pleasant when I didn't have to wear hats!"[20]

Figure 27 Jacqueline Kennedy (L) and Mamie Eisenhower (R) outside the White House, 1960. Photo by Ed Clark/The LIFE Picture Collection via Getty Images.

The new First Lady did wear hats, but her pillbox sat on the back of her head upstaged by her carefully constructed hairstyle. Mrs. Kennedy's hairstyle was created by Kenneth, who became a celebrity due to his association with her. Kenneth's bouffant style was achieved by backcombing the hair and securing it with hairspray so it could be shaped and styled. He also invented extra-large rollers to stretch the hair out and create waves. The hairstyle was so important that great care was taken not to crush it when Mrs. Kennedy would arrive at the Bergdorf Goodman millinery salon staffed by Halston, a young milliner who began his career in New York working for Lilly Daché. She would not try the hats on there but would work with a sketch artist to get the right style. The pillbox Halston created for her would be worn perched on the back of her head secured by two or three hat pins or small combs set into the inside hatband. These would keep the hat in place without flattening her hair. The First Lady would wear other styles including Bretons and cloches with deep crowns also strategically placed on the back of her head.[21]

Kenneth was not the only influential hairstylist in the 1960s. Hairstyling became a huge industry. Hairstylists had not been so influential since the days of

Figure 28 Milliner Halston shows hats to Actress Virna Lisi at Bergdorf Goodman's Milliner Studio in 1964. Bettman Archive via Getty Images.

Monsieur Leonard in the court of Marie Antoinette. Kenneth's bouffant was only one of the many styles for women that evolved in the decade.

Chicago hairdresser Margaret Heldt invented the beehive in 1960, a towering column of hair with a French twist in back held firmly in place with hairspray. Ironically, the new style was based on the shape of her favorite hat, a fez-like toque. Women loved the style because the hairspray would keep the style in place for a week. Celebrities adopted the style quickly, including the girl group the Ronettes and Audrey Hepburn, who appeared in the beehive in "Breakfast at Tiffany's."[22]

Milliners had already tried to fight fashion's casual trend in the 1950s by establishing secondary, less expensive lines aimed at younger women, but the new proportions of clothing and the towering hairdos shellacked with hairspray baffled them. Fashion journalist Eugenia Shepherd pointed out milliners were stymied.

> Over the past few years most of the milliners reacted in the worst possible way. Trying to put up a bold front, they countered hatlessness by creating what they laughingly called the hattier hat. Many of the hattier hats, believe me, were downright gruesome. There wasn't anything they didn't do to

caricature the face. They certainly helped to plunge millinery to rock bottom, which it hit during the years of the bouffant hairdo.[23]

Hats expanded to fit over the new bouffant hair. They shrank to wisps of netting and flowers. This would cut costs, but eliminate possible customers. No matter what milliners tried—wig hats, space age helmets, draped scarves, and turbans—women still rejected hats.

> At the millinery show which opened the New York couture group's semiannual Press Week activities, one speaker suggested the word "hat" be substituted by something more "zingy" since teen-agers don't understand the "square" term.
>
> The designers of the top-notch fashions admit they are wooing the young because they are desperate. Making up half the female population is a hair-conscious, hatless generation that may grow into hatless adults unless they get them ready about headgear very soon.
>
> Worse, daughters have stopped imitating the way their mothers dress. Mothers imitate them—including the no-hat bit.[24]

Women did buy babushkas or snoods to cover rollers when they went out. Halston produced a padded headband that could be worn under headscarves to protect the hairstyle. It was a best seller at Bergdorf's.[25]

Wigs that could be styled in advance became fashionable. *Newsweek* reported at least half a million women were wearing wigs or hairpieces by 1962.[26] Bill Cunningham saw wigs taking over from millinery in the late 1950s:

> The final blow to milliners came when Givenchy showed wigs on his models in Paris. Their hair was being ruined each time they changed clothes during his shows, and they didn't have time to redo their hair, so he put wigs on them. All the newspapers reported it as a big joke; no one took it seriously. But I knew that instant that the wig or the coiffured head would replace the hat for the next generation.[27]

Wigs and hairpieces were the tools used by designer Ara Gallant to create fantastical hairstyles in the pages of *Vogue*. Working with photographer Richard Avedon, Gallant used huge hairpieces of the synthetic Dynel to create long hairstyles that seemed to fly through the air around the dancing models.[28] Vreeland used these layouts to bombard her readers with a dreamlike fashionable world where they, too, could have luxuriant hair that would float around their heads too.

Another stylist with a different approach to hair rose to prominence. Vidal Sassoon cut hair into short caps with geometric sharp angles. His five-point cut soon became famous and became part of the look cultivated by Mary

Quant and prominent models like Grace Coddington. Unlike the bouffant and the beehive, Sassoon's cuts were easy to maintain since they did not require hairspray or rollers to give them shape. The simple cut gave its wearer a youthful look, the perfect topping for Quant's short dresses. Quant later described how his cut, uniquely flattered the individual's face: "Hair could be cut into shapes and textures that not only flattered the character and the texture of the hair, but projected the best qualities of the head and face—pointing out the cheekbones and focusing on the eyes and making the maximum impact on the Individuality of the face and personality."[29] Quant was photographed getting a Sassoon cut and his style became completely identified with her look.

Sassoon was quickly discovered by Americans. *Vogue* editor Grace Mirabella met the stylist on a trip to London in 1965 and urged him to contact formidable Editor-in-Chief Diana Vreeland. The meeting was fortuitous since Sassoon was getting ready to bring his look to the United States.[30] Though Vreeland was skeptical at first, Sassoon won her over. It was the beginning of a career that would spawn salons across the country and a line of hair care products that would eventually earn him $100 million a year.[31]

Hairstyles did not just convey the Youthquake message. The Black Power movement in the United States led African American women and men to evaluate their hairstyles and opt for a natural look free of straighteners. The "Afro" became the symbol of the movement.

The new movement known as "Hippies" sought to distinguish themselves and establish a counterculture. Men and women grew their hair long. For men this meant controversy. Students who wore long hair to school were expelled which led to lawsuits. For women, the long straight hair was less controversial, but not everyone had hair of the right texture. Thousands of young women would straighten their hair themselves by stretching it out on an ironing board and ironing it. The Millinery Institute was still trying to fight the wave of change and bring women back to buying at least eight hats a year. The odds were against them. Fashion writer Muriel Fisher reported on the mood in Manhattan's millinery district in 1964. One man summed up the feelings of the industry, succinctly, if not eloquently:

Today you're lucky if you see any hat. My mother wore a hat every day of her life, may she rest in peace. Those were the days when a woman wouldn't go to the butcher without a hat. It's all this fuss with the hair. Mark my words, in ten years they'll be balder than the eagle.[32]

To cut costs and try to attract women to hats at the lowest price point, the industry also made an incomprehensible decision. Hats would be stamped out for the mass market in only one size.

Tatiana of Saks was fired in 1965. Sally Victor closed her shop in 1967.[33] Even though Lilly Daché had many other attractions in her East 56th Street building, including a beauty salon that once employed Kenneth Battele, she closed her business in 1968. When she died in 1990 at the age of ninety-seven, her obituary described her as "Creator of Hats for the Fashion Set of Yesteryear."[34]

Mr. John had a dim view of the fashion wave away from hats to hair, calling new styles "orthopedic hairdos and French fried curls." He managed to hang on the longest. He closed his 57th Street Salon in 1970 though he continued to work for private clients till his death in 1993.[35]

Other milliners found new lines of work. Adolfo began to show clothes to go with his hats in 1962 after learning dressmaking skills from Cuban designer Anna Marie Berrero.[36] He was quite successful. In an interview with the *New York Times* when he retired in 1993, he claimed he never enjoyed making hats, but working as a milliner was a good way to meet future clients for his dress line.[37]

Halston, who had made his name designing hats for Mrs. Kennedy, turned to clothing design in 1966. His designs would define the 1970s. *New Yorker* fashion critic Kennedy Fraser wrote: "The success of Halston—which may owe something to his background as a milliner and consequent freedom from pre-conceptions about how to construct clothes—signaled the end of designing in the way the old-guard Famous Designer understood it."[38]

Bill Cunningham closed his salon in 1962. He would go on to a career in journalism as a photographer chronicling the fashion world in New York City for *Women's Wear Daily* and then, the *New York Times* where he worked for forty years. Still, the closing of his salon was wrenching even though he had seen the end coming long before: "I closed the doors of William J., and it was really quite sad, all rather like a divorce. My childhood love affair didn't die, it just vanished. Women had stopped wearing hats."[39]

EPILOGUE

Figure 29 Boy delivering hats. Bleecker Street, New York City, 1912. Library of Congress.

Twenty years ago, I was a guest at a wedding in Great Britain. The groom was American. The bride was English. It was easy to tell the Americans from the English guests. The Americans were bareheaded, relying on their carefully styled hair to stand out, while the English guests wore an assortment of hats and fascinators that made an individual statement for each woman. The Americans were confused. For them, the hat had passed into fashion irrelevance. Gone were the hat bars that were present in many department stores in the 1940s and 1950s. Even if one of them had wanted to wear a hat, it would have been difficult to find one, even in New York City, the former capital of millinery in America. And yet, it's wise not to say "never" in the fashion world. Items that were thought to be hopelessly archaic have a way of returning, not in the same form or with the same meaning, but with a new relevance for a new generation.

By the 1970s, *New Yorker* fashion writer Kennedy Fraser wrote "hats, like white gloves, are boring and dispensable. Heads go uncovered to weddings, let alone luncheons. As a social object, the hat has ceased to be; as a decorative accessory, it long ago ceased to evolve."[1]

Hat wearing had definitely declined among white Americans. Fashion historian Colin McDowell says the decline of the hat was a result of the informality that swept the fashion world:

> By the early 1960s it [the hat] had received the ageist kiss of death: young women felt hats were irrelevant to their fast-moving new freedoms and were suitable only for the stiff formality of the life of an older woman. No items of clothing can recover its former position once it has been assigned to the ghetto of middle-aged and elderly wear, and the formal hat was no exception.[2]

Even women in the Roman Catholic Church began to stop wearing hats or "chapel veils" in the 1970s despite a 1917 edict in the Code of Canon Law that women's heads much be covered during Mass. The ban was finally lifted by Pope John Paul II in 1983. The pope gave no explanation for the change in policy. It seems the church was catching up to the times.[3]

There was one prominent American hat wearer in the 1970s, but she was definitely not a fashion icon. Bella Abzug was elected to Congress in 1970 to represent a district on New York City's Upper West Side. She was fifty, a brash, outspoken woman who quickly acquired the nickname "Battling Bella." Her hats were her trademark. She explained that she wore them because women lawyers were extremely rare when she began practicing law in 1947. So, she wore a hat in court so men would know she was not a secretary. As she explained, "In those days professional women in the business world wore hats."[4] When she died in 1998, one of her obituaries said she was best known as the "The Woman Who Wore Hats."[5]

However, there was one large group of Americans who wore hats faithfully. If Kennedy Fraser had ventured uptown to Harlem, she would have found African American women wearing hats to church every Sunday. Hats were a source of pride for these women, stemming from the days when they could not wear hats to work since their jobs were domestic help and cooking. So, Sunday was the day to dress well and wear the wonderful hat. Bill Cunningham commented that he had enormous support for his millinery work from *Jet* and *Ebony*, two national magazines for African American readers. Cunningham staged hat shows in Harlem and described them as "some of the most exciting ever given; the audience truly appreciated creative ideas. . . . Those ladies know how to wear a hat like you've never seen, the more exciting it is, the better they appreciate it."[6]

Hats were more than a fashion statement for these women. They were a way to define themselves in a hostile culture. In 2000, Michael Cunningham and Craig Marberry published *Crowns: Portraits of Black Women in Church Hats*, a book of photographs and reminiscences by women of all ages on the power they feel their hats gave them. When the National Museum of African American History and Culture opened in 2016, it featured a recreation of Mae's Millinery. The shop opened in 1942 in downtown Philadelphia and remained a fixture of the community until 1997. The exhibit is a tribute to the many millinery shops run by African Americans across the country, places that would serve them in the Jim Crow era. Today women come into the exhibit and linger, exchanging stories and pictures of hats they loved and hats their mothers and aunts were especially proud of. Harlem is still a place to find millinery shops. Some of them have been in business for over twenty years.

When President Barak Obama was inaugurated in 2009, Aretha Franklin opened the ceremony by singing "My Country Tis' of Thee" wearing a gray felt pillbox with a huge bow edged in Swarovski crystals. Her milliner, South Korean immigrant Luke Song of Detroit, had made hundreds of hats for Franklin over the years. Song recalled the moment years later: "When I saw her wearing it, I probably had two minutes of appreciation and then my phone started ringing. It was an incredible moment. I still can't grasp what happened even to this day. I shared in one of our country's biggest events, and I'm so privileged to have shared it with Miss Franklin."[7]

The art and craft of millinery survives and seems to have new energy today. The British seem to have a more durable millinery tradition, perhaps due to the fact that their culture offers more opportunities to "dress up." The influence of the royal family cannot be discounted and recent royal weddings have placed the guests' hats in the public eye.[8] The late Isabella Blow, a fashion tastemaker, was known for her fanciful hats. For Blow hats were a necessity: "I don't use a hat as a prop, I use it as a part of me."[9]

Here in the United States, the special skills of millinery survive. Fashion Institute of Technology (FIT) in New York City offers training for aspiring milliners as it has since it was founded in 1944. Prominent milliners like Patricia Underwood, Lisa Schaub, Rob Keenan, Lola Erlich, and Julia Emily Knox have trained there. There are also self-trained milliners like Amy Downs whose quirky styles have a large group of fans. The city has an active Milliners' Guild[10] that promotes the art and craft of millinery through events like the annual celebration of St. Catherine, the patron saint of milliners, every November and displays of hats in such places as the Museum Shop of the Metropolitan Museum of Art.

Most Americans are still hat-adverse, but for those who wear hats, they are a way to express one's individuality in public. In 2011, an article on the influential "Style" page of the *New York Times* highlighted a new type of milliner, one who views a hat as wearable sculpture and who doesn't recreate the old familiar shapes like the fedora and cloche. As Patricia Underwood puts it, "Wearing a hat takes confidence because it is a choice. Society says we have to wear clothes, life says we have to wear shoes, but YOU [original emphasis] have to choose to wear a hat."[11] Rock stars like Lady Gaga appear on stage frequently in hats that enable them to stand out. So, the hat has gone from a necessity dictated by etiquette to a strong individual statement. One of the millinery's new generation summed up the hats' new appeal succinctly: "I think hats were an area of style that had been neglected for a long time. People forgot their power."[12]

One woman who knew their power was Mimi Weddell, who died in 2009 at the age of ninety-four. Her obituary in the *New York Times* said she was never seen without a hat and owned 150 of them: "Mrs. Weddell excelled, above all, at striking glamorous attitudes, waving her cigarette holder and sporting one of the 150 or so hats she regarded less as a style statement than as a physical necessity, like oxygen."[13] Her daughter, apparently not a hat wearer, said her mother could embarrass her when she walked down the street in her hat waving a cigarette on a long holder. But, Mimi Weddell probably expressed the joy of wearing a hat better than anyone: "Hats give you a frame," she told the *Times* in 2008. "However dreary you feel, if you put on a hat, by golly, you've changed everything. I keep telling my daughter, my granddaughter, everybody, 'If you don't wear a hat, you're missing it.'"[14] Perhaps she put her finger on why hats survive. They can give one joy in our modern world.

NOTES

Introduction

1 Edith Wharton, *The House of Mirth* in *Novels* prepared by R. W. B. Lewis (New York: The Library of America, 1985), 299 (all subsequent references are to this edition).

2 Mary van Kleeck, *A Seasonal Industry: A Study of the Millinery Trade in New York* (New York: Russell Sage Foundation, 1917), 29.

3 Ibid., 62.

4 Wharton, *House of Mirth*, 301.

5 Ibid.

6 Nancy F. Cott, *The Bonds of Womanhood: "Woman's Sphere" in New England 1780-1835*, 2nd ed. (New Haven and London: Yale University Press, 1997), 128–9.

7 Wendy Gamber, *The Female Economy: The Millinery and Dressmaking Trades, 1860-1930* (Urbana and Chicago: University of Illinois Press, 1997), 73.

8 Ibid., 89.

9 Virginia Penny, *The Employments of Women: A Cyclopedia of Women's Work* (Boston: Walker, Wise and Company, 1863), 318.

Chapter 1

1 Susie Hopkins, *Milliners*, The Berg Fashion Library, London, England http://www.berg fashionlibrary.com/bazf/bazf00399.xml.

2 William Shakespeare, *Henry IV, Part 1*. Act I, Scene III, lines 37–41.

3 Susan Watkins, *Elizabeth and Her World* (New York: Thames and Hudson, 2007), 75.

4 Valerie Steele, *Paris Fashion: A Cultural History* (London: Bloomsbury Academic, 1998), 26.

5 Jennifer M. Jones, *Sexing la Mode: Gender, Fashion and Commercial Culture in Old Regime France* (London: Berg, 2004), 21.

6 Anne Hollander, *Seeing Through Clothes* (1993; repr., Berkeley and Los Angeles: University of California Press, 1975), 352.

7 Joan DeJean, *The Essence of Style: How the French Invented High Fashion, Fine Food, Chic Cafes, Sophistication, and Glamour* (New York: Free Press, 2006), 42–3.

8 Kimberly Chrisman-Campbell, *Fashion Victims: Dress at the Court of Louis XVI and Marie Antoinette* (New Haven and London: Yale University Press, 2015), 52.

9 Ibid., 54.

10 Jones, *Sexing la Mode*, 92.

11 Ibid.

12 Ibid., 57.

13 Ibid., 92.

14 Baroness Oberkirch as quoted in Philippe Séguy, "Costume in the Age of Napoleon," in Katell Le Bourhis, ed., *The Age of Napoleon: Costume from the Revolution to Empire: 1789-1815*, exh. cat. (New York: Metropolitan Museum of Art, 1989), 34.

15 A. Varron, "Paris Fashion Artists of the 18th Century," *CIBA Review,* volume 25 (Basle, Switzerland: CIBA Ltd, September 1939), 892.

16 Steele, *Paris Fashion*, 39.

17 Chrisman-Campbell, *Fashion Victims*, 54.

18 Jones, *Sexing La Mode*, 94.

19 Séguy, "Costume in the Age of Napoleon," 48.

20 *CIBA Review*, 897.

21 Steele, *Paris Fashion*, 50.

22 Ibid.

23 *The London Tradesman* (1747) as quoted in Aileen Ribeiro, *Dress in 18th C Europe 1715-1789* (London: B.T. Batsford Ltd., 1984), 57.

24 Randolph Trumbach, "Man-Milliners and Macaronis: Clothes, Same Sex Desire, and the 18th Century Origins of the Modern Sexual System," paper presented at Museum at FIT Symposium, New York, NY, November 9, 2013.

25 Ibid.

26 Ibid.

27 *Webster's Revised Unabridged Dictionary*. S.v. "Man milliner." Retrieved September 16, 2019, from https://www.thefreedictionary.com/Man+milliner

28 Patricia Cleary, *Elizabeth Murray: A Woman's Pursuit of Independence in 18th C America* (Amherst: University of Massachusetts Press, 2000), 42.

29 Ibid., 93–4.

30 "The Straw Shop," *Inventive Women of America*, https://thestrawshop.com/inventive-women-of-america/.

31 Ibid.

32 Marla R. Miller, *The Needle's Eye: Women and Work in the Age of Revolution* (Amherst and Boston: University of Massachusetts Press, 2006), 180.

33 Ibid., 71.

34 Ibid., 72.

35 Linda K. Kerber, *Women of the Republic: Intellect and Ideology in Revolutionary America* (Chapel Hill: University of North Carolina Press, 1980), 36.

36 Diary of Elizabeth Sandwich Drinker, as quoted in Ibid., 44.

37 Kerber, *Women of the Republic,* 45.

38 Benjamin Rush, "Thoughts Upon Female Education, Accomplished to the Present State of Society, Manners and Government in the United States of America" (Philadelphia, 1781) as quoted in Kerber, *Women of the Republic*, 204.

39 Cott, *The Bonds of Womanhood,* 104–5.

40 Jodi Campbell, "Benjamin Rush and Women's Education: A Revolutionary's Disappointment, A Nation's Achievement," *John and Mary's Journal*, Number 13, Dickinson College, 2000. http://chronicles.dickinson.edu/johnandmary/JMJVol ume13/campbell.htm (Accessed January 2018).

41 Michele Majer, "American Women and French Fashion," in Le Bourhis, ed., *The Age of Napoleon: Costume from the Revolution to Empire: 1789-1815*, 223.

42 David Ramsey, *The History of South Carolina from Its first Settlement in 1670 to the Year 1808*, as quoted in Ibid., 224.

43 Betsy [Metcalf] Baker February 11, 1858, letter as quoted in Louise Hall Tharp, "Bonnet Girls," *New England Galaxy* 1, no. 3 (Spring 1960), 5.

44 Anne L. MacDonald, *Feminine Ingenuity: Women and the Invention of America* (New York: Ballantine Books, 1992), 6.

45 "The Straw Shop," https://thestrawshop.com/inventive-women-of-america/.

46 Erin Blakemore, "Meet Mary Kies, America's First Woman to Become a Patent Holder," Smithsonian.com May 5, 2016. https://www.smithsonianmag.com/smar t-news/meet-mary-kies-americas-first-woman-become-patent-holder-180959008/? no-ist (Accessed January 2018).

47 Melissa Josefiak, "Sophia Woodhouse's Grass Bonnets," Wethersfield Historical Society, 2003, http://www.wethersfieldhistory.org/articles-from-the-community/so phia_woodhouses_grass_bonnets/.

48 Linda K. Kerber, *No Constitutional Right to Be Ladies: Women and the Obligations of Citizenship* (New York: Hill and Wang, 1998), 34.

Chapter 2

1 Sarah Grimké, "Letters on the Equality of the Sexes," in Mark Perry, ed. Intro, *On Slavery and Abolitionism: Essays and Letters* (New York: Penguin Books, 2014), 35–6.

2 Cott, *The Bonds of Womanhood*, 39–40.

3 Sir William Blackstone, *Commentaries on the Laws of England in Four Books*, 2 vols., 2nd ed., ed. Thomas M. Cooley (Chicago: Callingham, 1879), I:44.

4 Countess de Carabrella, *The Ladies' Science of Etiquette by an English Lady of Rank (to Which Is Added, the Ladies' Handbook of the Toilet: A Manual of Elegance and Fashion)* (Philadelphia: T.B. Peterson, 1853), 26.

5 Grimké, *On Slavery and Abolitionism*, 89.

6 *The Female Instructor; Or Young Woman's Companion* (Liverpool, UK: Nuttall, Fisher, and Dixon, c. 1811), 27.

7 Miss Leslie, *The Behavior Book: A Manual for Ladies*, 3rd ed. (Philadelphia: Willis P Hazard, 1853), n99.

8 Ibid.

9 Penny, *The Employments of Women*, vi.

10 Ibid., v.

11 Louisa Mae Alcott, *Work: A Story of Experience* (1873; repr. New York: Penguin Books, 1994), 117.

12 *The Female Instructor; Or Young Woman's Companion*, 27.

13 Beth Harris, ed., Introduction to *Famine and Fashion: Needlewomen of the Nineteenth Century* (Burlington, VT: Ashgate Publishing Company, 2005), 4.

14 William Burns, *Female Life in New York City* (Philadelphia: T B Peterson, 185?), 15.

15 The most famous hatter today is The Mad Hatter, a character in Lewis Carroll's classic *Alice In Wonderland*. The character's erratic behavior was based on "Mad Hatter's Disease," which was caused by exposure to mercury fumes used in making fur felt. Inhaling these fumes caused neurological problems like tremors, memory loss, and organ failure. Carroll was born in Stockport, a hat-making center, so he would have been familiar with men with this disease. Malcolm Smith, *Hats: A Very Unnatural History* (East Lansing, MI: Michigan State University Press, 2020), 21–2.

16 Penny, *The Employments of Women*, 318.

17 Burns, *Female Life in New York City*, 15.

18 Ibid., 16.

19 Gamber, *The Female Economy*, 12.

20 H., "History of the Hat," Godey's Ladies' Book, August 1834, 91.

21 Amy Simon, "She Is So Neat and Fits so Well": Garment Construction and the Millinery Business of Eliza Oliver Dodds, 1821-1833, Master's thesis, University of Delaware, 1993, p. 76.

22 Ibid., 77.

23 Lorinda Perry Ph.D., *Millinery as a Trade for Women* (London, Bombay and Calcutta: Longmans, Green, and Company, 1916), 14.

24 Ibid., 20.

25 Ibid., 107.

26 Burns, *Female Life in New York City*, 7.

27 Ibid., 8.

28 Ibid.

29 Ibid., 315.

30 Alison Matthews David, *Fashion Victims: The Dangers of Dress Past and Present* (London and New York: Bloomsbury Visual Arts, 2015), 74–85.

31 Ibid., 92.

32 Perry, *Millinery as a Trade for Women*, 107.

33 Rohan McWilliam, "The Melodramatic Seamstress: Interpreting a Victorian Penny Dreadful," in Harris, ed. *Famine and Fashion*, 106.

34 Penny, *The Employments of Women*, 315.

35 Beth Harris, "All That Glitters Is Not Gold: The Show-Shop and the Victorian Seamstress," in Harris, ed., *Famine and Fashion*, 116.

36 Thomas Hood, "The Song of the Shirt" (1843), http://www.bartleby.com/246/246.html.

37 Ibid.

38 *The Milliner's Girl or Authentic and Interesting Adventures of Fanny Bilson, a Country Clergyman's Daughter Describing the Circumstances Which Induced Her to Leave Her Father, Her Journey to London, and Remarkable Occurrence at the Inn; with Her Preservation from Ruin, and Further Particulars of Her Marriage* (Derby: Thomas Richardson; Simpkin, Marshall, and Co, London [1840?]), 9.

39 Ibid., 15.

40 Ibid.

41 Ibid., 19.

42 "Mrs. Slimmen's Window," *Godey's*, January 1859, 40.

43 Ibid.

44 Penny, *The Employments of Women*, 815.

45 Catherine Beecher and Harriet Beecher Stowe, *Principles of Domestic Science* (New York: J. B. Ford and Company, 1871), 279.

46 U.S. Bureau of the Census, *Comparative Occupation Statistics 1870-1930* (Washington, DC: Government Printing Office, 1940), 107.

47 Leslie, *The Behavior Book: A Manual for Ladies*, 78–9.

48 Penny, *The Employments of Women*, 316.

49 Division Street on New York's Lower East Side was, even then, the center of an immigrant neighborhood. It would remain an important millinery street into the twentieth century.

50 Ibid., 317.

51 Ibid.

52 Christine Stansell, *City of Women: Sex and Class in New York 1789-1860* (New York: Alfred A. Knopf, 1986), 107–8.

53 Luc Sante, Low Life: Lures and Snares of Old New York (1991; repr., New York: Vintage Departures, 1992), 77–80.

54 Ibid., 16.

55 Cott, *The Bonds of Womanhood*, 22.

56 Penny, *The Employments of Women*, 16.

57 Grimké, *On Slavery and Abolitionism*, 65.

58 Edwin G. Burrows and Mike Wallace, *Gotham: A History of New York City to 1898* (New York: Oxford University Press, 1999), 604.

59 Mrs. Jenkins as quoted in *Godey's*, 1852, 373.

60 Ibid.

61 Frank Leslie, *Frank Leslie's Ladies; Gazette of Fashion* (New York: Frank Leslie, 1857), 127.

62 Penny, *The Employments of Women*, 317.

63 Ibid., 317.

64 Ibid.

65 Dr. William Sanger, *The History of Prostitution: Its Extent, Causes, and Effects Throughout the World*, 1859 as quoted in Timothy J. Guilfoyle, *City of Eros: New York City, Prostitution, and the Commercialism of Sex, 1790-1920* (New York and London: W.W. Norton and Company, 1992), 59.

66 Burns, *Female Life in New York City*, 15.

67 Catherine Beecher, *A Treatise on Domestic Economy for the Use of Young Ladies at Home and at School*, revised ed. (New York: Harper & Brothers 1855), 30.

68 Sarah Josepha Buell Hale, *Manners; Or, Happy Homes and Good Society All the Year Round* (Boston: JE Tilton and Company, 1868), 358.

69 Leslie, *The Behavior Book*, 199.

Chapter 3

1 Drew Gilpin Faust, Preface to *This Republic of Suffering: Death and the American Civil War* (New York: Alfred A. Knopf, 2008), xi–xii.

2 Penny, Preface to *The Employments of Women*, v.

3 Nina Silber, *Daughters of the Union: Northern Women Fight the Civil War* (Cambridge, MA and London: Harvard University Press, 2005), 43.

4 Ibid., 40.

5 Dorothea Dix in Ibid., 114.

6 Silber, *Daughters of the Union*, 35.

7 Ibid., 66.

8 Stephen B. Oates, *A Woman of Valor: Clara Barton and the Civil War* (New York: The Free Press, 1994), 125.

9 Silber, *Daughters of the Union*, 63.

10 Ibid., 186.

11 William Tecumseh Sherman as quoted in Anne L. MacDonald, *No Idle Hands: The Social History of American Knitting* (New York: Random House, 1988), 112.

12 Penny, Preface to *Employments of Women*, vi.

13 George Fitzhugh (1854) as quoted in Drew Gilpin Faust, *Mothers of Invention: Women of the Slaveholding South in the American Civil War* (Chapel Hill and London: The University of North Carolina Press, 1996), 6.

14 Faust, *Mothers of Invention*, 78.

15 Ibid., 88–9.

16 Ibid., 109.

17 *Savannah Daily Morning News*, August 18, 1864. Macdonald, *No Idle Hands*, 122.

18 Burrows and Wallace, *Gotham*, 878.

19 "The Fortunes of War," July 1864 and "The Russian Ball," November 21, 1863, in Silber, *Daughters of the Union*, 35.

20 Joan Severa, *Dressed for the Photographer: Ordinary Americans and Fashion 1840-1900* (Kent, OH and London: The Kent State University Press, 1995), 188.

21 Clara Barton as quoted in Silber, *Daughters of the Union*, 158.

22 *Godey's*, March 1861 as quoted in Severa, *Dressed for the Photographer*, 189.

23 Nancy Dymond, 1863 as quoted in Severa, *Dressed for the Photographer*, 193.

24 Silber, *Daughters of the Union*, 108.

25 Faust, *Mothers of Invention*, 221.

26 Ibid., 47.

27 Ibid., 48.

28 Valerie Steele, *Fashion and Eroticism* (New York and London: Oxford University Press, 1985), 75.

29 Faust, *This Republic of Suffering*, 148–53.

30 Wharton, *The House of Mirth*, 297.

31 Charles Butler, *The American Lady* (Philadelphia: Hogan & Thompson, 1836), 142.

32 Wharton, *The House of Mirth*, 298.

33 Ibid., 299.

34 Perry, *Millinery as a Trade for Women*, 20.

35 Ibid., 20.

36 Wharton, *House of Mirth*, 299–300.

37 Perry, *Millinery as a Trade for Women*, 21

38 Gamber, *The Female Economy*, 179.

39 Perry, *Millinery as a Trade for Women*, 21.

40 Ibid., 21.

41 Ibid., 22.

42 Ibid., 22.

43 Penny, *The Employments of Women*, 315.

44 Wayne E. Reilly, ed., Introduction to *The Diaries of Sarah Jane and Emma Ann Foster: A Year in Maine During the Civil War* (1864), by Sarah Jane and Emma Ann Foster (Rockport, ME: Picton Press, 2002), x.

45 Sarah Jane became a teacher of newly freed slaves after the war. In her first post in Harper's Ferry, WV, she braved angry mobs for associating with her students. She died of yellow fever in 1868 shortly after leaving her second teaching job on South Carolina's Gullah Islands.

46 Gamber, *The Female Economy*, 13.

47 Emma Foster, diary entry dated April 27, 1864, as quoted in Reilly, ed. *The Diaries of Sarah Jane and Emma Ann Foster*, 86.

48 Emma Foster, diary entry dated May 6, 1864, as quoted in Reilly, ed. *The Diaries of Sarah Jane and Emma Ann Foster*, 92.

49 Ibid., 93.

50 Emma Foster, diary entry dated May 7, 1864, as quoted in Reilly, ed. *The Diaries of Sarah Jane and Emma Ann Foster*, 94.

51 Ibid.

52 "Straw Bonnets," *Harper's New Monthly Magazine* XXIX (June to November, 1864), 580.

53 Reilly, ed., Introduction to *The Diaries of Sarah Jane and Emma Ann Foster*, xix.

54 Emma Foster, diary entry dated June 11, 1864, as quoted in Ibid., 114.

55 Emma Foster, diary entry dated July 20, 1864, as quoted in Reilly, ed. *The Diaries of Sarah Jane and Emma Ann Foster*, 133.

56 Emma Foster, diary entry dated September 2, 1864, as quoted in Reilly, ed. *The Diaries of Sarah Jane and Emma Ann Foster*, 161.

57 Emma Foster, diary entry dated November 14, 1864, as quoted in Reilly, ed. *The Diaries of Sarah Jane and Emma Ann Foster*, 194.

58 Gamber, *The Female Economy*, 117–80.

59 Penny, *The Employments of Women*, 315.

60 Emma Foster, diary entry dated June 7, 1864, as quoted in Reilly, ed. *The Diaries of Sarah Jane and Emma Ann Foster*, 112.

61 Ibid.

62 September 3, 1864, 162.

63 September12, 1864, 166.

64 October 25, 1864, 182.

65 November 12, 1864, 192.

66 December 14, 1864, 210.

67 Edith Wharton, "Bunner Sisters," in Maureen Howard, ed., *Collected Stories 1911-1937* (New York: The Library of America, 2001), 167.

68 Emma Foster poem as quoted in Reilly, ed., *The Diaries of Sarah Jane and Emma Ann Foster*, 219.

69 Faust, *Mothers of Invention*, 81.

70 Emmala Reed, *A Faithful Heart: The Journals of Emmala Reed, 1865 and 1866*, ed. Robert Oliver (Columbia, SC: University of South Carolina Press, 2004), 30.

71 Silber, *Daughters of the Union*, 245.

72 Tara Hunter, *To Joy My Freedom: Southern Black Women's Lives and Labors After the Civil War* (Cambridge, MA and London: Harvard University Press, Reprint 1998), 26.

73 Silber, *Daughters of the Union*, 267.

Chapter 4

1 Sarah Josepha Hale as quoted in Paul Quigley, "The Birth of Thanksgiving," *New York Times*, November 28, 2013.

2 Holly Pyne Connor, *Off the Pedestal: New Women in the Art of Homer, Chase, and Sargent*, ed. Holly Pyne Connor (New Brunswick, NJ and London: Rutgers University Press, 2006), 3.

3 Howard Zinn, *A People's History of the United States* (New York: Harper Perennial Classics, 2005), 240–1.

4 Anonymous Labor Organizer as quoted in Gamber, *The Female Economy*, 89.

5 Virginia Penny, *Think and Act: A Series of Articles Pertaining to Men and Women Work and Wages* (Philadelphia: Claxton, Remsen & Haffelfinger, 1869), 85.

6 Belle Otis [Caroline H. Woods], *The Diary of a Milliner* (New York: Hurd and Houghton, 1867), v.

7 Otis, *The Diary of a Milliner*, 2.

8 Ibid, 2.

9 Ibid. 2.

10 Ibid., 32.

11 Ibid., 9–10.

12 Ibid., 14.

13 Ibid., 167.

14 Gamber, *The Female Economy*, 104.

15 Penny, *Think and Act*, 193.

16 Ibid., 129.

17 Ibid., 3.

18 Ibid., 5.

19 Pyne, *Off the Pedestal*, 3.

20 Claudia B. Kidwell and Margaret C. Christman, *Suiting Everyone: The Democratization of Clothing in America* (Washington, DC: Smithsonian Institution Press, 2nd printing 1975), 63, 155.

21 *Millinery Trade Review*, March 1876, 25.

22 Ibid., 129.

23 Burrows and Wallace, *Gotham*, 945.

24 Kidwell and Chrisman, *Suiting Everyone*, 157.

25 Susan Porter Benson, *Counter Cultures: Saleswomen, Managers, and Customers in American Department Stores, 1890-1940* (Urbana, IL and Chicago: University of Illinois Press, 1986), 20.

26 Philippe Perot, *Fashioning the Bourgeoise: A History of Clothing in the Nineteenth Century*, trans. Richard Bienvenue (Princeton, NJ: Princeton University Press, 1994), 59.

27 Ibid., 59.

28 Benson, *Counter Cultures*, 23.

29 Louis Hyman, "How Sears Helped Oppose Jim Crow," *New York Times*, October 20, 2018.

30 Richard White, *Railroaded: The Transcontinentals and the Making of America* (New York: W.W. Norton, 2012).

31 Penny, *Think and Act*, 29.

32 Jo Chimes, "'Wanted 1000 Spirited Young Milliners': The Fund for Promoting Female Emigration," in Harris, ed., *Famine and Fashion*, 229.

33 Ibid., 229.

34 Helen Campbell, *Prisoners of Poverty* (Boston: Roberts Brothers, 1889), 101–2.

35 "Go West, Young Woman," *Millinery Trade Review*, October 1880, 132.

36 "Millinery among Mormons," *Millinery Trade Review,* January 1886, 29.

37 Ibid., 29.

38 Ibid.

39 Lara Vapnek, *Breadwinners: Working Women & Economic Independence 1865-1920* (Urbana and Chicago: University of Illinois Press, 2009), 42.

40 "Trade in the Far West," *Millinery Trade Review*, October 28, 1879, 152.

41 "Business Notes," *Millinery Trade Review,* January 1881, 10.

42 Ibid.

43 "Peroxide of Barnum," *Millinery Trade Review*, April 1886, 149–50.

44 Ibid.

45 Ibid.

46 Campbell, *Prisoners of Poverty*, 18.

47 Ibid., 214.

48 Ibid.

49 Burrows and Wallace, *Gotham*, 1116.

50 Severa, *Dressed for the Photographer*, 386.

51 Kathy Peiss*, Cheap Amusements: Working Women and Leisure in Turn-of-the-Century New York* (Philadelphia, PA: Temple University Press, 1986), 63 (Rose Pasternak-oral history).

52 Sophie Abrams as quoted in Elizabeth Ewan, *Immigrant Women in the Land of Dollars: Life and Culture on the Lower East Side 1890-1925* (New York: Monthly Review Press, 1985), 68.

53 Nan Enstad, *Ladies of Labor, Girls of Adventure: Working Women, Popular Culture, and Labor Politics at the Turn of the Twentieth Century* (New York: Columbia University Press, 1999), 9.

54 Anzia Yeziersha, *Breadgivers* (1925; repr. New York: Persea Books, 2003), 4–5.

55 Gino Speranza, "The Italian in Congested Districts," *Charities and Commons* (1908) quoted in Ewan, *Immigrant Women in the Land of Dollars,* 68.

56 Enstad, *Ladies of Labor, Girls of Adventure*, 9.

57 *Lillian Wald*, The House on Henry Street (1915) (New York: Henry Holt and Company, Reprint 1931), 193.

58 John H. Young, *A Guide to the Manners, Etiquette, and Deportment of the Most Refined Society* (New York: Lyons Press, 2001; Reprint 1879), 321.

59 Ibid., 322.

60 Steele, *Fashion and Eroticism*, 71.

61 Gamber, *The Female Economy*, 205.

62 Perry, *Millinery as a Trade for Women*, 40–1.

63 Gamber, *The Female Economy*, 188.

64 Ibid.

65 *Milliner* 27 (September 1916) n.p. (inside back cover) as quoted in Ibid., 183.

66 These dyes probably did not contain radium. It was extremely expensive. However, there was a "craze" for radium in the early twentieth century since it was considered a wonder drug; so many manufacturers in a wide variety of industries used the name to cash in. *Kate Moore, Radium Girls: The Dark Story* (Napierville, IL: Sourcebooks, 2017), 6.

67 "How to Turn Dead Stock into Money," *Illustrated Milliner*, February 1914, 136.

68 Perry, *Millinery as a Trade for Women*, 108.

69 Peiss, *Cheap Amusements*, 42.

70 "Hat Block," *Millinery Trade Review*, February 1880, 30.

71 "Scalping a Hat Trimmer," *Millinery Trade Review*, September 1881, 136.

72 "Hanson Advertisement," *Millinery Trade Review*, 1882, 5.

73 "Foreign Clippings," *Millinery Trade Review*, 1882, 61.

74 Catharine Beecher, *The Duty of American Women to Their Country* (New York: Harper & Brothers, 1845), 65.

75 Young, *Guide to the Manners*, 234.

76 Alice Kessler-Harris, *Women Have Always Worked* (Old Westbury, NY: Feminist Press/NY: McGraw-Hill Company, 1981), 96.

77 Burrows and Wallace, *Gotham*, 1177.

78 Young, *Guide to Manners*, 1879, 331.

79 Ibid., 332.

80 "Bicycling for Ladies," *Staten Island Historian*, Fall 2011, 2.

81 "This Month," *Millinery Trade Review*, December 1881, 165–6.

82 Kessler-Harris, *Women Have Always Worked*, 99–100.

83 "Women in the Trade," *Millinery Trade Review*, December 1901, 104.

Chapter 5

1 Linton Weeks, "Hats Off to the Women Who Saved the Birds," NPR, July 15, 2015, https://www.npr.org/sections/npr-history-dept/2015/07/15/422860307/hats-off-to-women-who-saved-the-birds.

2 Migratory Bird Treaty Act Explained, National Audubon Society, January 26, 2018, https://www.audubon.org/news/the-migratory-bird-treaty-act-explained

3 Enstad, *Ladies of Labor, Girls of Adventure*, 27.

4 Karen Halttunen, *Confidence Men and Painted Women: A Study of Middle-Class Culture in America, 1830-1870* (New Haven, CT: Yale University Press, 1982), 95.

5 Bertha Richardson as quoted in Enstad, *Ladies of Labor, Girls of Adventure*, 77–8.

6 (Tape I-132 [side A]), Immigrant Labor History Collection of the CCNY Oral History Project, Robert F Wagner Archives, Tamiment Institute Library, New York University.

7   Anzia Yezierska, *Salome of the Tenements* (1923; Reprint, Urbana and Chicago: University of Illinois Press, 1995), 23.

8   Van Kleeck, *A Seasonal Industry,* 4.

9   Ibid., 156.

10 Elizabeth Riedell, "School Training for Milliners in Boston," in Perry, *Millinery as A Trade for Women*, 122.

11 Ibid., 124–5.

12 Ibid., 127.

13 Van Kleeck, *A Seasonal Industry*, 15 (footnote).

14 Ibid., 14.

15 Ibid., 28.

16 Perry, *Millinery as a Trade for Women*, 40–1.

17 Van Kleeck, *A Seasonal Industry*, 58.

18 Irving Lewis Allen, *The City in Slang: New York Life and Popular Speech* (New York and Oxford: Oxford University Press, 1999), 201.

19 Yezierska, *Salome of the Tenements*; Introduction by Gay Wilentz, 13–14.

20 Elizabeth Beardsley Butler, *Women and the Trades: Pittsburgh 1907-1908* (Pittsburgh, PA: University of Pittsburgh Press, 1984; Reprint 1909), 26.

21 Perry, *Millinery as a Trade for Women*, 93.

22 Ibid.

23 Van Kleeck, *A Seasonal Industry*, 68.

24 Ibid.

25 Mary van Kleeck, *Artificial Flower Makers* (New York: Survey Associates, Inc., 1913), 35.

26 Ibid. 37.

27 Ibid., 23.

28 Van Kleeck, *A Seasonal Industry*, 129.

29 Ibid., 128.

30 Perry, *Millinery as a Trade for Women*, 14.

31 Van Kleeck, *A Seasonal Industry*, 170.

32 Ibid., 170.

33 Ibid., 168.

34 Ibid.

35 Ibid., 126.

36 Ibid., 95.

37 Mrs. Z. B. Dexter, "Wafted from the Workroom," *The Illustrated Milliner*, February 1901, 77.

38 Susan M. Kingsbury, Director, Department of Research, Women's Educational and Industrial Union in Perry, *Millinery as a Trade for Women*, vii–viii.

39 Van Kleeck, *A Seasonal Industry*, 142.

40 Enstad, *Ladies of Labor, Girls of Adventure*, 142.

41 Perry, *Millinery as a Trade for Women*, 107.

42 "Leader Tells Why 40,000 Girls Struck," *New York Evening Journal*, November 26, 1909 (11–12).

43 May Allison, "Dressmaking as a Trade for Women in Massachusetts," Washington, Government Printing Office 1913 (United States Bureau of Labor Statistics, Bulletin 193), 79.

44 Alice Kessler-Harris, *A Woman's Wage: Historical Meanings and Social Consequences* (Lexington, KY: University Press of Kentucky, 1990), 14–44.

45 Enstad, *Ladies of Labor, Girls of Adventure*, 113.

46 Mary Anderson, "Letter," *Life and Labor* (December 1911) as quoted in Enstad, *Ladies of Labor, Girls of Adventure*, 115.

47 Van Kleeck, *A Seasonal Industry*, 134.

48 Wall Text, *Mad Hatters: New York Hats and Hatmakers*, City Lore Gallery, 2016.
The CHCMW merged with the Amalgamated Clothing and Textile Workers Union in 1983. Later the combined union merged again with the International Ladies Garment Works in 1995 to form UNITE (Union of Needle Trades, Industrial and Textile Employees).

49 "Talks on Labor," *American Federalist* 12 (November 1905), 846.

50 Van Kleeck, *A Seasonal Industry*, 135.

51 Ibid., 109.

52 Ibid., 98.

53 Parsons School of Design-The New School, New York, NY, "Parsons' History," https://www.newschool.edu/parsons/history/.

54 Van Kleeck, *A Seasonal Industry*, 166.

55 New York State Factory Investigation Commission as quoted in Ibid., 178–81.

56 Ibid., 180.

57 Ibid., 192.

58 "A Woman Who Is the Greatest Millinery Success in America," *Illustrated Milliner*, January 1902, 34.

59 Ibid.

60 *New-York Tribune*, New York, NY, July 1902. Chronicling America: Historic American Newspapers. Library of Congress, https://chroniclingamerica.loc.gov/lccn/sn83030214/1921-02-26/ed-1/seq-1/.

61 "The Road to Fortune—Madame Wallman!" *Illustrated Milliner*, June 1909, 45.

62 Ibid.

Chapter 6

1 *Illustrated Milliner* (New York: The Baldwin Syndicate, January 1900), 3.

2 Ibid., 41.

3   Ibid., 23.

4   Ibid., 71.

5   Ibid., 30–1.

6   "Why Are There No Millinery Millionaires?" *Illustrated Milliner*, April 1900, 70.

7   Ibid., 71.

8   *Illustrated Milliner*, January 1900, 71.

9   "100 Years: Alexander Hamilton U.S. Custom House, New York City," http:// oldnycustomhouse.gov/history/ (Accessed May 18, 2010).

10 "How Millinery Materials Made Abroad Get Through the US Custom House," *The Illustrated Milliner*, January 1901, 55.

11 Ibid.

12 *Illustrated Milliner*, January 1900, 55.

13 Ibid.

14 Ibid.

15 *Illustrated Milliner*, November 1907, 22.

16 *Illustrated Milliner*, January 1900, 37.

17 *Illustrated Milliner*, January 1901, 41.

18 Ibid.

19 Ibid.

20 Ibid.

21 *Illustrated Milliner*, May 1912, 63.

22 *Illustrated Milliner*, April 1913, 21.

23 Karen Abbott, "'The Hatpin Peril' Terrorized Men Who Couldn't Handle the Twentieth Century Woman," Smithsonian.com, April 24, 2014, http://www.smithsonianmag .com/history/hatpin-peril-terrorized-men-who-couldnt-handle-20th-century-woman- 180951219/#0QZ5U1A4lKdl8QuM.99.

24 Ibid.

25 "Notes & Comments," *Illustrated Milliner*, June 1913, 15.

26 *Illustrated Milliner*, January 1914, 26.

27 Ibid., 29.

28 Testimony of Robert Howard, Mule-Spinner in Fall River Cotton Mills, before the U.S. Senate Committee on Labor, 1883 cited in Louis D. Brandeis and Josephine Goldmark, *Women in Industry: Decision of the U.S. Supreme Court in Curt Muller vs. State of Oregon Upholding the Constitutionality of the Oregon Ten Hour Law for Women and Brief for the State of Oregon* (New York: National Consumers' League, 1908).

29 "Notes & Comments," *Illustrated Milliner*, April 1914, 27.

30 Ibid.

31 Ibid.

32 *Illustrated Milliner*, September 1914, 7.

33 Ibid., 14.

34 Ibid., 7.

35 "The World's Fashion Center in Days of War," *Illustrated Milliner*, October 1914, 7.

36 Ibid.

37 "Shopping Economy," *Illustrated Milliner*, October 1914, 3.

38 "A Plea for Paris," *Illustrated Milliner*, November 1914, 13.

39 Ibid.

40 "Simplicity the Keynote in Paris Spring Styles," *Illustrated Milliner*, January 1915, 13.

41 Ibid.

42 "Millinery and Prosperity," *Illustrated Milliner*, June 1915, 19.

43 "Lady Duff Gordon's Interpretation of Prevalent Millinery Styles," *Illustrated Milliner*, May 1915, 109.

44 Ibid.

45 "Coiffures Up to Date," *Illustrated Milliner*, June 1915, 58.

46 "Notes and Comments," *Illustrated Milliner*, January 1916, 15M.

47 Ibid.

48 Ibid.

49 "Comments," *Illustrated Milliner*, January 1916, 11M.

50 "Help the Red Cross Work," *Illustrated Milliner*, May 1917, 15.

51 "Novelties of the Month," *Illustrated Milliner*, July 1917, 13.

52 Ibid., 113M.

53 "This Means You!" *Illustrated Milliner*, September 1917, 80.

54 "Keep Knitting," *Illustrated Milliner*, September 1917, 95M.

55 "Business Must Be as Usual," *Illustrated Milliner*, January 1918, 135.

56 Ibid.

57 "Legislation to Restrict Employment," *Illustrated Milliner*, April 1918, 96M.

58 *Illustrated Milliner*, May 1918, 75M.

59 *Illustrated Milliner*, July 1981, 158M.

60 "The New Mourning Hat: A Thing of Exquisite Beauty," *Illustrated Milliner*, June 1918, 64–5.

61 "Influenza Epidemic Is Great Slump to Business," *Illustrated Milliner*, November 1918, 83M.

62 John Barry, *The Great Influenza: The Epic Story of the Deadliest Plague in History* (New York: Viking, 2004), 4–5.

63 "Great Slump to Business," *Illustrated Milliner*, November 1918, 83M.

64 "Complimentary Lunch for the Ladies," *Illustrated Milliner*, August 1919, 55.

65 "Past, Present, Future," *Illustrated Milliner*, January 1920.

66 Ibid.

67 Ibid.

68 "Millinery Firms Using Crippled Workers," *Illustrated Milliner*, February 1920, 9M.

69 Ibid.

70 Ibid.

71 "Proposed Remedies for the Labor Shortage," *Illustrated Milliner*, July 1920, 15M.

72 "After All, It's Not the Hat, but the Way It's Worn, Illustrated Milliner, December 1920, 60.

73 This was an effort to reproduce a New York city working class accent.

74 Ibid.

75 Ibid.

76 Ibid.

Chapter 7

1 Richmond Pearson Hobson, "The Truth About Alcohol," Speech in the House of Representatives, December 22, 1914 (Washington, DC: U.S. Government Printing Office, 1914), 20.

2 The Day in History, January 16, https://www.history.com/this-day-in-history/prohibition-ratified.

3 The Day in History, August 26, https://www.history.com/topics/womens-history/19th-amendment-1.

4 "The Voice of the Trade," *The Illustrated Milliner*, October 1920, 3M.

5 Jack London, *John Barleycorn* (New York: Oxford University Press, 1998), 1.

6 Ibid., 3.

7 Ibid., 2.

8 "Shortage of Female Help in Factories," *The Illustrated Milliner*, December 1920, 86.

9 *The Illustrated Milliner*, March 1922, 69.

10 Kelly J. Baker, "Make America White Again?" *The Atlantic*, March 12, 2016, https://www.theatlantic.com/politics/archive/2016/03/donald-trump-kkk/473190/.

11 Cecil Beaton, *The Glass of Fashion* (London: Cassell, 1989), 118.

12 Ibid., 124.

13 Ibid., 125.

14 Suzanne Lussier, *Art Deco Fashion* (London: V&A Publishing, 2003), 20.

15 Martin Pei and Terence Pepper, *1920s Jazz Age: Fashion and Photographs* (London: Unicorn Publishing, 2018), 19 and Valerie Mendes and Amy de la Haye, *Fashion Since 1900*, 2nd ed. (London: Thames and Hudson, 1999 and 2010), 65.

16 Frederick Lewis Allen, *Only Yesterday: An Informal History of the 1920s* (New York: Harper Perennial, 2010; Reprint 1931), 80.

17 F. Scott Fitzgerald, *This Side of Paradise* (New York: A.L. Burt, 1920), 188.

18 *Chicago Tribune*, 1930 as quoted in Joshua Zeitz, *Flapper: A Madcap Story of Sex, Style, Celebrity and the Women Who Made America Modern* (New York: Crown Publishing, 2006), 148.

19 Long, "Tables for Two," *The New Yorker*, September 12, 1925, 32–3.

20 Dale Kramer, *Ross and The New Yorker* (Garden City, NY: Doubleday and Company, Inc. 1951), 83.

21 Emmanuelle Dirix, "Feathers and Fringes: The Spectacular Modern Flapper: Ode to a Changing Icon," in Kenneth Ramaekers, ed., *Jazz Age: Fashion in the Roaring 20s* (Ghent-Courtrai: Snoeck Publishers, 2015), 118.

22 Lois Long, *The New Yorker*, December 12, 1925 as quoted in Zeitz, *Flapper*, 193.

23 Ibid.

24 Ibid.

25 Evans, Caroline, *The Mechanical Smile: Modernism and the First Fashion Shows in France and America 1900-1929* (New Haven and London: Yale University Press, 2013), 125.

26 Victoria Sherrow, *Encyclopedia of Hair: A Cultural History* (Westport, CT: Greenwood Press 2006), 65.

27 Clarence Darrow, "Liberty, Equality, Fraternity" (December 1926), in Graydon Carter, ed., *Bohemians, Bootleggers, Flappers, and Swells: The Best of Early Vanity Fair* (New York: Penguin Press, 2014), 265.

28 Ibid.

29 Ibid.

30 Ibid., 266–7.

31 Ibid., 267.

32 Carolyn Rennolds Milbank, *New York Fashion: The Evolution of American Style* (New York: Harry N. Abrams, 1989), 80.

33 Clair Hughes, *Hats* (New York and London: Bloomsbury Publishing, 2017), 2–231.

34 Madeleine Ginsburg, *Hat: Trends and Traditions* (Hauppauge, NY: Barron's, 1990), 114.

35 Susie Hopkins, *The Century of Hats: Head-Turning Style of the Twentieth Century* (Edison, NJ: Chartwell Books, 1989), 29.

36 Perry, *Millinery as a Trade for Women*, 44.

37 Hopkins, *The Century of Hats*, 42.

38 *Harper's Bazaar*, October 1923 as quoted in Milbank, *New York Fashion*, 79.

39 Dilys Blum, *Ahead of Fashion: Hats of the Twentieth Century* (Philadelphia, PA: Philadelphia Museum of Art, 1993), 10.

40 *The Illustrated Milliner*, February 1922, 63.

41 Ibid.

42 Edna Woolman Chase as quoted in Ginsberg, *The Hat*, 115.

43 Pei and Pepper, *1920s Jazz Age*, 42.

44 Jane Bradbury and Edward Maeder, *American Style and Spirit: Fashions and Lives of the Roddis Family, 1850-1995* (London: V&A Publishing, 2016), 119.

45 Helen Landon Cass (radio announcer), June 6, 1923, as quoted in William Leach, *Land of Desire: Merchants, Power, and the Rise of a New American Culture* (New York: Vintage Books, 1993), 298.

46 Leach, *Land of Desire*, 293.

47 Ibid.

48 *The Illustrated Milliner*, 1922, 13.

49 Alice Kessler-Harris, *Out to Work: A History of Wage-Earning Women in the United States* (New York: Oxford University Press, Reprint 2003), 226.

50 Brandeis and Goldmark, *Women in Industry*, 21.

51 Secretary of Labor James David. 1926 was quoted in Cott, *The Grounding of Modern Feminism,* 137.

52 Ibid.

53 Kessler-Harris, *Out to Work*, 152.

54 *American Federationist* (February 1896) as quoted in Kessler-Harris, *Out to Work*, 153.

55 Samuel Gompers, *American Federationist* (January 1906) as quoted in Kessler-Harris, *Out to Work*, 153.

56 Kessler-Harris, *Women Have Always Worked*, 100.

57 The American blockers were still subject to exposure to mercury. Hatter's disease was called "Danbury Shakes" in the United States, a reference to Danbury, Connecticut, center of the hatmaking industry. David, *Fashion Victims*, 44.
     Though France banned mercury in hat-making in 1898, the United States did not ban its use until the 1940s due to the pressure of powerful manufacturers on lawmakers. They blamed drunkenness, not mercury poisoning, produced the neurological symptoms in their workers. Smith, *Hats: An Unnatural History*, 22.

58 Gamber, *The Female Economy*, 213.

59 Milbank, *New York Fashion*, 80.

60 Ibid., 89–90.

61 Ibid., 90.

62 Gamber, *The Female Economy*, 227.

63 Joseph Adna Hill, *Women in Gainful Occupations, 1870 to 1920* (Washington, DC: U.S. Government Printing Office, 1929), 33.

64 1929 UCHCMW Convention Proceedings, *United Hatters, Cap and Millinery Workers International Union Files on Microfilm. 5755 Mf. Kheel Center for Labor-Management Documentation and Archives*, Martin P. Catherwood Library, Cornell University., n.d. 11.

65 Ibid.

66 Ibid.

67 "No More Flappers," *New York Times*, February 28, 1928, 22.

68 Charles H. Green, *The Headwear Workers: A Century of Trade Unionism* (New York: United Cap and Millinery Workers International Union, 1944), 175–6.

Chapter 8

1 Patricia Mears and Bruce Boyer, *Elegance In the Age of Crisis: Fashions of the 1930s* (New Haven and London: Yale University Press, 2014), 141.

2 Emmanuelle Dirix, *Dressing the Decades: Twentieth-Century Vintage Style* (New Haven and London: Yale University Press, 2016), 83.

3 Adrian was surprised by the popularity of the Eugenie and very upset that his design was widely copied. Three years after *Romance* was released he told a reporter, "The French designers can sell their models for huge prices, but ours are just pirated. Look what happened when we designed the Eugénie hat for Garbo in Romance . . . ugh?" Howard Gutner, *Gowns by Adrian: The MGM Years 1928-1941* (New York: Harry N. Abrams, Inc., 2001), 81.

4 "France: Empress Eugénie Again," *Time*, August 3, 1931, http://search.time.com.

5 Ernestine Carter, *The Changing World of Fashion: 1900 to the Present* (New York: G.P. Putnam's Sons, 1977), 81.

6 Palmer White, *Elsa Schiaparelli: Empress of Paris Fashion* (London: Aurum Press, 1995), 69.

7 Kohle Yohannan and Nancy Nolf, *Claire McCardell: Redefining Modernism* (New York: Harry N. Abrams, Inc., 1998), 45 and 46 (picture).

8 Jody Shields, *Hats: A Stylish History and Collector's Guide* (New York: Clarkson, Potter, 1991), 44 and 49.

9 The cloche style of the 1920s was called "nude" because it hugged the shape of the head.

10 *Contemporary Modes*, Early Fall, 1936, 9.

11 "Findings and Recommendations of the Special Board of the Millinery Industry," Max Meyer Papers #5221. Kheel Center for Labor-Management Documentation and Archives, Cornell University Library.

12 Ibid.

13 Marx Lewis, *A Half Century of Achievement: The History of Millinery Workers' Union Local 24* (New York: Millinery Workers' Union, Local 24, 1960), 19.

14 In 1936, a new national organization, the Congress of Industrial Organizations (CIO) would challenge the AFL. Unions in the CIO were organized on the principle of "industrial unionism"; that is, all workers in an industry are organized into one union regardless of the skill or craft they practice.

15 Biennual Convention Proceedings, United Hatters, Cap, and Millinery Workers, 1925, Kheel Center for Labor-Management Documentation and Archives, Cornell University Library.

16 Annalise Orleck, *Common Sense and a Little Fire: Women and Working-Class Politics in the United States 1900-1965*, 2nd ed. (Chapel Hill: University of North Carolina Press, 1991, 2017), 42.

17 Lewis, *Half Century of Achievement*, 96–113.

18 David B. Robinson, *Spotlight on a Union: The Story of the United Hatters, Cap and Millinery Workers* (New York: The Dial Press, 1948), 160–1.

19 Jack "Legs" Diamond is one gangster whose name has been mythologized in American literature. Pulitzer Prize-winning author William J. Kennedy wrote a fictional biography of Legs in 1975. It was the first in his "Albany Cycle."

20 Okent, *Last Call*, 243.

21 Green, *Headwear Workers*, 177.

22 Ibid., 177–81 and Lewis, *A Half Century of Achievement*, 121–38.

23 William Manchester, *The Glory and the Dream: A Narrative History of American 1932-1972* (New York: Bantam Books, 1990 [Orig. pub. 1974]), 88–9.

24 Ibid., 89.

25 Ibid., 131.

26 *Fibre and Fabric* as quoted in Ibid., 131.

27 Robinson, *Spotlight on a Union*, 216–17.

28 Ibid., 217.

29 Edward L. Fries, Label Review Officer, Compliance Division NRA, Radio Address, February 21, 1935. Kheel Center for Labor-Management Documentation and Archives, Cornell University Library.

30 Ibid.

31 Apparel Codes LabeL Council, Max Meyers Papers. Kheel Center for Labor-Management Documentation and Archives, Cornell University Library.

32 "Planning and Education Program for the Millinery Industry," Max Meyers Papers, Kheel Center for Labor-Management Documentation and Archives, Cornell University Library.

33 Ibid.

34 Katherine A. Klein, Livingston Brothers, San Francisco, CA, as quoted in "Planning and Education Program for the Millinery Industry," Max Meyers Papers, Kheel Center for Labor-Management Documentation and Archives, Cornell University Library.

35 "Planning and Education Program for the Millinery Industry," Max Meyers Papers, Kheel Center for Labor-Management Documentation and Archives, Cornell University Library.

36 "Report to Assistant Attorney General Thurman Arnold," 1938, Max Meyers Papers, Kheel Center for Labor-Management Documentation and Archives, Cornell University Library.

37 Ibid., 6.

38 Ibid., 9.

39 Susan Ware, *Beyond Suffrage: Women in the New Deal* (Cambridge, MA: Harvard University Press, 1981), 6.

40 Margaretta Byers with Consuelo Kamholz, *Designing Women: The Art, Technique, and Cost of Being Beautiful* (New York: Simon and Schuster, 1938), 153.

41 Ibid., 179.

42 Ibid., 193.

43 Executive Board Minutes, August 29, 1935. United Hatters, Cap and Millinery Workers International Union Files on Microfilm. 5755 Mf. Kheel Center for Labor-Management Documentation and Archives, Martin P. Catherwood Library, Cornell University., n.d.

44 Ibid.

45 Ibid.

46 Ibid.

47 Robinson, *Spotlight on a Union*, 252.

48 Ibid., 253.

49 "Anything Goes in a Hat for a Woman," *Life*, November 22, 1947, 81.

50 Ibid.

51 "Madame Has a Funny Hat," *Vogue*, January 1, 1938, 56.

52 "A Fashion for Odd-Looking Veils Makes the World Look Different," *Life*, October 18, 1937, 53–5.

53 "Now the Fad Is Dolls' Hats/ Did the Comics Inspire These Pee-Wees?" *Life*, July 4, 1938, 54.

54 Ibid., 55. The hat would cost $264.78 today, http://www.westegg.com/inflation/infl.cgi.

55 "Sneers for Snoods," *Time*, September 25, 1939, http://search.time.com.

56 "Cold Ears and Wind-Blown Hair Bring the Medieval Wimple," *Life*, January 2, 1939, 52.

57 "Letters to the Editor," *Life*, January 16, 1939, 2.

58 Ibid.

59 Ibid.

60 Ibid.

61 "Fancy Dress and Fashion," *Vogue*, August 1, 1935, 35.

62 "Nets Go to Your Head," *Vogue*, February 1, 1939, 136.

63 Marcel Vertès with Byran Holme, *Art and Fashion*, trans. George Davis (New York and London: The Studio Publications, 1944), 84.

64 Sandra Stansbery Buckland, "Promoting American Designers, 1940–44: Building Our Own House," in Linda Welters and Patricia Cunningham, eds., *Twentieth Century American Fashion* (New York: Berg, 2005), 111.

65 Carolyn Hall, *The Thirties in Vogue* (New York: Harmony Books, 1985), 130.

66 *Vogue*, February 1, 1939, 101.

67 Lilly Daché, ed. Dorothy Roe Lewis, *Talking Through My Hats* (New York: Coward-McCann, Inc., 1946), 219.

68 Executive Board Minutes, November 13, 1939. United Hatters, Cap and Millinery Workers International Union Files on Microfilm. 5755 Mf. Kheel Center for Labor-Management Documentation and Archives, Martin P. Catherwood Library, Cornell University., n.d.

69 Ibid.

70 Sally Victor quoted in untitled and undated article *c.* 1935, Sally Victor Papers, Special Collections, Gladys Marcus Library, Fashion Institute of Technology, New York, NY.

71 Fiorello LaGuardia (1940) as quoted in Sandra Stansbery Buckland, "Promoting American Designers, 1940-44: Building Our Own House," 109–10.

72 "The Best Dressed Women—and Why," *Vogue*, February 1, 1938, 153.

73 Carmel Snow as quoted in Fashion Group Bulletin, October 1940, 2.

74 Eileen Ford's interview as quoted in Penelope Rowlands, *A Dash of Daring: Carmel Snow and Her Life in Fashion, Art and Letters* (New York: Atria, 2005), 288.

75 William Manchester, *The Glory and the Dream* (1974; Reprint, New York: Bantam Books, September 1975), 129.

76 *Harper's Bazaar*, May 1938, 70.

77 Nikolas Murray, "Keep 'It' Under Your Hat," *Contemporary Modes*, August 1940, 11.

78 Russell Patterson as quoted in Ibid.

79 "Half a Hat Is Better Than None," *Vogue*, December 15, 1940, 43.

80 Ibid.

81 "Vogue's Eye View of Nominations," *Vogue*, July 15, 1940, 15.

Chapter 9

1 Edna Woolman Chase, "Fashion in 1914 and 1939," speech to meeting of Fashion Group International, New York, NY, September 27, 1939.

2 Rowlands, *A Dash of Daring*, 266–8.

3 Bettina Ballard, *In My Fashion* (New York: David McKay and Company, 1960), 154.

4 Jonathan Walford, *Forties Fashion* (London: Thames and Hudson, 2008), 144.

5 M. D. C. Crawford, *The Ways of Fashion* (New York: G.P. Putnam's Sons, 1941), 4.

6 "Clothes: Home Styles," *Time*, August 19, 1940, http://www.time.com/time/magazine/article/0,9171,764436,00.html.

7 Virginia Pope, "Mayor Has Plan to Aid Fashion Bid," *New York Times (1857-Current file)*, August 22, 1940, http://www.proquest.com/ (accessed January 17, 2010).

8 Ibid.

9 Ibid.

10 Ibid.

11 Ibid.

12 Wolford, *Forties Fashion*, 61.

13 Buckland, "Promoting American Designers, 1940-44: Building Our Own House," 111.

14 "Display Ad—37 No Title," *New York Times (1857-Current file)*, September 5, 1940, http://www.proquest.com/ (accessed January 23, 2010).

15 Ibid.

16 Ibid.

17 Ibid.

18 "Paris Still Held Center of Fashion," *New York Times (1857-Current File)*, September 25, 1940, http://www.proquest.com/ (accessed January 17, 2010).

19 Ibid.

20 Ibid.

21 "10 Billion Involved in 'Fashion Futures,'" *New York Times (1857-Current file)*, December 10, 1940, http://www.proquest.com/ (accessed January 17, 2010).

22 "Fashion Show Sold Out," *New York Times (1857-Current file)*, December 24, 1940, http://www.proquest.com/ (accessed January 17, 2010).

23 Times Wide World, "Mayor, as Expert on New Styles, Inspects Fabrics and Models for Big Show Here," *New York Times (1857-Current file)*, December 28, 1940, http://www.proquest.com/ (accessed January 17, 2010).

24 Ibid.

25 Ibid.

26 Ibid.

27 Virginia Pope, "New York: Twofold Fashion Center," *New York Times (1857-Current file)*, January 5, 1941, http://www.proquest.com/ (accessed January 17, 2010).

28 "Women: Fit to Be Tied," *Time*, December 12, 1940, http://search.time.com.

29 Colin McDowell, *Hats: Status, Style and Glamour* (New York: Rizzoli, 1992), 149.

30 *Lilly Daché: Glamour at the Drop of a Hat* (exhibit brochure), The Museum at FIT, Fashion Institute of Technology (March 13–April 21, 2007), 13.

31 Daché, *Talking Through My Hats*, 4.

32 The team broke up in 1948. Mr. John established his own studio and continued as one of the most famous milliners in the country until his retirement in 1970. Frederic Hirst, the second team member, passed from the public eye.

33 Daché, *Talking Through My Hats*, 207.

34 Stein, Gail, "Mr. John, 'Emperor of Fashion,'" *Dress* 27 (2000): 39.

35 Fay Hammond as quoted in Oliver, Myrna (1993), *Los Angeles Times* obituary, June 29.

36 Amy Sullivan, "Million-Dollar Milliner," *Harper's Bazaar*, 124.

37 M-G-M press release as quoted in Herb Bridges and Terryl Boodman, *Gone with the Wind: The Definitive Illustrated History of the Book, the Movie, the Legend* (New York: Simon and Schuster, 1989), 65.

38 H. Stanley Marcus, "The Future of Fashion," *Fortune*, November 1940, 80.

39 Ibid.

40 Aline Fruehauf, "Some American Designers," *Vogue*, October 15, 1940, 63.

41 Keene, *Boston Evening Transcript*, November 4, 1933, Sally Victor Papers.

42 "Business: Sally Victor," *Time*, March 30, 1959, http://www.time.com/time/magazine/article/0,9171,892459,00.html.

43 Grace Davidson, "Says Men Prefer Hats on Women," *Boston Post*, December 3, 1941, Sally Victor Papers.

44 Eugenia Sheppard, "Priorities Give Fashion Industry Its Second Big Beating in Year," *New York Herald Tribune*, August 25, 1941, Sally Victor Papers.

45 "How to Knit," *Life*, November 24, 1941, 110.

46 Ibid., 113.

47 Maud Moody, *Women's Wear Daily*, speech to the Fashion Group International, New York, NY, November 17, 1941.

48 *Hats*, March 1941, 2.

49 Damon Runyon, "The Brighter Side," *Hats*, November 1941, inside back cover.

50 Ibid.

51 *Women's Wear Daily*, October 21, 41, Sally Victor Papers.

52 Ibid.

53 "Women Buy Warm, Useful Clothes to be Prepared for War's Rigors," *New York Times*, December 12, 1941, Sally Victor Papers.

54 "Hats That Hold On," *Vogue*, March 1, 1940.

55 "First Black-Out Hat," *New York Herald Tribune*, December 15, 1941, Sally Victor Papers.

56 Ibid.

57 "Air Raid Hat for Civilians—Designed by Sally Victor," *Women's Wear Daily*, December 16, 1941, Sally Victor Papers.

58 Franklin D. Roosevelt, Radio address on December 1941, quoted in "Mobilizing for War," *The Price of Freedom: Americans at War*, Smithsonian National Museum of American History, http://americanhistory.si.edu/militaryhistory/exhibition/flash.html.

59 Ibid.

60 Bettie J. Morden, Center for Military History, United States Department of the Army, *The Women's Army Corps, 1945-1978*, 2000, http://www.history.army.mil/books/wac/index.htm.

61 Walford, *Forties Fashion*, 37–57.

62 H. Stanley Marcus, *Minding the Store: A Memoir* (Boston, MA: Little, Brown and Company, 1974), 115.

63 "The Untrimmed Look: Hats Are Voluntarily Simple . . . Decorative. Undecorated," *Vogue*, July 15, 1942, 19.

64 Ibid.

65 "Fashion in America Now," *Vogue*, February 1, 1942, 50.

66 "Beautiful Hats . . . Dutiful Hats," *Vogue*, January 15, 1942, 43.

67 "Hair Style for Safety WWII," http://www.youtube.com/watch?v=mgpvKXLTwr8.

68 Ibid.

69 Ibid.

70 Ibid.

71 Ibid.

72 "More Beauty. More Work," *Vogue*, November 1, 1942, 76.

73 Ibid.

74 Ibid.

75 "Wartime Headgear," *New York Times*, October 4, 1942, Sally Victor Papers.

76 Ibid.

77 Dorothy Roe, "Wartime Styles Go to Work," *AP Features*, March 18, 1943, Sally Victor Papers.

78 "Welder's Snood," *Clinton (IA) Herald*, November 20, 1942. Sally Victor Papers.

79 "Arc Welding Supplies," General Electric brochure, 1942, Sally Victor Papers.

80 *Harper's Bazaar*, November 1943, cover.

81 Still a substantial investment since $10 in 1942 is equal to $130.71 today. http://www.westegg.com/inflation/infl.cgi.

82 "Homemade Hats," *Life*, March 23, 1942, 82–3.

83 Ibid.

84 "Sally Victor Tells How to Make Your Easter Hat: Triple Trio Patterns," *Woman's Home Companion*, c. 1942, Sally Victor Papers.

85 "Vertès Handkerchiefs . . . a Fold, a Twist, a Triumph," *Harper's Bazaar*, June 1942, 52.

86 Maud Moody, *Women's Wear Daily*, "What Questions Are Buyers Asking?" speech to the Fashion Group International, New York, NY, February 26, 1942.

87 Ibid.

88 Peggy Parker, "How to Pick a Hat to Win a Husband, a Job or to Boost Morale," *Times-Herald*, c. 1942, Sally Victor Papers.

89 Blum, *Ahead of Fashion*, 32.

90 Daché, *Talking Through My Hats*, 209.

91 "Look Your Best While You Do Your Best," *Vogue*, March 1, 1943, 62.

92 *Vogue*, September 1, 1943.

93 Alistair Horne, *Seven Ages of Paris* (2002; repr., New York: Vintage Books, 2004), 348.

94 "Wider Aid Sought by Jewish Appeal," *New York Times* (1923-Current File), September 4, 1943, http://www.proquest.com/ (accessed February 15, 2010).

95 Francine du Plessix Grey, *Them: A Memoir of Parents* (New York: Penguin Press, 2003), 46.

96 "New Hats Demand a Haughty Carriage," *New York Times (1857-Current file)*, March 2, 1945, http://www.proquest.com/ (accessed November 12, 2009).

97 Ibid.

98 Ibid., 300.

99 Ibid., 381.

100 Columbe Pringle, *Roger Vivier* (New York: Assouline Publishing, 2004), 9.

101 Ibid., 9.

102 Ibid., 10.

103 Virginia Pope, "Special Showings Open New Hat Shop," *New York Times (1857-Current file)*, January 8, 1943, http://www.proquest.com/ (accessed November 28, 2009).

104 Virginia Pope, "Breton, Fedora and Beret Themes Are Stressed in Fall Hat Showing," *New York Times (1857-Current file)*, July 1, 1943, http://www.proquest.com/ (accessed November 28, 2009).

105 Roger Vivier as quoted in Pringle, *Vivier*, 11.

106 Paid Notice: Deaths Rémy. Suzanne, New York, *New York Times*, April 1, 2001, Master File Premier, http://search.ebscohost.com/login.aspx?direct=true&db=f5h&AN=28934341&site=ehost-live (accessed November 28, 2009).

107 Joan Gardner, "War Limitations Result in Accessory Sets," *Binghamton (NY) Press*, October 26, 1943, Sally Victor Papers.

108 "Much Ado About Hats: They Assume Large Proportions on the Head and in the News," *Vogue*, May 5, 1944, 74–5.

109 Ibid.

110 Eve Keelher, "Here Is What They Are Doing in Paris," *Cleveland (OH) News*, April 21, 1944, Sally Victor Papers.

111 Ibid.

112 Sgt. Mickey Thurgood to his wife, April 9, 1945.

113 *A Pocket Guide to France: Instructions for American Servicemen in France During WWII* (1944, Repr., Chicago, IL: University of Chicago Press, 2008), 22.

114 Ibid.

115 Edward R. Murrow was an American war correspondent who reported for CBS from Europe during the war, known for his coverage of the bombing of London. Manchester, *The Glory and the Dream*, 513–14.

116 The three houses of couture mentioned here did manage to stay open during the Occupation. However, the couturiér Edward Molyneux, a British citizen, escaped to London in June 1940 and remained there during the war. Elsa Schiaparelli spent the war years in the United States, returning to Paris in1945. Jeanne Lanvin remained in Paris. Crawford, *The Ways of Fashion*, 318–19.

117 Manchester, *The Glory and the Dream*, 333.

118 "Teen Age Girls: They Live in a Wonderful World of Their Own," *Life,* December 11, 1944, 91.

119 Ibid., 305.

120 *Life*, December 11, 1944, 91.

121 Evelyn Green, Beauty Editor of *Vogue* "Hair Today—Hair Tomorrow," speech to Fashion Group International, January 9, 1944.

122 Prunella Wood, President of Fashion Group International, speech to Fashion Group International, October 25, 1944.

123 Lilly Daché as quoted in Ibid.

124 Daché Hair Net advertisement, *Vogue*, March 15, 1944.

125 Blanche Krause, "A Salute to American Designers: What Is the Future of American Design?" Sally Victor Papers.

126 Morris, "Designers Who Make the 'American Look,'" *Detroit News*, January 28, 1945, Section C.

127 Mary Morris, "Off with the Old—On with the New," *Detroit News*, February 16, 1947, Section C.

128 Ibid.

129 Ibid.

130 Mary Morris, "Movement Is Started Against 'Skullduggery' in Millinery," *Detroit News*, February 20, 1947.

131 Anonymous reader (1947) quoted in Morris, *Detroit News*, February 20, 1947.

132 Ibid.

133 "Easter Lays a Small Egg," *Time*, March 31, 1947, http://www.time.com/time/magazine/article/0,9171,793530,00.html (accessed December 12, 2009).

134 Ibid., Hattie Carnegie's hats averaged $55.00, equal to $524.70 today.

135 Kay Sullivan, speech to the Fashion Group International, Hotel Astor, New York, NY, December 15, 1947.

136 Bettina Ballard, speech to the Fashion Group International, Hotel Astor, New York, NY, September 15, 1948.

Chapter 10

1 John Updike, Introduction to "Fourth Decade: 1954-64," in *Complete Cartoons of the New Yorker* (New York: Black Dog & Leventhal, 2004), 240.

2 David Halberstam, *The Fifties* (New York: Fawcett Books, 1993; Ballantine Books, 1994), 497.

3 Barbara Heggie, "Back on the Pedestal, Ladies," *Vogue*, January 15, 1946, 78.

4 Ibid.

5 Thorstein Veblen quoted in William Leach, *Land of Desire* (New York: Pantheon Books, 1993), 92.

6 *Dry Goods Economist* (August 15, 1903) as quoted in Leach, *Land of Desire*, 92.

7 "This Is Your Wife" (Bell Telephone advertisement) in *Life*, September 9, 1957, 93.

8 Anne Fogarty as quoted in Introduction to *Wifedressing*, Rosemary Feitelberg, ed., viii.

9 Ibid., 10.

10 Halberstam, *The Fifties*, 593.

11 Ibid., 509–10.

12 Kathell le Bourhis, "The Elegant 50s: When Fashion Was Still a Dictate," in Fine Arts Museums, San Francisco, *New Look to Now: French Haute Couture, 1947-1987* (New York: Rizzoli, 1989), 20.

13 The increased control of the designers in the creation of their own hats led to a decline in the influence of the modistes after the war. Ballard, *In My Fashion*, 91.

14 Christian Dior, *Christian Dior and I*, trans. Antonia Fraser (New York: E.P. Dutton and Company, Inc., 1957), 111.

15 Christian Dior, *Little Dictionary of Fashion* (London: Cassell and Company, 1954), 54.

16 Karal Marling, *As Seen on TV: The Visual Culture of Everyday Life in the 1950s* (Boston: Harvard University Press, 1996), 21.

17 Dorothy Parnell, "Look What's Become of Sally!" *Milwaukee Sentinel*, July 20, 1956.

18 Marling, *As Seen on TV*, 33.

19 Ibid.

20 Ibid., 32.

21 Milbank, *New York Fashion*, 175.

22 Bill Cunningham, *Fashion Climbing* (New York: Penguin Press, 2018), 133.

23 "Business: Sally Victor," *Time*, March 30, 1959, http://www.time.com/time/magazine/article/0,9171,892459,00.html (accessed April 4, 2008).

24 Ibid.

25 Ibid.

26 Ibid.

27 "Joan Crawford," http://www.imdb.com/name/nm0001076/, "Irene Dunne, http://www.imdb.com/name/nm0002050/ "Merle Oberon," http://www.imdb.com/name/nm0643353/, IMDb.com (accessed December 22, 2009).

28 George Dugan, "Sally Victor, 83, a Hat Designer with Many 'Firsts' in Fashions," *New York Times (1857-Current file)*, May 16, 1977, http://www.proquest.com/ (accessed January 5, 2010).

29 Morris, "Lilly Daché, 97, Creator of Hats for the Fashion Set of Yesteryear," *New York Times*, January 2, 1990, http://www.nytimes.com/1990/01/02/obituaries/lilly-dache-97-creator-of-hats-for-the-fashion-set-of-yesteryear.html?scp=2&sq=lilly%20dache,%20turbans&st=cse and Anne-Marie Schiro, "Mr. John, 91, Hat Designer for Stars and Society," *New York Times*, June 29, 1993, http://www.nytimes.com/1993/06/29/obituaries/mr-john-91-hat-designer-for-stars-and-society.html (accessed April 4, 2008).

30 Kathy Peiss, *Hope in a Jar: The Making of America's Beauty Culture* (New York: Henry Holt and Company, 1998), 238.

31 Barbara Brady, *Dallas Morning News*, January 12, 1954 in Sally Victor Papers, 1953–1954.

32 Peiss, *Hope in a Jar*, 244.

33 Jane Pavitt, *Fear and Fashion in the Cold War* (London: V&A Publishing, 2008), 33.

34 "Corporations: The Wizards of Wilmington," *Time*, April 15, 1951, http://www.time.com/time/magazine/article/0,9171,814737,00.html (accessed December 22, 2009).

35 Ibid.

36 Richard Corson, *Fashions in Makeup: From Ancient to Modern Times* (London: Peter Owen Limited, 1972), 546.

37 Ibid., 536.

38 "Business: Records All Around," *Time*, February 6, 1956, http://www.time.com/time/magazine/article/0,9171,893334,00.html (accessed December 22, 2009).

39 "Modern Living: The Pink Jungle," *Time*, June 15, 1958, http://www.time.com/time/magazine/article/0,9171,863523,00.html/ (accessed January 6, 2010).

40 "Business: Sally Victor," *Time*, March 30, 1959, http://www.time.com/time/magazine/article/0,9171,892459,00.html (accessed April 4, 2008).

41 "Modern Living: The Pink Jungle," *Time*, June 15, 1958, http://www.time.com/time/magazine/article/0,9171,863523,00.html/ (accessed January 6, 2010).

42 The Inflation Calculator, http://www.westegg.com/inflation/ (accessed January 6, 2010).

43 "Business: Sally Victor," *Time*, March 30, 1959.

44 The Inflation Calculator, http://www.westegg.com/inflation/ (accessed January 6, 2010).

45 "Tonettte and Toni Home Perm," http://www.boominback.com/archives/features/tonihomeperms0906.html/ (accessed January 3, 2010).

46 "This Lady Is Dying Her Hair," *Life*, November 27, 1950, 113.

47 Ibid.

48 Ibid., 115.

49 Inflation Calculator, http://www.westegg.com/inflation/ (accessed January 6, 2010).

50 Rose Weitz, *Rapunzel's Daughters: What Women's Hair Tells Us About Women's Lives* (New York: Farrar, Straus and Giroux, 2004), 21.

51 Malcolm Gladwell, "Annuals of Advertising: True Colors," *The New Yorker*, March 22, 1999, http://www.gladwell.com/1999/19990322acolors.html/ (accessed December 22, 2009).

52 "Hairstyles: Poodle vs. Horsetail," *Life*, January 7, 1952, 1.

53 "A Big Bulge in Hair: A 'Bouffant' Style Is Summer's Replacement for the Outsized Hat," *Life*, July 9, 1956.

54 Ibid., 59.

55 "Modern Living: The Pink Jungle," *Time*, June 16, 1958, http://www.time.com/time/magazine/article/0,9171,863523,00.html/ (accessed December 27, 2009).

56 Schiro, "Mr. John, 91, Hat Designer for Stars and Society."

57 "Shift to Green," *Mademoiselle*, April 1958, 86.

58 Cunningham, *Fashion Climbing*, 117.

59 Ibid., 114.

60 Cecil Beaton, *The Glass of Fashion* (Garden City, NY: Doubleday and Company, Inc., 1954), 21.

61 Ibid., 23.

Chapter 11

1 Dirix, *Dressing the Decades*, 123–4.

2 Rudi Gernreich as quoted by Marylou Luther in Peggy Moffit and William Claxton, *The Rudi Gernreich Book* (New York: Rizzoli International Publications, 1991), 12.

3 Sally Tuffin as quoted in Valerie Steele, *Fifty Years of Fashion: New Look to Now* (New Haven and London: Yale University Press, 1997), 50.

4 Marnie Fogg, *Boutique: A '60s Phenomenon* (London: Octopus Publishing, 2003), 8.

5 Ibid., 8.

6 Patricia Stacey as quoted in Jenny Lister, ed., *Mary Quant* (London: V & A Publishing, 2019), 29.

7 Fogg, *Boutique*, 22.

8 Andre Courrèges as quoted in Steele, *Fifty Years of Fashion*, 52.

9 Steele, *Fifty Years of Fashion*, 52.

10 James Wedge as quoted in Fogg, *Boutique*, 47.

11 Ibid., 109 and 113–14.

12 Ibid., 114.

13 Ibid., 117.

14 *Vogue*, January 1, 1969, 79.

15 Richard Donovan, "That Friend of Your Wife's—Mr. Dior," *Collier's* (June 10, 1955), 37.

16 Sally Victor as quoted in Patricia Shelton, "Fewer Hats but Business Good," *Christian Science Monitor*, September 30, 1966.

17 Cunningham, *Fashion Climbing*, 159.

18 Diana Vreeland as quoted in Hamish Bowles, "Defining Style," in *Jacqueline Kennedy: The White House Years* (Boston: Little, Brown and Company, 2001), 17.

19 *Ladies' Home Journal* as quoted in Bowles, *Jacqueline Kennedy: The White House Years*, 17.

20 Jacqueline Kennedy as quoted in Bowles, "Hats," *Jacqueline Kennedy: The White House Years*, 179.

21 Bowles, *Jacqueline Kennedy: The White House Years*, 179.

22 Bruce Webber, "Margaret Heldt, Who Built the Beehive, Dies at 98," *New York Times*, June 13, 2016.

23 Eugenia Shepherd, "Hats Come Back in Fashion," *Hutchinson [KS] News*, January 20, 1964.

24 "Milliners Woo Teens," *Allentown Morning Call*, January 4, 1965.

25 Bowles, *Jacqueline Kennedy: The White House Years*, 179.

26 McDowell. *Hats: Status, Style and Glamour*, 179.

27 Cunningham, *Fashion Climbing*, 114.

28 Amanda Mackenzie Stuart, *Empress of Fashion: A Life of Diana Vreeland* (New York: HarperCollins, 2012), 208.

29 Mary Quant as quoted in Regina Blaszczyk, "Into the Big Time," Jenny Lister, ed., *Mary Quant*, 104.

30 Stuart, *Empress of Fashion*, 204.

31 Bruce Weber, "Vidal Sassoon Hairdresser and Trendsetter Dies at 84," *New York Times*, May 9, 2012.

32 Muriel Fisher, "Passion and Piracy Pervade the Street Where Hats Are Made" (no newspaper credited). Sally Victor Papers, 1964.

33 George Dugan, "Sally Victor, 83, a Hat Designer with Many 'Firsts' in Fashion," *New York Times*, May 16, 1977.

34 Bernardine Morris, "Lilly Dache 97, Creator of Hats for the Fashion Set of Yesteryear," *New York Times*, January 2, 1009.

35 Anne-Marie Shiro, "Mr. John, 91, Hat Designer for Stars and Society," *New York Times*, June 23, 1993.

36 Milbank, *New York Fashion*, 212.

37   Anne-Marie Shiro, "Adolfo Decides to Quit Designing," *New York Times*, March 19, 1993.

38   Kennedy Fraser, *The Fashionable Mind* (New York: Alfred A Knopf, 1974), 113.

39   Cunningham, *Fashion Climbing*, 160.

Epilogue

1   Kennedy Fraser, *The Fashionable Mind: Reflections on Fashion 1970-1981* (New York: Alfred A. Knopf, Inc., 1981), 56.

2   McDowell, *Hats: Status, Style and Glamour*, 177.

3   Brian Baker, "Hats in Church: A Heady Issue," *U.S. Catholic*, June 13, 2016, http://www.uscatholic.org/articles/201606/hats-change-30665.

4   Bella Abzug as quoted in "Hats Off," *People Magazine*, April 13, 1998.

5   Ibid.

6   Cunningham, *Fashion Climbing*, 160.

7   Luke Song as quoted in Tom Teenan, "How I Made Aretha Franklin's Famous Obama Inauguration Hat," *The Daily Beast*, October 8, 2018, https://www.thedailybeast.com/luke-song-how-i-made-aretha-franklins-famous-obama-inauguration-hat.

8   Oriele Cullen, "Stephen Jones and Britishness," in Geert Brulout and Kaat Debo, eds., *Stephen Jones and the Accent of Fashion* (Tielt, Belgium: Lannoo Publishers, 2010), 150–7.

9   Isabella Blow as quoted in Bibby Sowray, "Isabella Blow," *Vogue* (UK), November 2011.

10   http://www.millinersguild.org

11   Patricia Underwood as quoted in Jeffery Banks and Doris de la Chapelle, *Patricia Underwood: The Way You Wear Your Hat* (New York and London: Rizzoli, 2015), 42.

12   Nasir Mazhar as quoted in Robb Young, "Millinery Madness: Hatmakers with an Attitude," *The New York Times*, October 3, 2001.

13   William Grimes, "Mimi Weddell, Model, Actress and Hat Devotee, Is Dead at 94," *The New York Times*, October 5, 2009.

14   Ibid.

BIBLIOGRAPHY

Alcott, Louisa May. *Work: A Story of Experience*. New York: Penguin Books, 1873. Reprint, New York: Penquin Books,1994.

Allen, Frederic Lewis. *Only Yesterday: An Informal History of the 1920s*.1931. Reprint, New York: Harper Perennials, 2010.

Allen, Irving Lewis. *The City of Slang: New York Life and Popular Speech*. New York and Oxford: Oxford University Press, 1993.

Allison, May. "Dressmaking as a Trade for Women in Massachusetts." Washington, Government Printing Office 1913. United States Bureau of Labor Statistics, Bulletin 193.

Amnéus, Cynthia. *A Separate Sphere: Dressmakers in Cincinnati's Golden Age 1877–1924*. Lubbock, TX: Texas Tech University Press, 2003.

Army Information Branch of the Army Special Forces, United States Army. Introduction by Rick Atkinson. *Instructions for American Servicemen in France During World War II*. 1944. Reprint, Chicago: University of Chicago Press, 2008.

Arnold, Rebecca. *The American Look: Fashion, Sportswear and the Image of Women in 1930s and 1940s New York*. London and New York: I.B. Tauris, 2009.

Ballard, Bettina. *In My Fashion*. New York: David McKay Company, Inc., 1960.

Barry, John. *The Great Influenza: The Epic Story of the Deadliest Plague in History*. New York: Viking, 2004.

Beaton, Cecil. *The Glass of Fashion*. London: Cassell, 1989.

Beecher, Catherine E. *The Duty of American Women to Their Country*. New York: Harper & Brothers, 1845.

Beecher, Catherine E. *A Treatise on Domestic Economy for the Use of Young Ladies at Home and at School*, revised ed. New York: Harper & Brothers, 1855.

Beecher, Catherine E. and Harriet Beecher Stowe. *Principles of Domestic Science*. New York: J. B. Ford and Company, 1871.

Benson, Susan Porter. *Counter Cultures: Saleswomen, Managers, and Customers in American Department Stores, 1890–1940*. Urbana, IL and Chicago: University of Illinois Press, 1986.

Biennual Convention Proceedings, United Hatters, Cap, and Millinery Workers, 1925 and 1927, Kheel Center for Labor-Management Documentation and Archives, Cornell University Library.

Blackstone, Sir William. *Commentaries on the Laws of England in Four Books*, 2 vols., 2nd ed. Edited by Thomas M. Cooley. Chicago: Callagham, 1879.

Blaszczyk, Regina Lee, ed. *Producing Fashion: Commerce, Culture, and Consumers*. Philadelphia, PA: University of Pennsylvania Press, 2009.

Blum, Dilys. *Ahead of Fashion: Hats of the Twentieth Century*. Philadelphia, PA: Philadelphia Museum of Art, 1993.

Bowles, Hamish. *Jacqueline Kennedy: The White House Years*. New York: Little, Brown and Company, 2001.

Bradbury, Jane and Edward Maeder. *American Style and Spirit: Fashions and Lives of the Roddis Family, 1850–1995*. London: V&A Publishing, 2016.

Brandeis, Louis D. and Josephine Goldmark. *Women in Industry: Decision of the U.S. Supreme Court in Curt Muller vs. State of Oregon Upholding the Constitutionality of the Oregon Ten Hour Law for Women and Brief for the State of Oregon*. New York: National Consumers' League, 1908.

Breward, Christopher, Edwina Ehrman, Caroline Evans. *The London Look: From Street to Catwalk*. New York and London: Yale University Press, 2004.

Brown, Carrie. *Rosie's Mom: Forgotten Women of the First World War*. Hanover and London: University Press of New England. 2002.

Burns, D. D., Jabez, ed. *Mothers Wise and Good*, 4th ed. Boston: Gould and Lincoln, 1851.

Burns, William. *Female Life in New York City*. Philadelphia: T B Peterson, 185?.

Burrows, Edwin G. and Mike Wallace. *Gotham: A History of New York City to 1898*. New York: Oxford University Press, 1999.

Butler, Elizabeth Beardsley. *Women and the Trades: Pittsburgh 1907–1908.* 1909. Reprint, Pittsburgh, PA: University of Pittsburgh Press, 1984.

Butler, Esq., Charles. *The American Lady*. Philadelphia: Hogan & Thompson, 1836.

Byers, Margaretta and Consuelo Kamholz. Designing Women: The Art, Technique, and *Cost of Being Beautiful*. New York: Simon and Schuster, 1938.

Cahan, Abraham. *The Imported Bridegroom and Other Stories of the New York Ghetto*. New York: Houghton, Mifflin and Company, 1898.

Cahan, Abraham. *The Rise of Devid Levinsky*. New York: Harper and Brothers, 1917.

Campbell, Helen. *Prisoners of Poverty*. Boston: Roberts Brothers, 1889.

Carter, Ernestine. *The Changing World of Fashion: 1900 to the Present*. New York: G. P. Putnam's Sons, 1977.

Carter, Graydon, ed. *Bohemians, Bootleggers, Flappers, and Swells: The Best of Early Vanity Fair*. New York: Penguin Press, 2014.

Chambers, Bernice G. *Color and Design in Apparel*. New York: Prentice-Hall, 1942.

Chambers, Bernice G. *Fashion Fundamentals*. Englewood Cliffs, NJ: Prentice-Hall, 1947.

Chase, Edna Woolman, and Ilka Chase. *Always in Vogue*. Garden City, NY: Doubleday and Company, Inc., 1954.

Chrisman-Campbell, Kimberly. *Fashion Victims: Dress at the Court of Louis XVI and Marie Antoinette*. New Haven and London: Yale University Press, 2015.

Cleary, Patrica. *Elizabeth Murray: A Woman's Pursuit of Independence in 18th C America*. Amherst: University of Massachusetts Press, 2000.

Cobb, Richard. *French and Germans, Germans and French: A Personal Interpretation of France Under Two Occupations, 1914-1918/1940-1944.* Hanover and London: University Press of New England, 1983.

Connor, Holly Pyne, ed. *Off the Pedestal: New Woman in the Art of Homer, Chase, and Sargent*. Newark, NJ: The Newark Museum: New Brunswick, NJ: Rutgers University Press, 2006.

Corson, Richard. *Fashions in Hair: The First Five Thousand Years*. London: Peter Owen, 1965.

Corson, Richard. *Fashions in Makeup: From Ancient to Modern Times*. London: Peter Owen Limited, 1972.

Cott, Nancy F. *The Grounding of Modern Feminism*. New York and London: Yale University Press, 1987.

Cott, Nancy F. *The Bonds of Womanhood: "Women's Sphere" in New England, 1789–1835*, 2nd ed. New Haven and London: Yale University Press, 1997.

Crawford, M. D. C. *The Ways of Fashion*. New York: G.P. Putnam's Sons, 1941.

Crawford, M. D. C. *The Ways of Fashion*. New York: Fairchild Publishing Company, 1948.

Crocker, H Matthew. *Observations on the Real Rights of Women*. Boston: Printed for the Author, 1818.

Cumming, Valerie. *The Visual History of Costume Accessories*. New York: Costume and Fashion Press, 1998.

Cunningham, Bill. *Fashion Climbing*. New York: Penguin Press, 2018.

Cunningham, Patricia A. and Susan Voso Lab, eds. *Dress and Popular Culture*. Bowling Green, OH: Bowling Green State University Popular Press, 1991.

Daché, Lilly and Dorothy Roe. *Talking Through My Hats*. New York: Coward-McCann, Inc., 1946.

Davis, Alison Matthews. *Fashion Victims: The Dangers of Dress Past and Present*. London and New York: Bloomsbury Visual Arts, 2015.

Davis, Fred. *Fashion, Culture, and Identity*. Chicago and London: The University of Chicago Press, 1992.

Day, Charles William. *Hints on Etiquette and the Usages of Society with a Glance at Bad Habits*. 1836. Reprint, New York: EP Dutton & Co, Inc., 1947.

de Carabrella, Countess. *The Ladies' Science of Etiquette by an English Lady of Rank (to Which Is Added, the Ladies' Handbook of the Toilet: A Manual of Elegance and Fashion)*. Philadelphia: T.B. Peterson, 1853.

DeJean, Joan. *The Essence of Style: How the French Invented High Fashion, Fine Food, Chic Cafes, Sophistication, and Glamour*. New York: Free Press, 2006.

Dior, Christian. *The Little Dictionary of Fashion*. London: Cassell and Company, 1954.

Dior, Christian. *Christian Dior and I*. Translated by Antonia Fraser. New York: E.P. Dutton and Company, Inc., 1957.

Dirix, Emmanuelle. *Dressing the Decades: Twentieth-Century Vintage Style*. New Haven and London: Yale University Press, 2016.

Drake, Nicholas. *The Fifties in Vogue*. New York: Henry Holt, 1987.

Emery, Joy Spanabel. *A History of the Paper Pattern Industry: The Home Dressmaking Fashion Revolution*. New York and London: Bloomsbury, 2014.

Enstad, Nan. *Ladies of Labor, Girls of Adventure: Working Women, Popular Culture, and Labor Politics at the Turn of The Twentieth Century*. New York: Columbia University Press, 1999.

Erwin, Mabel D. *Clothing for Moderns*. New York: MacMillian Company, 1943.

Erwin, Mabel D. and Lila A. Kinchen. *Clothing for Moderns*, 3rd ed. New York: MacMillian Company, 1964.

Etiquette for Ladies; with Hints on the Preservation, Improvement, and Display of Female Beauty. Philadelphia: Carey, Lea & Blanchard, 1838.

Evans, Caroline. *The Mechanical Smile: Modernism and the First Fashion Shows in France and America 1900–1929*. New Haven and London: Yale University Press, 2013.

Ewan, Elizabeth. *Immigrant Women in the Land of Dollars: Life and Culture on the Lower East Side 1890–1925*. New York: Monthly Review Press, 1985.

Faust, Drew Gilpin. *Mothers of Invention: Women of the Slaveholding South in the American Civil War*. Chapel Hill and London: University of North Carolina Press, 1996.

Faust, Drew Gilpin. *This Republic of Suffering: Death and the American Civil War*. New York: Alfred A. Knopf, 2008.

Feely, Mildred and Charlotte Wright Wilkerson. *A Wonderful You!: A Modern Women's Guide to Poise, Charm and Beauty*. New York: Greenberg, 1947.

The Female Instructor; or Young Woman's Companion. Liverpool, UK: Nuttall, Fisher, and Dixon, c. 1811.

Fenston, Gretchen. *Millinery from 1945 to 1995: Industry in Crisis or Business as Usual*. Thesis. New York: Fashion Institute of Technology, 1995.

Fitzgerald, F. Scott. *This Side of Paradise*. New York: A.L. Burt, 1920.

Fogarty, Anne. Introduction by Rosemary Feitelberg. *Wife Dressing: The Fine Art of Being the Well-Dressed Wife*. New York: L. Messner, 1959. Reprint, New York: Glitterati Incorporated, 2008.

Fogg, Marnie. *Boutique: A '60s Phenomenon*. London: Octopus Publishing, 2003.

Foster, Sarah Jane and Emma Ann. *The Diaries of Sarah Jane and Emma Ann Foster: A Year in Maine Curing the Civil War*. Edited by Wayne E. Reilly. Rockport, ME: Picton Press, 2002.

Gamber, Wendy. *The Female Economy: The Millinery and Dressmaking Trades, 1860–1930*. Urbana and Chicago: University of Illinois Press, 1997.

Ginsburg, Madeleine. *Hat: Trends and Traditions*. Hauppauge, NY: Barron's, 1990.

Green, Charles H. *The Headwear Workers: A Century of Trade Unionism*. New York: United Cap and Millinery Workers, 1944.

Grey, Francine du Plessix. *Them: A Memoir of Parents*. New York: The Penguin Press, 2005.

Grimke, Sarah and Angelina. *On Slavery and Abolitionism: Essays and Letters*. Edited by Mark Perry. New York: Penguin Books, 2014.

Guglielmo, Jennifer. *Living the Revolution: Italian Women's Resistance and Radicalism in New York City, 1880–1945*. Chapel Hill, NC: University of NC Press, 2010.

Guilfoyle, Timothy J. *City of Eros: New York City, Prostitution, and the Commercialism of Sex, 1790–1920*. New York and London: W.W. Norton and Company, 1992.

Gutner, Howard. *Gowns by Adrian: The MGM Years 1928–1941*. New York: Harry N. Abrams, Inc., 2001.

Halberstram, David. *The Fifties*. New York: Fawcett Books, 1993; Ballantine Books, 1994.

Hale, Sarah Josepha Buell. *Manners; Or, Happy Homes and Good Society All the Year Round*. Boston: JE Tilton and Company, 1868.

Hall, Carolyn. *The Forties in Vogue*. London: Octopus Books, 1985.

Hall, Carolyn. *The Thirties in Vogue*. New York: Harmony Books, 1985.

Halttunen, Karen. *Confidence Men and Painted Women: A Study of Middle-Class Culture in America, 1830–1870*. New Haven, CT: Yale University Press, 1982.

Harris, Beth, ed. *Famine and Fashion: Needlewoman in the Nineteenth Century*. Burlington, VT: Ashgate Publishing Company, 2005.

Harrison, Mrs Burton. *The Well-Bred Girl in Society (Ladies' Home Journal Girls' Library)*. Philadelphia: Curtis Publishing Company, 1898.

Hawes, Elizabeth. *Fashion Is Spinach*. New York: Random House, 1938.

Henderson, Debbie. *The Handmade Felt Hat*. Yellow Springs, OH: Wild Goose Press, 2001.

Herndon, Boonton. *Bergdorf's on the Plaza*. New York, Alfred A. Knopf, 1956.

Hill, Joseph Adna. *Women in Gainful Occupations, 1870 to 1920*. Washington, DC: U.S. Government Printing Office, 1929.

Hobson, Richmond Pearson. "The Truth About Alcohol." Speech in the House of Representatives, December 22, 1914. Washington, DC: U.S. Government Printing Office, 1914.

Hollander, Anne. *Seeing Through Clothes*. Reprint, Berkeley and Los Angeles: University of California Press, 1993.

Hollander, Anne. *Sex and Suits*. New York: Kodansha International, 1995.

Hollander, Anne. *Feeding the Eye: Essays*. New York: Farrar, Straus and Giroux, 1999.

Hopkins, Susie. *The Century of Hats: Head-Turning Style of the Twentieth Century*. Edison, NJ: Chartwell Books, 1989.

Horne, Alistair. *Seven Ages of Paris*. New York: Random House, 2002 (Reprint, New York: Vintage Books, 2004).

Howell, Georgina. *In Vogue: Seventy-Five Years of Style*. London: Conde Nast Books, 1991.

Hughes, Clair. *Hats*. New York and London: Bloomsbury Publishing, 2017.

Hunter, Tara. *To Joy My Freedom: Southern Black Women's Lives and Labors After the Civil War*. Cambridge, MA and London: Harvard University Press, Reprint 1998.

Isenberg, Nancy. *Sex and Citizenship in Antebellum America*. Chapel Hill and London: University of North Carolina Press, 1998.

Janney, Paulena Stevens, 1859-1866. *The Civil War Period Journals of Paulena Stevens Janney 1859–1866*. Edited by Christie Hill Russell. Baltimore, MD: Gateway Press, 2007.

Jones, Jennifer M. *Sexing La Mode: Gender, Fashion and Commercial Culture in Old Regime France*. London: Berg, 2004.

Jones, Stephen and Oriole Cullen. *Hats: An Anthology by Stephen Jones*. London: V & A Publishing, 2009.

Kasson, John F. *Rudeness & Civility: Manners in 19th Century America*. New York: Hill and Wang, 1990.

Kaye, Georgina Kerr. *Millinery for Every Woman*. 1926. Reprint, Berkeley, CA: Lacis Publications, 1992.

Kerber, Linda K. *Women of the Republic: Intellect and Ideology in Revolutionary America*. Chapel Hill: University of North Carolina Press, 1980.

Kerber, Linda K. *No Constitutional Right to Be Ladies: Women and the Obligations of Citizenship*. New York: Hill and Wang, 1998.

Kessler-Harris, Alice. *Women Have Always Worked*. Old Westbury, NY: Feminist Press/NY: McGraw-Hill Company, 1981.

Kessler-Harris, Alice. *A Woman's Wage: Historical Meanings and Social Consequences*. Lexington, KY: University Press of Kentucky, 1990.

Kessler-Harris, Alice. *Out to Work: A History of Wage-Earning Women in the United States*. New York: Oxford University Press, Reprint 2003.

Kidwell, Claudia B. and Margaret C. Christman. *Suiting Everyone: The Democratization of Clothing in America*. Washington, DC: Smithsonian Institution Press, 2nd printing 1975.

Koda, Harold and Andrew Bolton, eds. *Poiret*. New Haven, CT and London: Yale University Press, 2007.

Kramer, Dale. *Ross and the New Yorker*. Garden City, NY: Doubleday and Company, Inc., 1951.

The Laws of Etiquette; Or, Short Rules and Reflections for Conduct in Society by a Gentleman. *New edition. With additions*. Philadelphia: Carey, Lea & Blanchard, 1836.

Leach, William. *Land of Desire: Merchants, Power, and the Rise of a New American Culture*. 1993. Reprint, New York: Vintage Books, 1994.

Le Bourhis, Katell, ed. *Fashion in the Age of Napoleon: Costume from Revolution to Empire 1789–1815*. New York: The Metropolitan Museum of Art, 1989.

Leslie, Miss. *The Behavior Book: A Manual for Ladies*, 3rd ed. Philadelphia: Willis P Hazard, 1853.

Leuchtenburg, William E. *The Perils of Prosperity 1914-1932*, 1958. Repint, Chicago and London: The University of Chicago Press, 1993.

Lewis, Marx. *A Half Century of Achievement: The History of Millinery Workers' Union Local 24*. New York: Millinery Workers' Union, Local 24, 1960.

Lewis, Susan Ingalls. *Unexceptional Women: Female Proprieters in Mid-Nineteenth Century Albany, New York, 1830–1885*. Columbus, OH: The Ohio State University Press, 2009.

Lilly Daché: Glamour at the Drop of A Hat. New York: The Museum at FIT, 2007. Published in conjunction with the exhibition "Lilly Daché: Glamour at the Drop of A Hat" shown at The Museum at FIT.

Lister, Jenny, ed. *Mary Quant*. London: V & A Publishing, 2019.

London, Jack. *John Barleycorn: Alcoholic Memoirs*. 1913. Reprint, New York: Oxford University Press, 1998.

Lussier, Suzanne. *Art Deco Fashion*. London: V&A Publishing, 2003.

MacDonald, Anne L. *No Idle Hands: The Social History of American Knitting*. New York: Random House, 1988.

MacDonald, Anne L. *Feminine Ingenuity: Women and Invention in America*. New York: Ballantine Books, 1992.

Mack, Susan. "Gifts to Be Cultivated: Training in Dressmaking and Millinery 1860–1930." Ph,D diss., University of St. Thomas, 2011.

Malkiel, Theresa H. *The Diary of a Shirtwaist Striker*. 1910. Ithaca, NY and London: ILR Press, 1990.

Manchester, William. *The Glory and the Dream: A Narrative History of American 1932–1972*. New York: Bantam Books, 1990 [Orig. pub. 1974].

Marcus, H. Stanley. *Minding the Store*. Boston; Little, Brown and Company, 1974.

Marling, Karal Ann. *As Seen On TV: The Visual Culture of Everyday Life in the 1950s*. Cambridge, MA: Harvard University Press, 1994.

Martin, Richard and Harold Koda. Christian Dior. New York: Metropolitan Museum of Art, 1996.

Martine, Arthur. *Martine's Hand-Book of Etiquette, and a Guide to True Politeness*. New York: Dick & Fitzgerald, 1866.

Max Meyers Papers. Kheel Center for Labor-Management Documentation and Archives, Cornell University Library.

McCardell, Claire. *What Shall I Wear?: The What, Where, When and How Much of Fashion*. New York: Simon and Schuster, 1956.

McDowell, Colin. *Hats: Status, Style and Glamour*. New York: Rizzoli, 1992.

Mears, Patricia and Bruce Boyer. *Elegance in the Age of Crisis: Fashions of the 1930s*. New Haven and London: Yale University Press, 2014.

Mendelson, Adam D. *The Rag Race: How Jews Sewed Their Way to Success in America and the British Empire*. New York and London: New York University Press, 2015.

Merceron, Dean L. *Lanvin*. New York: Rizzoli, 2007.

Milbank, Carolyn Rennolds. *New York Fashion: The Evolution of American Style*. New York: Harry N. Abrams, 1989.

Miller, Marla R. *The Needle's Eye: Women and Work in the Age of Revolution*. Amherst and Boston: University of Massachusetts Press, 2006.

The Milliner's Girl, or Authentic and Interesting Adventures of Fanny Bilson, a Country Clergyman's Daughter Describing the Circumstances Which Induced Her to Leave

Her Father, Her Journey to London, and Remarkable Occurrence at the Inn; with Her Preservation from Ruin, and Further Particulars of Her Marriage. Derby: Thomas Richardson; Simpkin, Marshall, and co., London, 1840?.

Moffit, Peggy and William Claxton. *The Rudi Gernreich Book*. New York: Rizzoli International Publications, 1991.

Moore, Kate. *The Radium Girls: The Dark Story*. Napierville, IL: Sourcebooks, Inc., 2017.

Morton, Grace Margaret. *The Arts of Costume and Personal Appearance*. New York: John Wiley and Sons, Inc. 1943.

Nienburg, Bertha M. *Conditions in the Millinery Industry in the United States*. United States. Women's Bureau, and United States. Department of Labor. Washington, DC: U.S. Government Print Office, 1939.

Oates, Stephen B. *A Woman of Valor: Clara Barton and the Civil War*. New York: The Free Press, 1994.

Okrent, Daniel. *Last Call: The Rise and Fall of Prohibition*. New York: Scribner, 2010.

Okrent, Daniel. *The Guarded Gate: Bigotry, Eugenics, and the Law That Kept Two Generations of Jews, Italians, and Other European Immigrants Out of America*. New York: Scribner, 2019.

Orleck, Annelise. *Common Sense and a Little Fire: Women and Working-Class Politics in the United States 1900–1965*, 2nd ed. Chapel Hill: University of North Carolina Press, 1991, 2017 (preface).

Otis, Belle [Caroline H. Woods] *The Diary of a Milliner*. New York: Hurd and Houghton, 1867.

Parker, Emma. *Important Trifles Chiefly Appropriate to Females on their Entrance to Society*. London: T Egerton, Military Library, Whitehall, 1817.

Pavitt, Jane. *Fear and Fashion in the Cold War*. London: V&A Publishing, 2008.

Pei, Martin and Terence Pepper. *1920s Jazz Age: Fashion and Photographs*. London: Unicorn Publishing, 2018.

Penny, Virginia. *The Employments of Women: A Cyclopaedia of Women's Work*. Boston: Walker, Wise and Company, 1863.

Penny, Virginia. *Think and Act: A Series of Articles Pertaining to Men and Women Work and Wages*. Philadelphia: Claxton, Remsen & Haffelfinger, 1869.

Peiss, Kathy. *Cheap Amusements: Working Women and Leisure in Turn-of-the-Century New York*. Philadelphia, PA: Temple University Press, 1986.

Peiss, Kathy. *Hope in a Jar: The Making of America's Beauty Culture*. New York: Henry Holt and Company, 1998.

Perrot, Philippe. *Fashioning the Bourgeoisie: A History of Clothing in the Nineteenth Century*. Translated by Richard Bienvenu. Princeton, NJ: Princeton University Press, 1994.

Perry, Lorinda, Ph.D. *Millinery as a Trade for Women*. London, Bombay and Calcutta: Longmans, Green, and Company, 1916.

Pochna, Marie-France. *Christian Dior: The Man Who Made the World Look New*. Translated by Joanna Savill. New York: Arcade Publishing, 1994.

Polle, Emmanuelle. *Jean Patou: A Fashionable Life*. Paris: Flammarion, SA, 2013.

Post, Emily. *Etiquette: The Blue Book of Social Usage*. New York: Funk and Wagnalls, 1947.

Pringle, Colombe. *Roger Vivier*. New York: Assouline Publishing, 2004.

Probert, Christine. *Hats in Vogue Since 1910*. New York: Abbeville Press, 1981.

Quant Mary. *Quant By Quant*. London: Cassell and Company, Ltd., 1966.

Ramaekers, Kenneth, ed. *Jazz Age: Fashion in the Roaring 20s*. Ghent-Courtrai: Snoeck Publishers, 2015.

Raushenbush, Winifred. *How to Dress in Wartime*. New York: Coward-McCann, Inc., 1942.

Reed, Emmala. *A Faithful Heart: The Journals of Emmala Reed, 1865 and 1866*. Edited by Robert Oliver. Columbia, SC: University of South Carolina Press, 2004.

Reid, Lillian. *Personality and Etiquette*. Boston: Little, Brown and Company, 1940.

Ribeiro, Aileen. *Dress in the Eighteenth Century Europe 1715–1789*. London: B.T. Batsford Ltd., 1984.

Robertson, Nancy MacDonell. "Miss Jazz Age: The Fashion Criticism of Lois Long, 1925–1969." Diss., Fashion Institute of Technology, 2017.

Robinson, Donald B. *Spotlight on a Union: The Story of the United Hatters, Cap and Millinery Workers*. New York: The Dial Press, 1948.

Rowlands, Penelope. *A Dash of Daring: Carmel Snow and Her Life in Fashion, Art, and Letters*. New York: Atria Books, 2005.

Rudofsky, Bernard. *Are Clothes Modern?: An Essay on Contemporary Attire*. Chicago, Paul Theobald, 1947.

Ryan, Mildred Graves and Velma Phillips. *Clothes for You*, 2nd ed. New York: Appleton-Century-Crofts, Inc., 1954.

Ryan, Mildred Graves and Velma Phillips. *Dress Smartly: A 100 Point Guide*. New York: Scribner's Sons, 1956.

Sante, Luc. *Low Life: Lures and Snares of Old New York*. 1991. Reprint, New York: Vintage Departures, 1992.

Schiaparelli, Elsa. *Shocking Life*. 1954. Reprint, V&A Publications, 2007.

Segrave, Kerry. *Beware the Masher: Sexual Harassment in American Public Places, 1880–1930*. Jefferson, NC: McFarland and Company, Inc., 2014.

Severa, Joan. *Dressed for the Photographer: Ordinary Americans and Fashion 1840–1900*. Kent, OH and London: The Kent State University Press, 1995.

Shakespeare, William. "Henry IV, Part, I." *The Oxford Shakespeare: The Complete Works of William Shakespeare*. Edited by W. D. Craig. London: Oxford University Press, 1914.

Shaw, Madelyn and Lynn Zacek Bassett. *Homefront and Battlefield: Quilts and Context in the Civil War*. Lowell, MA: American Textile History Museum, 2012.

Shelton, Amanda, 1864. *Turn Backward, O Time: The Civil War Diary of Amanda Shelton*. Edited by Kathleen Hanson. Edinburgh, UK: Edinburgh University Press, 2006.

Sherrow, Victoria. *Encyclopedia of Hair: A Cultural History*. Westport, CT: Greenwood Press, 2006.

Shields, Jody. *Hats: A Stylish History and Collector's Guide*. New York: Clarkson Potter Publishers, 1991.

Silber, Nina. *Daughters of the Union: Northern Women Fight the Civil War*. Cambridge, MA and London: Harvard University Press, 2005.

Simon, Amy Catherine. "'She Is So Neat and Fits So Well': Garment Construction and the Millinery Business of Eliza Oliver Dodds, 1821–1833." MA thesis, University of Delaware, 1993.

Simon, Linda. *Lost Girls: The Invention of the Flapper*. London: Reaktion Books Ltd., 2019.

Smith, Malcolm. *Hats: A Very Unnatural History*. East Lansing, MI: Michigan State University Press, 2020.

Soohoo, Pamela. *Fashions for Victory: Regulation, Improvisation and Innovation in American Women's Fashion 1940–1946*. Thesis, Fashion Institute of Technology, New York, 2004.

Stansell, Christine. *City of Women: Sex and Class in New York 1789–1860*. New York: Alfred A. Knopf, 1986.

Steele, Valerie. *Fashion and Eroticism*. New York and London: Oxford University Press, 1985.

Steele, Valerie. *Paris Fashion*: *A Cultural History*. New York: Oxford University Press, 1988.

Steele, Valerie. *Women of Fashion: Twentieth-Century Designers*. New York: Rizzoli, 1991.

Steele, Valerie. *Fifty Years of Fashion: New Look to Now*. New Haven and London: Yale University Press, 1997.

Stein, Sarah Abrevaya. *Plumes: Ostrich Feathers, Jews, and a Lost World of Global Commerce*. New Haven: Yale University Press, 2008.

Steinberg, Neil. *Hatless Jack: The President, the Fedora, and the History of an American Style*. New York: Penguin Books, 2004.

Story, Margaret. *Individuality and Clothes*. New York and London: Funk and Wagnalls Company, 1930.

Stuart, Amanda MacKenzie. *Empress of Fashion: A Life of Diana Vreeland*. New York: HarperCollins, 2012.

Thurgood, Sgt. Mickey. Sgt. Mickey Thurgood to His Wife, Paris, France, April 9, 1945.

Tractenberg, Alan. *The Incorporation of America: Culture and Society in the Gilded Age*. 1982. Reprint, New York: Hill & Wang, 1994.

Train, Susan, ed. *Theatre de la Mode*, rev. 2nd ed. Portland, OR: Palmer/Pletsch Inc., 2002.

Trollope, Frances. *Domestic Manners of the Americans*. 1832. Reprint, Mineola, NY: Dover Publications, 2003.

Twain, Mark (Samuel Langhorne Clemens) and Charles Dudley Warner. *The Gilded Age: A Tale of Today*. 1873. Reprint, New York: Penguin Group, 2001.

Underwood, Josie (1861). *Josie Underwood's Civil War Diary*. Edited by Nancy Disher Baird. Lexington, KY: University of Kentucky Press, 2009.

United Hatters, Cap and Millinery Workers International Union Files on Microfilm. 5755 Mf. Kheel Center for Labor-Management Documentation and Archives, Martin P. Catherwood Library, Cornell University, n.d.

U.S. Bureau of the Census. *Comparative Occupation Statistics 1870–1930*. Washington, DC: Government Printing Office, 1940.

Van Kleeck, Mary. *Artificial Flower Makers*. New York: Survey Associates, Inc., 1913.

Van Kleeck, Mary. *A Seasonal Industry: A Study of the Millinery Trade In New York*. New York: Russell Sage Foundation, 1917.

Vapnek, Lara. *Breadwinners: Working Women & Economic Independence 1865–1920*. Urbana & Chicago: University of Illinois Press, 2009.

Veillon, Dominique. *Fashion Under the Occupation*. Translated by Miriam Kochan. New York: Berg, 2002.

Vincent, Susan J. *Hair: An Illustrated History*. London and New York: Bloomsbury Visual Arts, 2018.

Wald, Lillian. *The House on Henry Street*. New York: Henry Holt and Company, 1931.

Walford, Jonathan. *Forties Fashion: From Siren Suits to the New Look*. London: Thames and Hudson, 2008.

Ware, Susan. *Beyond Suffrage: Women in the New Deal*. Cambridge, MA: Harvard University Press, 1981.

Watkins, Susan. *Elizabeth I and Her World*. New York: Thames and Hudson, 2007.

Weitz, Rose. *Rapunzel's Daughters: What Women's Hair Tells Us About Women's Lives*. New York: Farrar, Straus and Giroux, 2004.

Welters, Linda and Patricia Cunningham, eds, *20th Century American Fashion*. New York: Berg, 2005.

Welther, Barbara. "The Cult of True Womanhood: 1820–1860." *American Quarterly*, 18, no. 2, Part 1 (Summer, 1966): 151–74.

Wharton, Edith. *The House of Mirth*, 1905 in *Novels*. Edited by R. W. B. Lewis. New York: The Library of America, 1985.

Wharton, Edith. "Bunner Sisters." In *Collected Stories 1911–1937*, edited by Maureen Howard. New York: The Library of America, 2001.

White, Palmer. *Elsa Schiaparelli: Empress of Paris Fashion*. London: Aurum Press, 1995.

White, Richard. *Railroaded: The Transcontinentals and the Making of America*. New York: W.W. Norton, 2012.

Wilson, Elizabeth. *Adorned in Dreams: Fashion and Modernity*. London: Virago Press, 1985; New Brunswick, NJ: Rutgers University Press, 2003.

Winterburn, Florence Hull. *Principles of Correct Dress*. New York and London: Harper and Brothers Publishers, 1914.

Yezierska, Anzia. *Salome of the Tenements*, 1923. Reprint, Urbana and Chicago: University of Illinois Press, 1995.

Yezierska, Anzia. *Breadgivers*, 1925. New York: Persea Books (Reprint 2003).

Yohannan, Kohle and Nancy Nolf. *Claire McCardell: Redefining Modernism*. New York: Harry N. Abrams, Inc., 1998.

Young, A. M., John H. *A Guide to the Manners, Etiquette, and Deportment of the Most Refined Society*. 1879. Reprint, New York: Lyons Press, 2001.

The Young Lady's Book: A Manual of Elegant Recreations, Exercises and Pursuits, 3rd ed. Boston: Lilly, Wait, Colman and Holden and Abel Bowen, 1833.

Zeitz, Joshua. *Flapper: A Madcap Story of Sex, Style, Celebrity and the Women Who Made America Modern*. New York; Crown Publishing. 2006.

Zinn, Howard. *A People's History of the United States*. New York: Harper Perennial Classics, 2005.

Magazines and Trade Journals

American Fabrics, 1948.
American Federationist 1896, 1905, 1906.
CIBA Review, Volume 25, September 1939.
Contemporary Modes, 1934–1941.
Godey's Ladies' Book, 1834–1859.
Fortune, 1934, 1940.
Frank Leslie's Ladies' Gazette of Fashion, 1854–1857.
Harper's Bazaar, 1935–1957.
Hats, 1941–1948.
The Illustrated Milliner, 1900–1922.
Ladies' Home Journal, 1938–1945.
Life, 1937–1952.
Millinery Trade Review, 1876–1899.
New England Galaxy volume 1, no. 3, Spring 1960.

New York Times, 2013, 2018.
Time, 1935–1959.
Town and Country, 1937–1943.
Vogue (U.K.), 2011.
Vogue (U.S.), 1935–1959.

Newspapers

Detroit News, 1945–1952.
The New York Times, 1936–1959.

Archives

Fashion Group International Records, c.1930–1950.
Kheel Center for Labor-Management Documentation and Archives, Cornell University.
Manuscripts and Archives Division, New York Public Library, New York, NY.
Max Meyer Papers, 1925–1979.
Report of Millinery Stabilization Commission, 1936–1937.
Sally Victor Papers, Special Collections, Gladys Marcus Library, Fashion Institute of
    Technology, New York, NY.

Audiovisual Material

The Women (1939) George Cukor, director, Warner Brothers DVD 2002.

Websites

Abbott, Karen, "'The Hatpin Peril' Terrorized Men Who Couldn't Handle the Twentieth
    Century Woman." Smithsonian.com, April 24, 2014. http://www.smithsonianmag
    .com/history/hatpin-peril-terrorized-men-who-couldnt-handle-20th-century-woman-1
    80951219/#0QZ5U1A4IKdl8QuM.99
Blakemore, Erin, "Meet Mary Kies, America's First Woman to Become a Patent Holder."
    Smithsonian.com May 5, 2016 https://www.smithsonianmag.com/smart-news/mee
    t-mary-kies-americas-first-woman-become-patent-holder-180959008/?no-ist
Campbell, Jodi, "Benjamin Rush and Women's Education: A Revolutionary's
    Disappointment, A Nation's Achievement." *John and Mary's Journal*, Number 13,
    Dickinson College, 2000. http://chronicles.dickinson.edu/johnandmary/JMJVolume13
    /campbell.htm
Jalou Gallery, Les Archives de L'Officiel de la Mode. http://patrimoine.jalougallery.com/
    lofficiel-de-la-mode-sommairepatrimoine-13.html

Josefiak, Melissa, "Sophia Woodhouse's Grass Bonnets." Wethersfield Historical Society, 2003 http://www.wethersfieldhistory.org/articles-from-the-community/sophia_woodh ouses_grass_bonnets/

Lessons From Bernard Rudofsky (Getty Center Exhibits). http://www.getty.edu/art/exhib itions/rudofsky/

Life Magazine. http://www.life.com/

New-York Tribune. (New York [N.Y.]), July 1902. *Chronicling America: Historic American Newspapers.* Library of Congress. https://chroniclingamerica.loc.gov/lccn/sn830 30214/1921-02-26/ed-1/seq-1/

Parsons School of Design-The New School "Parsons History." https://www.newschoo l.edu/parsons/history/

Teeman, Tom, "Luke Song: How I Made Aretha Franklin's Famous Obama Inauguration Hat." *The Daily Beast*, October 18, 2018, https://www.thedailybeast.com/luke-song-how-i-made-aretha-franklins-famous-obama-inauguration-hat

"The Straw Shop." *Inventive Women of America*. https://thestrawshop.com/inventive-women-of-america/

Trumbach, Randolph, "Man-Milliners and Macaronis: Same Sex Desire, and the 18th Century Origins of the Modern Sexual System." Queer History of Fashion Symposium, Museum at FIT, December 12, 2013. https://www.youtube.com/watch? v=-9UkKR6d4RM

YouTube: Hair Styles for Safety WWII. http://www.youtube.com/watch?v=mgpvKXLTwr8

INDEX

Note: Page numbers in italics refers to figures.

www.ingramcontent.com/pod-product-compliance
Lightning Source LLC
Chambersburg PA
CBHW050426280326
41932CB00013BA/2005